NONVERBAL

COMMUNICATION

NONVERBAL

COMMUNICATION

ALBERT MEHRABIAN

UNIVERSITY OF CALIFORNIA, LOS ANGELES

ALDINE · ATHERTON | CHICAGO · NEW YORK

ABOUT THE AUTHOR

Albert Mehrabian received his B.S. and M.S. from Massachusetts Institute of Technology in 1961 and a Ph.D. in Psychology from Clark University in 1964. He is Associate Professor of Psychology and Chairman of the personality area of Psychology at UCLA. He has contributed widely to professional journals and is presently a consulting editor for the *Journal of Psycholinguistic Research*.

First published 1972 by
Aldine · Atherton, Inc.
529 South Wabash Avenue
Chicago, Illinois 60605

ISBN 0-202-25091-1
Library of Congress Catalog Number 72-172859

Printed in the United States of America

To
My Dear Friend and Colleague
Morton Wiener

Preface

This volume deals with nonverbal communication and, more specifically, with the subtle ways in which people convey their feelings. People are discouraged, generally, from an overt (linguistic) expression of their feelings, so they convey them in less consensual and less easily recognizable forms. Examples are subtle variations in speech, such as the speech errors noted by Freud, vocal qualities of speech, such as sarcasm, and various postures, movements, and gestures.

In contrast to the well-defined codes that are available for languages, the codes for these more subtle communications remain implicit. Nevertheless, experimental findings show some consensus in the encoding as well as the decoding of nonverbal signals. In examining the basis of this common, though unverbalized, consensus, our approach will emphasize feelings, attitudes, and evaluations as the basic referents of nonverbal behavior. The thesis is that, as is the case when examining verbal concepts, more than half the variance in the significance of nonverbal signals can be described in terms of a three-dimensional framework: positiveness, potency or status, and responsiveness. It is also recognized that the unaccounted variance bears on other facets of nonverbal communication, such as its regulative function in social interaction.

One important way in which this approach differs from that employed in most available studies in the nonverbal communication literature is noteworthy here. Any attempt at a comprehensive description of findings in the study of nonverbal communication has to include the large numbers of behavioral cues that are studied (e.g., eye contact, distance, leg and foot movements, facial expressions, voice qualities). Further, the description should also account for (1) the relationships among these cues, (2) the relationships between these cues and the feelings, attitudes, and personalities of the communicators, and (3) the qualities of the situations in which the communications occur. Describing all of these relationships for each behavioral cue would yield an enormous compendium of facts, with little possibility for integration. Such a collection of facts would become all the more confusing because of inconsistencies in results from different studies that could be due to differences in subject populations and experimental methods. A catalogue of findings, then, would fail to provide the conceptual economy of a scientific enterprise.

To arrive at a parsimonious description of the large numbers of facts, our approach uses a three-dimensional framework that allows a succinct characterization of the referents of nonverbal communication, and provides a basis for the consistent formulation and study of the diverse phenomena in this area. Thus, the presentation of the various studies and results is more in terms of the proposed three-dimensional framework (positiveness, potency or status, and responsiveness) than in terms of specific cues, although experimental results are of course always based on the observation of specific cues.

The generality of the proposed framework is evident from the fact that individual differences in nonverbal communication can be specifically described in terms of a characteristic ability and preference for communicating a certain level of positiveness, potency, and responsiveness to others. Also, communication behaviors can be grouped in terms of the referents that they most effectively convey. Finally, inconsistent communications can be defined and measured in terms of the degree of discrepancy that is implied by different behaviors simultaneously produced by a speaker. Thus, total inconsistency for any two channels can be measured in terms of the distance in the three-dimensional space between the referent of one channel and that of the other.

I hope that sufficient data is provided from diverse social situations to show the relevance and value of the proposed three-dimensional scheme for studies of nonverbal communication. One of the by-products of this approach is that it provides the background for an empirical description of social interaction. This description, explored later in the book, provides some measures of social behavior that can be of value to investigators in the social and personality areas.

Portions of this book have previously been published in a different form in "Nonverbal Communication," in *Nebraska Symposium on Motivation, 1971,* edited by James K. Cole (Lincoln: University of Nebraska Press, 1972). I am grateful to the University of Nebraska Press, as well as to the Academic Press, the American Psychological Association, Appleton-Century-Crofts, Duke University Press, Psychonomic Society, and Wadsworth Publishing Company for their kind permission to use materials from my previous publications.

The research that is reported in this volume would not have been possible without the many sources of human and financial assistance that I received. Initial small grants from the University of California (grant

2189 and National Science Foundation grant 89) allowed me to begin most of this work. Subsequent funding from grants MH 12629 and MH 13509 from the United States Public Health Service, and GS 2482 from the National Science Foundation, provided the support needed to rapidly accelerate our work in this area. The Federal Work-Study program was another important, though indirect, source of funds. It was particularly gratifying to employ students in this program. This group included some of the most conscientious and promising students with whom I have ever had occasion to come in contact.

Even though a listing of names is hardly adequate to express my appreciation, I do, nevertheless, want to mention the following students who assisted me with the experiments: Niki Boon, Jerry Brennan, Nancy Burke, Ira Ellenbogen, Sandy Finkelman (Goldhaber), Carey Fox, Laurie Gompert, Carolyn Goren, David Humphrey, James Lane, Pelayo Lasa, Robert Law, Allan Lowe, Ernie Nathan, Sylvia Norman, Harold Reznick, Peter Rodriguez, Laurie Snow, Stanley Sue, Larry Wentink, Charles West, and Tony Zannini. I want to especially thank my colleagues and graduate students who were actively involved in the design and conceptualization of some of the experiments: Nancy Beakel, Shirley Diamond, Norman Epstein, John Friar, Sheldon Ksionzky, Henry Reed, James Russell, Morton Wiener, Martin Williams, and Susan Ferris (Zaidel). Finally, I am most grateful to Sherry Leffell, Kathleen Dalzen, and particularly to Lena Chow, who helped with the editing, and to Dr. Starkey Duncan, Jr. for his helpful reactions to an earlier version of the manuscript.

Contents

A Semantic Space For
Nonverbal Behavior

Defining Nonverbal Behavior and its Functions

The last decade has seen a tremendous upsurge in research and popular interest in the phenomena of nonverbal communication. Whenever any topic stimulates a rapid accumulation of research evidence, periodic overview and integration become essential to continued progress and understanding. Such is the attempt of this volume, to review the more subtle aspects of human communication and to provide a conceptual integration for one segment of recent findings on the subject.

In its narrow and more accurate sense, "nonverbal behavior" refers to actions as distinct from speech. It thus includes facial expressions, hand and arm gestures, postures, positions, and various movements of the body or the legs and feet (Birdwhistell, 1952, 1970; Efron, 1941; Ekman and Friesen, 1969b; Exline and Winters, 1965; Hall, 1959, 1963, 1966; Kendon, 1967a; Mehrabian, 1971c, 1972; Scheflen, 1964, 1965, 1966; Sommer, 1969).

In the broader sense in which the concept has been used traditionally, however, the term "nonverbal behavior" is a misnomer, for a variety of subtle aspects of speech frequently have been included in discussions of nonverbal phenomena. These include paralinguistic or vocal phenomena, such as fundamental frequency range and intensity range, speech errors or pauses, speech rate, and speech duration (for example, Boomer, 1963; Crystal and Quirk, 1964; Davitz, 1964; Dittmann and Llewellyn, 1969; Duncan, 1969; Goldman-Eisler, 1968; Huttar, 1967; Mahl and Schulze, 1964; Matarazzo, Wiens, and Saslow, 1965; Mehrabian, 1965; Pittenger and Smith, 1957; Rubenstein and Cameron, 1968; Starkweather, 1964;

This chapter includes rewritten segments from my article, "A Semantic Space for Nonverbal Behavior," *Journal of Consulting and Clinical Psychology*, 35 (1970), 248–57, copyright (1970) by the American Psychological Association. Reproduced by permission.

Trager, 1958). In our discussions, we shall refer to these vocal qualities as "implicit" aspects of speech.

Also included in discussions of nonverbal behavior are complex communication phenomena, such as sarcasm, where inconsistent combinations of verbal and nonverbal behavior take on special significance in subtly conveying feelings (Argyle, Salter, Nicholson, Williams, and Burgess, 1970; Beakel and Mehrabian, 1969; Haley, 1963; Mehrabian, 1970e; Schuham, 1967; Weakland, 1961).

It is more the subtlety, then, of a communication form than its verbal versus nonverbal quality which determines its consideration within the nonverbal literature. Nonverbal behaviors *per se* form the backbone of this literature. Their subtlety can be attributed to the lack of explicit coding rules for these behaviors in most cultures. Whereas verbal cues are definable by an explicit dictionary and by rules of syntax, there are only vague and informal explanations of the significance of various nonverbal behaviors. Similarly, there are no explicit rules for encoding or decoding paralinguistic phenomena or the more complex combinations of verbal and nonverbal behavior in which the nonverbal elements contribute heavily to the significance of a message.

Despite the absence of explicit coding rules, there is some degree of consistency both within and between cultures (Ekman, 1972; Ekman and Friesen, 1971) in the use of subtle behaviors to convey a certain state, relation, or feeling (encoding), and in the inference of another's state, relation, or attitude from such behaviors (decoding). Although the exact degree of this consistency cannot be established readily because it differs for different persons, situations, and types of behaviors, it is nevertheless legitimate to consider such behaviors *communicative*.

The explicit-implicit dichotomy seems quite suited for distinguishing these subtle communication phenomena from verbal-linguistic cues. Usually, an idea or feeling is made explicit with words, and remains implicit when the speaker refrains from talking, or when he says the words in a voice that conveys a subtle, or even contradictory, shade of meaning. The explicit-implicit dichotomy also reminds us of the idea that the coding rules for verbal-linguistic phenomena are explicit and that the coding rules for subtle communication phenomena are implicit. In this volume, then, the concept of implicit communication is used in preference to the misnomer, nonverbal communication.

SOME FUNCTIONS OF IMPLICIT BEHAVIORS

Although this book focuses primarily on the ways in which implicit communication behaviors relate to feelings and attitudes, these behaviors also serve other functions. A case in point is the occurrence of *uh-huh* or head nods in conversations. Along with Krasner (1958) and Matarazzo, Wiens, and Saslow (1965), we shall focus primarily on how such behaviors convey respect toward, and agreement with, a listener; that is, serve as social reinforcers. These cues might also be used to regulate another's speech—suggest that the speaker continue, or prompt the listener to take over when the speaker stops talking.

Ekman and Friesen (1969b) proposed five major categories of nonverbal behavior that illustrate some of these other functions. The first category, *emblem*, refers to the small class of nonverbal acts that can be accurately translated into words (for example, a handshake, shaking a fist at someone, a smile, a frown). The second category, *illustrator*, is very much a part of speech and serves the function of emphasis. Examples are head and hand movements that occur more frequently with primary-stressed words (Dittmann and Llewellyn, 1969), pointing gestures, or other movements that redundantly draw a picture of the linguistic referent. Included in this category are those movements that seem to serve as added punctuation or emphases, such as pointing with the hand or with a turn of the head, or tracing the contour of an object or person referred to verbally.

The third major category, *affect display*, deals with the function we shall be discussing most. However, our approach will be different. Instead of focusing on primary affects (happiness, anger, surprise, fear, disgust, sadness, and interest), we shall use a multidimensional scheme that subsumes these primary affects and their combinations, as well as many others. The fourth category, *regulator*, refers to acts that help to initiate and terminate the speech of participants in a social situation. These regulators might suggest to a speaker that he keep talking, that he clarify, or that he hurry up and finish. The last category, *adaptor*, refers to acts that are related to the satisfaction of bodily needs, such as moving into a more comfortable position, or scratching.

Several investigators have dealt with the various functions of implicit behavior. For instance, studies of illustrators are exemplified by Boomer's (1963) experiment, which showed a direct correlation between speech disturbance (particularly the filled pause) and a composite measure of head, hand, and foot movements of a patient. In a more elaborate and precise study, Dittmann and Llewellyn explored the differential occurrence of movements at various positions of a phonemic clause—"a string of words, averaging five in length, in which there is one and only one primary stress and which is terminated by a juncture" (1969, p. 99). Head and hand movements occurred more frequently with primary-stressed words, but this relationship accounted for only 7 percent of the variance in body movement. This finding suggested that "if a person wishes to convey the idea that what he is expressing is important or difficult to conceptualize or exciting, he will introduce movements along with his speech to get this extra information across. The timing of these movements will tend to follow the pattern of timing he is familiar with: that is, early in encoding units or following hesitations in speech" (p. 105).

One implication of the small amount of variance that was accounted for in Dittmann and Llewellyn's results is that there are other determinants of movement besides the structural qualities of the statements that they accompany. According to Condon and Ogston (1966, 1967) and Kendon (1967b), one such source of movements is the synchronous quality of interpersonal interaction. These investigators attempted a microanalysis of movement sequences of participants in a conversation. Some of the forms of synchrony were *punctuation,* as in the Dittmann and Llewellyn (1969) study, *movement mirroring,* and *speech analogous* movements.

> There is a small amount of research which suggests that when subjects are exposed to an input that has a rhythmic organization, such as music, they tend to move in time to it . . . and that if they are already performing some activity, such as tapping, or typing, they may bring the rhythm of this activity into relation with the rhythm of the input. . . . We have seen here, both from the data we have reported on, and also very strikingly from the data reported by Condon and Ogston, that the synchrony of the listener's behavior to that of the speaker may be very precise indeed. The precision of the synchrony suggests that the listeners are responding to a rhythm with which they are thoroughly familiar. This rhythm is of course, largely the rhythm of speech, the rhythmical character of the syllabic pulse, and for those who have a given language in common this rhythm must be familiar. . . . It seems plausible, thus, that the minute synchrony observable between interactants is a product of their attention to an input where rhythmical structuring is highly familiar to them. (Kendon, 1967b, pp. 36–37)

The work of Condon and Ogston (1966, 1967) has dealt with synchronous relations of a speaker's verbal cues to his own and his addressee's nonverbal behaviors. One implication of their work is the existence of a kind of coactive regulation of communicator-addressee behaviors which is an intrinsic part of social interaction and which is certainly not exhausted through a consideration of speech alone. Kendon (1967a) recognized these and other functions that are also served by implicit behaviors, particularly eye contact. He noted that looking at another person helps in getting information about how that person is behaving (that is, to monitor), in regulating the initiation and termination of speech, and in conveying emotionality or intimacy. With regard to the regulatory function, Kendon's (1967a) findings showed that when the speaker and his listener are about to change roles, the speaker looks in the direction of his listener as he stops talking, and his listener in turn looks away as he starts speaking. Further, when speech is fluent, the speaker looks more in the direction of his listener than when his speech is disrupted with errors and hesitations. Looking away during these awkward moments implies recognition by the speaker that he has less to say, and is demanding less attention from his listener. It also provides the speaker with some relief to organize his thoughts.

The concept of regulation has also been studied by Scheflen (1964, 1965). According to him, a communicator may use changes in posture, eye contact, or position to indicate that (1) he is about to make a new point, (2) he is assuming an attitude relative to several points being made by himself or his addressee, or (3) he wishes to temporarily remove himself from the communication situation, as would be the case if he were to select a great distance from the addressee or begin to turn his back on him. There are many interesting aspects of this regulative function of nonverbal cues that have been dealt with only informally.

In addition to studying the emotion-conveying, regulating, or body-adaptation functions, investigators have also focused on the structural qualities of implicit communications, irrespective of any functions that these might have in the communication process. Duncan (1969) provided a review of such studies that "sought to identify fundamental elements (or units) of nonverbal behaviors, and to explore the systematic relationships among these units . . . the questions are: (*a*) Out of all behaviors which are possible to perform, which ones actually occur in communication? and (*b*) Do these selected communicative behaviors occur in characteristic sequences or clusters with other behaviors in the same or a different modality?" (p. 121). Accordingly, one primary hope and goal of studies of the structural qualities of implicit communications was to discover how "the pieces are organized into standard units . . . recognizable at a glance and recordable with a stroke" (Scheflen, 1966, p. 277).

In some studies of this kind, investigators have succeeded in showing some sequential dependencies or correlated behaviors in different channels. The studies of Boomer (1963) and Dittmann and Llewellyn (1968, 1969) exemplify such an approach. However, their findings fall far short of identifying structural hierarchies similar to those used by linguists working with verbal behaviors. Indeed, in a recent review Dittmann (1971) showed that the probe into these structural notions, for which Birdwhistell (1952, 1970) must be given primary credit, has been quite disappointing and has not led to the identification of any major organizational units.

Other studies that relate to the structural approach are purely descriptive (McQuown, 1957; Pittenger, Hockett, and Danehy, 1960; Pittenger and Smith, 1957; and Trager, 1958, for phonemic and paralinguistic transcription systems; Birdwhistell, 1952, 1970, for kinesic behavior). A notation system that was designed for dance is by far the most comprehensive method available for recording body movements (Hutchinson, 1970). Its detailed signs allow the recording of such diverse movements as those of the eyes and other parts of the face and those of the toes, together with the possibility of specifying the speed of movements. Such notation systems were devised for various facets of implicit behavior. No attempt was made to relate the categories of each to the functions which these categories might serve in interpersonal processes. Wiener and Mehrabian (1968) argued that such notation and category systems generally have failed to relate meaningfully to communicator states, feelings, emotions, communicator characteristics, relations among communicators, or other communication behaviors. Therefore, the systems are seldom used by other investigators. In contrast, the categories that have been elaborated with a view to their significance in the communication process (as exemplified by the proxemic categories of Hall, 1963) have been far more productive in generating research interest and empirical findings for understanding the communication process.

CULTURAL DIFFERENCES

Recent literature also contains some consideration of the cultural differences in implicit communication codes. Hall (1959, 1966) was one of the first researchers to point out the difficulties encountered during an interaction between members of different cultures. Such difficulties can be accounted for by the unquestioned and implicit assumptions people make when they try to interpret the behaviors of others, whether the latter be from their own, or from a different, culture. There is unfortunately very little experimental evidence to document the differences in the communication codes of various cultures or subcultures. The available studies are reviewed briefly below.

Efron's (1941) early observations of Jewish and Italian immigrants in the United States showed a greater preference for closeness and touching among the Jews. Whereas the Jews made more frequent use of emphasis-type illustrators, the Italians had a greater preference for those illustrators that redundantly describe the shape of the object that is being referred to with words.

Differential preferences of proxemic (Hall, 1963, 1964) or immediacy (Mehrabian, 1967a; Wiener and Mehrabian, 1968) cues have been the major focus of the available studies of cultural communication codes. Immediacy behaviors are those which increase the mutual sensory stimulation between two persons. Several studies have shown consistent cultural and subcultural differences in immediacy-related behavior. Watson and Graves (1966) found Arab students more immediate in their implicit social behaviors vis-à-vis each other than American students. The Arabs oriented more directly toward each other, were closer, touched more, had more eye contact, and talked louder. In comparing the preferred immediacy levels of a set of five cultures, Little (1968) requested subjects of various national groups to position dolls relative to one another to portray a variety of social situations. His findings indicated that, averaging over the different social situations, Greeks, Americans, Italians, Swedes, and Scots, in that order, assigned increasing distances between communicators.

There are also two studies of immediacy preferences of various subcultures in the United States. Among his American subjects, Willis (1966) found that blacks greeted others at greater distances than did whites; this was especially the case when the persons being greeted were also blacks. Baxter (1970) replicated this finding in the most thorough experiment of immediacy preferences among various ethnic groups available to date. His observations of pairs of subjects visiting at a zoo showed that Mexicans stood closest to one another and Anglos next closest. Blacks selected the most distant positions.

To summarize, the present approach makes the traditional distinction between verbal-linguistic communication and the phenomena of nonverbal communication. However, the subtle aspects of social interaction that are discussed in the nonverbal communication literature should more appropriately and generically be termed *implicit* behaviors, distinct from verbal-linguistic, or explicit, behaviors. The word *implicit* is used below when the entire realm of phenomena is the referent, and the concept *nonverbal* is reserved for special instances when actions, rather than words, are the referent. Although it is recognized that implicit behaviors have several functions, the work described below deals primarily with only one of these functions—the affect or attitude communication value. (The other functions have been detailed by Argyle, 1969; Duncan, 1969; and Ekman and Friesen, 1969b). Since people differ in their characteristic emotional reactions to others, the present approach readily provides a means for studying individual differences in implicit communication. These individual differences are therefore a frequent object of study in the following chapters.

Categorizing Implicit Behaviors from the Standpoint of Their Referents

One of the most troublesome aspects of research in any relatively unexplored area of study is the determination of basic categories or dimensions that cut across most of the phenomena of interest. In the study of implicit behaviors, this has been an ever present problem. Numerous categories can be selected from the following realms: communication behaviors, such as facial expressions, verbalizations, movements, or postures; referents, such as feelings or attitudes; communicator or addressee attributes, such as personality, psychological well-being, age, sex, or status; or communication media, such as face-to-face, telephone, or video interactions.

What are the important behaviors to explore in studying implicit communication? Although any behavior is in principle communicative—since it is observable and has some significance—certain behaviors are more a part of communication than others (for example, facial expressions in contrast to foot movements). The selection of implicit cues for study has sometimes been based on expressive qualities—that is, pathology-related attributes (Braatoy, 1954; Deutsch, 1947, 1952; Deutsch and Murphy, 1955; or Reich, 1945) or personality-related attributes (Allport and Vernon, 1967). Such psychoanalysts as Braatoy or Reich interpreted postural rigidity to indicate obsessional tendencies and greater resistance to change. Some clinicians were also interested in the identification of particular moods or feelings from specific behaviors (Fromm-Reichmann, 1950). Experimental investigations led to the identification of seven affects that were consensually coded into facial and vocal expressions, but failed to provide a general framework for the classification of nonverbal behavior (for example, findings reviewed by Davitz, 1964; Ekman, 1972; Tomkins and McCarter, 1964; or Woodworth and Schlosberg, 1954, Chapter 5).

In our present approach, the basic categories are developed from a detailed consideration of the referents, and not of the communication behaviors or the communicator-addressee attributes. The dimensions that are used to characterize the referents in turn provide a framework for classifying and studying the effects of the latter factors. Referents were chosen as the starting point because the existing implicit communication literature provides adequate evidence to characterize them in a quite general way. Considering some of this evidence, the referents are described in terms of a three-dimensional framework: evaluation, potency or status, and responsiveness. Positive evaluation is communicated by facial and vocal cues (which express variations in liking) and also by several postures and positions (a closer position, a greater forward lean, increased eye contact, and more direct orientation). Postural relaxation conveys potency or status, and increasing implicit activity (such as facial or vocal activity) expresses responsiveness to another person.

FACIAL AND VOCAL EXPRESSIONS

One of the first attempts for a more general characterization of the referents of implicit behavior and, therefore, possibly of the behaviors themselves, was made by Schlosberg (1954). He suggested a three-dimensional framework involving pleasantness-unpleasantness, sleep-tension, and attention-rejection. Any feeling could be assigned a value on each of these three dimensions, and different feelings would correspond to different points in this three-dimensional space. This shift away from the study of isolated feelings and their corresponding nonverbal cues and toward a characterization of the general referents of nonverbal behavior on a limited set of dimensions was seen as beneficial. It was hoped that it could aid in the identification of large classes of interrelated nonverbal behaviors.

Recent factor-analytic work by Williams and Sundene (1965) and Osgood (1966) provided further impetus for characterizing the referents of implicit behavior in terms of a limited set of dimensions. Williams and Sundene (1965) found that facial, vocal, or facial-vocal cues can be categorized primarily in terms of three orthogonal factors: general evaluation, social control, and activity.

For facial expression of emotions, Osgood (1966) suggested the following dimensions as primary referents: pleasantness (joy and glee versus dread and anxiety), control (annoyance, disgust, contempt, scorn, and loathing versus dismay, bewilderment, surprise, amazement, and excitement), and activation (sullen anger, rage, disgust, scorn, and loathing versus despair, pity, dreamy sadness, boredom, quiet pleasure, complacency, and adoration).

> One would expect to find a close relation between the dimensions operating here and those repeatedly found with the semantic differential technique . . . applied to linguistic signs. Pleasantness and Activation appear to be semantically identical with Evaluation and Activity, two of the three major factors in the general semantic space; what we have called the Control dimension is similar in semantic tone to the Potency factor—*scorn, sullen anger* and the like seem to imply strength and *bewilderment, surprise* and the like weakness— but the relation is not as compelling. (Osgood, 1966, p. 27)

HAND GESTURES

In one of the few studies available in the area of hand gesturing, Gitin (1970) presented 36 photographs of hand gestures to subjects who rated each of the photographs on 40 semantic differential scales. Her first three factors were characterized by the following sets of scales:

Factor I: active-passive, sharp-dull, interesting-uninteresting, tense-sleepy, exciting-boring, curious-indifferent, meaningful-senseless, and intentional-unintentional.

Factor II: pleasant-unpleasant, friendly-unfriendly, good-bad, and beautiful-ugly.

Factor III: submissive-dominant, weak-strong, unarmed-armed, doubtful-certain, shy-brave, and slow-fast.

Gitin's first factor corresponds to our responsiveness dimension, which is referred to as *activation* or *activity* in other studies. Her second factor is the counterpart of our evaluation dimension. Her third factor relates to the potency or status dimension. The semantic differential scales corresponding to these three factors further help clarify the referential significance of an important aspect of nonverbal behavior (hand gestures), as well as other implicit behaviors in general.

It is interesting to find that, at least for facial, vocal and manual expression, similar dimensions characterize the referents of implicit as well as explicit verbal behaviors. Such a correspondence is reassuring, for it confirms the expected similarity for cognitive categories despite the dissimilarity of communication channels. The similarities further suggest the possibility—as with verbal communications—of identifying other classes of implicit communication that relate primarily to one of the three referential dimensions. This indeed seems to be the case for those aspects of social interaction involving stationary postures and positions.

POSTURE AND POSITION

Scheflen (1964, 1965, 1966) provided detailed observations of an informal quality on the significance of postures and positions in interpersonal situations. Along similar lines, Kendon (1967a) and Exline and his colleagues explored the many-faceted significance of eye contact with, or observation of, another (Exline, 1962, 1963, 1972; Exline and Eldridge, 1967; Exline, Gray, and Schuette, 1965; Exline and Winters, 1965). These investigators consistently found, among same-sexed pairs of communicators, that females generally had more eye contact with each other than did males; also, members of both sexes had less eye contact with one another when the interaction between them was aversive (Exline, Gray, and Schuette, 1965). In generally positive exchanges, males had a tendency to decrease their eye contact over a period of time, whereas females tended to increase it (Exline and Winters, 1965).

One very distinctive aspect of the methodologies employed by Exline and his colleagues in some of their studies should be carefully considered in interpreting their findings. These investigators' experimental confederates behaved in specified ways with subjects whose behaviors were the dependent measures in the various situations. Specifically, the confederates were instructed to either look at the subject with a steady gaze (100 per cent eye contact) or to look away (zero eye contact). Such extreme variations in the visual behavior of the confederate can facilitate the experimental control of his behaviors and are likely to maximize the effects of eye contact on the various dependent measures. However, the drawback of the method used in these studies (for example, Exline and Eldridge, 1967) was that the visual behavior of the confederate was quite unusual, rarely occurring in everyday social interactions. For instance, extensive data provided by Kendon (1967a) showed that observation of another person during a social exchange varied from about 30 per cent to 70 per cent, and that corresponding figures for eye contact ranged from 10 per cent to 40 per cent.

Mehrabian (1968d, 1969b) reviewed experimental findings relating to the communication of attitudes (evaluation and liking) and status (potency or social control) via posture and position cues. Physical proximity, touching, eye contact, a forward lean rather than a reclining position, and an orientation of the torso toward rather than away from an addressee have all been found to communicate a more positive attitude toward him. A second set of cues that indicates postural relaxation includes asymmetrical placement of the limbs, a sideways lean and/or reclining position by the seated communicator, and specific relaxation measures of the hands or neck. This second set of cues relates primarily to status differences between a communicator and his addressee: there is more relaxation with an addressee of lower status, and less relaxation with one of higher status. Although the relaxation cues are intercorrelated and have been extracted as factors in some experiments (Mehrabian and Williams, 1969), the proxemic (Hall, 1963, 1966) or immediacy (Mehrabian, 1967a; Wiener and Mehrabian, 1968) cues are not intercorrelated. However, insofar as the set of immediacy cues (1) do together reflect a more positive attitude toward an addressee, (2) can be conceptually related as increasing the physical proximity between a communicator and his addressee, and (3) increase the mutual sensory stimulation between the communicators, there is some basis for grouping the cues as part of a single nonverbal dimension.

In sum, the findings from studies of posture and position and subtle variations in verbal statements (Wiener and Mehrabian, 1968) show that immediacy cues primarily denote evaluation, and postural relaxation cues denote status or potency in a relationship. It is interesting to note a weaker effect: less relaxation of one's posture also conveys a more positive attitude toward another. One way to interpret this overlap in the referential significance of less relaxation and more immediacy in communicating a more positive feeling is in terms of the implied positive connotations of higher status in our culture. A respectful attitude (that is, when one conveys that the other is of higher status) does indeed have implied positive connotations. Therefore it is not surprising that the communication of respect and of positive attitude exhibits some similarity in the nonverbal cues that they require. However, whereas the communication of liking is more heavily weighted by variations in immediacy, that of respect is weighted more by variations in relaxation.

The results for posture and position cues reviewed above were not obtained within the framework presently being proposed; rather, the framework evolved from these studies. The general correspondence of these findings with those of Gitin (1970), Osgood (1966), Osgood, Suci, and Tannenbaum (1957), and of studies reported in Snider and Osgood (1969) and Williams and Sundene (1965) suggested further exploration of the approach for other implicit cues. Therefore, this framework is used below to discuss various aspects of communication, such as facial movement, vocal expressions, and verbalizations.

MOVEMENTS AND IMPLICIT ASPECTS OF VERBALIZATION

Mahl, Danet, and Norton (1959) suggested that movement information complements verbal messages by anticipating, contradicting, or being concurrent with the referents of the verbal channel. More specific work by Ekman (1964, 1965) and Ekman and Friesen (1967) on the referents of movements of various body parts showed that stationary positions communicate gross affects (that is, attitudes), whereas movements and facial expressions communicate specific emotions.

Rosenfeld (1966a, 1966b) used a role-playing paradigm in which his subjects were requested to interact with someone and elicit varying degrees of liking from him. The implicit behaviors of the subjects were the dependent measures. Higher speech rates, lengthier communications, frequent verbal reinforcers to the addressee, gesticulation, smiling, positive head nods, and less frequent self references were found to be associated with the attempt to elicit more liking.

In the two studies described below, it was assumed that in certain interpersonal situations the implicit communication of attitudes is either more appropriate or a necessary concomitant of the communicator's affect. For instance, Zaidel and Mehrabian (1969) found that communicators were able to express variations in negative affect better than variations in positive affect, whether using facial or vocal channels. Perhaps implicit expressions of negative attitude are practiced more than are positive ones, because it is seldom appropriate to express negative feelings openly. Thus, negative feelings are delegated to these subtle channels more frequently than are positive feelings, and people become proficient at implicitly expressing their negative feelings rather than their positive feelings.

In stress situations, implicit channels once again may become salient indicators, particularly when the communicator is unwilling to express his feelings explicitly. Early psychoanalytic interest in nonverbal behavior was primarily motivated by this assumption (for example, Deutsch and Murphy, 1955). The recent interest in the detection of deceit from implicit behaviors also seems to be related (Ekman and Friesen, 1969a).

The importance of implicit behaviors is highlighted in situations in which unfamiliar persons interact, with one seeking to influence the other (as in political speeches or advertising). Verbal expression of feelings toward another is less permissible in these situations than is an argument or information relating to the topic in question. In the experiments summarized below, the interactions involved dyads, mostly of peers. One member of each dyad was a confederate of the experimenter. This member exhibited a prearranged set of behaviors designed to seem "normal" for that situation. The other member of the dyad, the actual subject, was observed through a one-way mirror. His or her behaviors were video recorded.

Perceived and Intended Persuasiveness. In the first two experiments reported by Mehrabian and Williams (1969), subjects presented messages to someone else, employing varying degrees of persuasion. The subjects' nonverbal, vocal, and verbal behaviors were recorded and analyzed. The movement cues rated were lateral swivels in a desk chair, rocking, head nodding, gesticulation, self-manipulation such as scratching or tapping one part of a hand with another, and leg and foot movements. Measures relating to the facial expressions included facial pleasantness and activity. Measures relating to verbalizations were length of communication in terms of number of words or duration, speech rate, the unhalting quality of speech, speech error rate, volume, and activity. The criteria for scoring these categories of implicit behavior are summarized in Appendix A.

The analyses of these data led to the postulation of an activity dimension for implicit behaviors. The variables grouped under this dimension included facial and vocal activity, speech volume, and speech rate. Whereas immediacy and relaxation indicate variations in liking and status respectively, activity communicates responsiveness (note Bentler's 1969 data for adjectives), and is a function of the salience of the addressee.

The findings from these persuasion studies showed that a communicator's activity increased with his intention to persuade, and the perceived persuasiveness of a message was correlated with the level of activity exhibited implicitly by the communicator. Both of the encoding experiments yielded this major effect relating activity and persuasion. A second, though weaker, relationship occurred between attempted persuasiveness and immediacy: communicators were more immediate to an addressee when they attempted to be more persuasive. Further, more immediate communications were also perceived as more persuasive in the two experiments.

Findings for the implicit concomitants of persuasion can be readily summarized: positive responsiveness to an addressee enhances the perceived persuasiveness of a message. When a person attempts to be persuasive, he exhibits more positive responsiveness to the addressee.

Deceit. Three of our experiments have explored the implicit behavioral concomitants of deceitful and truthful communications (Mehrabian, 1971a). A variety of paradigms were used in which a subject communicated deceitfully or truthfully to someone else. All the behaviors noted in the preceding discussion of perceived and intended persuasiveness were recorded and scored.

Findings from two of the Mehrabian (1971a) experiments indicated that immediacy toward an addressee is greater when one is truthful than deceitful. In the first experiment, the subject was either promised a reward for successful deceit or threatened that he would receive an electric shock if his deceit was detected. Subjects who were promised reward were more immediate when truthful than when deceitful, but there was no corresponding significant difference when subjects were threatened with shock. The second experiment involved role-playing of deceit versus role-playing of truth. Subjects were found to be more immediate while they were role-playing at being truthful than at being deceitful.

Relaxation was not a discriminator between deceit and truth in any of the experiments. Subjects in the first experiment who anticipated possible reward were more relaxed than those who anticipated possible shock. The second experiment indicated that males were generally more relaxed than females. Finally, in the third experiment, the subjects were induced to cheat in an ESP study by a confederate, so that their motivation to be deceitful in a subsequent interview with the experimenter was maximized. In this case, extroverts were found to be more relaxed than introverts.

Thus, these deceit studies provided further validity for the relaxation cues, and suggested a relationship between immediacy of postures and deceitful versus truthful communication, while not providing any relationship between activity level and deceit.

The experimental data reviewed thus far provided a preliminary basis for grouping nonverbal and implicit verbal communication cues, and indicated the primary significance of each of three sets of cues in a variety of social situations. These three sets of cues provide a way of objectively characterizing social interaction. To facilitate further exploration of the interrelationships among these cues and their relation to the personality of participants and the social situations in which they interact, the following section touches on the theoretical significance of these groupings.

Summary and Rationale for the Choice of Semantic Dimensions

Why did the three proposed referential dimensions—positiveness, potency or status, and responsiveness—emerge as particularly relevant in nonverbal communication? Our answer is based on the premise that non-verbal behavior is a developmentally earlier and more primitive form of communication which man shares with animals (for example, Werner, 1957; Werner and Kaplan, 1963). Such a premise implies that nonverbal behaviors reflect very basic social orientations that are correlates of major categories in the cognition of social environments (Piaget, 1960). Positive-negative affect and evaluation are basic cognitive distinctions made from early infancy and retained in adult life—they determine approach and avoidance tendencies toward objects or persons. The evaluation of objects and persons is a crucial aspect of intelligent functioning and even of survival. It is therefore not surprising that people possess behavioral correlates for this cognitive distinction—the immediacy cues—which are ever-present in social interaction.

The second dimension, status or potency, relates to social control. It is particularly salient in the social life of animals, as observed in the phenomenon of territoriality (for example, Calhoun, 1962), and is a major determiner of social interaction patterns among humans. This is especially evident in the highly stratified, authoritarian cultures but can be seen in even the most democratic societies (for example, Hall, 1966).

Responsiveness is conceptualized as the nonverbal-social counterpart of the orienting reflex (for example, Maltzman, 1967). As such it is another elementary and basic aspect of social life. The degree of responsiveness one person displays toward another indicates the other's salience for him. It is elicited by nonneutral events or persons (extreme instances being unusually reinforcing or threatening ones). In cognition (as in responsiveness), unusual events of either positive or negative quality are grouped and reacted to similarly, as exemplified by the concept of *mana* in many primitive cultures (for example, Cassirer, 1953–57). The differential responsiveness of humans or animals to various aspects of their social environment distinguishes them from the inanimate world and, together with the preceding two cognitive distinctions (evaluation and judgment of social power), is a basic aspect of intelligent (adaptive, *à la* Piaget, 1960) functioning.

The rather general quality of these cognitive and behavioral dimensions for both animal and human social systems provides a plausible basis for using data obtained from the social interaction of animals. Primates, in particular, can provide complementary information about certain aspects of affect and attitude communication in humans. For instance, Sommer (1967) summarized some of the research that related the spatial arrangement of persons in a variety of social situations to their social status. A number of the studies Sommer reviewed were motivated by observations of the more familiar phenomenon of territoriality in animals (Ardrey, 1966; Lorenz, 1966; McBride, 1964). Even an informal observation of chimpanzees living together provides impressive differences in the postures, positions, movements, and facial expressions of dyads differing in status. Since status or potency is readily specified in terms of size or strength in such animal social systems, investigation of the nonverbal correlates of potency is considerably simplified and may yield nonverbal interaction cues that have transcultural relevance. More generally, the observation of animal social interactions can complement the study of individuals of a single culture, such as American college students, and provide corroboration for identified dimensions of social interaction.

The Language of Posture and Position

The Historical Context

It was in contexts where overt expressions of feelings were not possible that psychoanalysts first noted the significance of nonverbal cues. Postures (for example, bodily relaxation or limb position) and positions (distance, orientation of the head and body, including eye contact) were used as a source of information about client's characteristics, attitudes, and feelings about themselves and others. Deutsch (1947, 1952) was among those who wrote informally on the subject. Based on case studies, he suggested that a client's posture reflected those motivations, attitudes, and intentions that might not have been verbalized. Deutsch also noted that characteristic postures were associated with the initiation and termination of speech. Deutsch and Murphy (1955) and Feldman (1959) provided several specific examples of how clients' feelings and attitudes could be inferred from their postures, mannerisms, and gestures. Feldman described some 200 mannerisms and gestures, and related these to maladjustment and the withholding of information.

Reich (1945) and Braatoy (1954) argued that postural rigidity or tension was an important measure of the difficulty a clinician would expect to encounter in trying to introduce changes in a client. In agreement with Reich and Braatoy, Lowen (1958) indicated that a client's characteristics were closely intertwined with his typical postures and gestures and, therefore, the modification of client characteristics could be enhanced through the manipulation of these nonverbal behaviors. Like Deutsch and Murphy (1955), Fromm-Reichmann (1950) used the changing postures of her clients to infer their feelings. She went further by imitating their postures herself in order to facilitate her own intuitive inference of their unverbalized feelings.

Unfortunately, although many psychoanalysts suggested a relationship between postural cues and feelings or attitudes, their observations for the most part remained informal. Thus, no specific hypotheses for such relationships were propounded or experimentally explored.

More recently, however, experimental evidence on the significance of posture and position cues in social situations has been accumulating rapidly. In reviewing and integrating these findings, the concept of "liking" will be used as an abbreviation for positive evaluation and/or preference of one person for another. A second important referent of postural cues has been identified as potency or status. The potency or status a person feels and communicates can be assessed with semantic differential scales such as the ones given in Tables A.1 of Appendix A (taken from Mehrabian and Russell, 1972). Alternatively, a satisfactory single index of status is occupational level (for example, as measured by Roe's scale, 1956), which is a correlate of both occupational and social prestige (Kahl, 1964). If social status is defined in terms of occupational level, then age, particularly in the range up to the late twenties, is a correlate of social status.

Ekman and Friesen (1967) considered the differential role of nonverbal cues in the communication of gross affect (for example, positive-negative attitude) versus specific affect (fear or elation). They presented a reformulation of Ekman's (1964, 1965) findings on the relative roles of bodily and facial cues in the communication of affect, and suggested that stationary facial expressions and postures are more likely to communicate gross affect (for example, liking), whereas facial and bodily movements are more likely to communicate specific emotions. The study of posture and position cues is thus useful for inferring liking, particularly when a communicator does not, or cannot, express his positive-negative emotions in the more readily recognized verbalizations or facial movements.

Although there is no general theory to relate posture and position cues to the communications of like-dislike and potency or status, a few concepts of broad relevance are available. A case in point is Hall's (1963) concept of proxemics, or the study of man's use of space as an aspect of his culture. Some proxemic variables are: distance between a speaker and his listener, the speaker's orientation (that is, the degree to which his body is turned toward, versus away from, his listener), touching, and eye contact between the speaker and the listener. Thus, the concept of proxemics subsumes variations in posture and distance and relates to the *immediacy* of interaction, which is the extent of mutual sensory stimulation between two persons (Mehrabian, 1967a; Wiener and Mehrabian, 1968). In addition to eye contact and directness of body orientation, Machotka (1965) noted that the accessibility of a speaker's body to the listener (such as the openness in the arrangement of his arms) also communicates varying degrees of liking. Such accessibility can also be construed as a proxemic variable.

Being an anthropologist, Hall (1959, 1963, 1964, 1966) used the concept of proxemics to describe characteristic spatial relationships (including territorial phenomena) among persons in various cultures, or within a given culture for different kinds of social occasions. His discussions relied on informal observations that related proxemic behaviors to other characteristics of the culture to form a meaningful whole. In discussing the Japanese, for instance, Hall (1966) noted how the nobility were arranged in concentric zones about Tokyo. Those nobles placed closest to the center were considered more intimate and loyal to the emperor. Hall also described how this concentric arrangement about an important center point was a pervasive aspect of Japanese culture. Thus, even though he focused on the broad cultural implications of proxemic and territorial phenomena, there were scattered throughout Hall's writings informal observations relating proxemic variables to liking. The preceding discussion of the arrangement of Japanese nobility, for instance, shows that the more liked and preferred nobles were allowed to assume a position more immediate to the emperor.

This relationship between liking and proxemics was formulated as the immediacy hypothesis by Mehrabian (1967a) and Wiener and Mehrabian (1968): more immediate postures and positions of a communicator are associated with his greater liking of the addressee, and lead the addressee to infer that the communicator likes him more. However, it is helpful to draw on Hall's (1964, 1966) observations to qualify this generalization. In his discussion of the significance of proxemic cues, Hall noted that each culture and/or subculture holds implicit norms regarding the permissible range of proximity between two speakers. In the case of distance, Hall (1966, p. 126) distinguished four zones: zero to 1½ feet for intimate; 1½ to 4 feet for personal; 4 to 10 feet for social-consultive; and 10 feet and over for public interactions among North Americans.

Hall suggested further that a communicator who violates these implicit distance limits will elicit negative feelings from his addressee. He described several interactions between communicators from various cultures where differences in the implicit norms for social distances led to misunderstandings about attitudes (Hall, 1959). In support of Hall's observations, Garfinkel (1964) found that violation of implicit norms regarding permissible physical closeness led to the bewilderment and embarrassment of an addressee and to his subsequent avoidance of the communicator. Felipe and Sommer (1966) also found that when someone assumed an inappropriately close position to another person, that person left his place earlier than he otherwise would have.

The implications of observations about implicit distance limits are that the immediacy hypothesis holds for variations in the distance that a communicator might assume within the acceptable range of distances for a given kind of social situation. Thus, standing one foot away from a stranger is inappropriate, since the relationship is not intimate, and leads to a negative, or avoidance, reaction (Felipe and Sommer, 1966). In general then, excessively immediate postures or positions (that is, those that exceed the implicit social norms of a subculture for a given situation) induce negative feelings.

An early experimental study by James (1932), which dealt with the feeling or attitude communicating significance of posture, is directly relevant to the immediacy hypothesis. Using photographs of a masked male model as stimuli, James asked three subjects what attitude was being expressed by each posture and which portions of the posture were most significant. In the 347 photographs James used, the positions of head, trunk, feet, knees, and arms were systematically varied—certain combinations being eliminated due to their awkward nature. He then selected 30 of these photographs on the basis of the highest judgment agreement among his subjects. Two additional experiments, in which other subjects interpreted this set of 30 selected postures, yielded four postural categories: (1) approach—an attentive posture communicated by a forward lean of the body; (2) withdrawal—a negative, refusing, or repulsed posture communicated by drawing back or turning away; (3) expansion— a proud, conceited, arrogant, or disdainful posture communicated by an expanded chest, erect or backward-leaning trunk, erect head, and raised shoulders; and (4) contraction—a depressed, downcast, or dejected posture communicated by a forward-leaning trunk, a bowed head, drooping shoulders, and a sunken chest. For each of these four generic categories, the head and trunk positions were found to be the most important indicators; however, specific discriminations within each category were determined by the position of hands and arms. In his third experiment, James found that a subject's conclusions in any given instance were generally the same whether he viewed the posture and interpreted it, or viewed and imitated the posture and then interpreted it. In addition, a decoder subject's inference was affected by the situation in which the posture occurred.

James' (1932) categories of approach and withdrawal relate to our immediacy variables, forward lean and body orientation. His findings showed that a forward lean conveyed greater liking whereas a backward lean or turning away showed a more negative attitude. The expansion category seems relevant to the communication of arrogance (that is, high status and slight dislike), whereas the contraction category seems to indicate a communicator's weakness (symbolizing low status) and unresponsiveness to others.

In the review of the more recent literature that follows, the findings for each cue are treated separately.

DISTANCE

National and ethnic differences in the preference for proximity or immediacy have been studied mainly in terms of characteristic interpersonal distance preferences. These studies, which were already discussed in Chapter 1, are reviewed briefly here. Watson and Graves (1966) found that Arab students assumed more immediate (for example, closer) positions relative to one another during social interaction than did North American students. Among his American subjects, Willis (1966) found that blacks greeted one another from farther distances than did whites. This result was replicated by Baxter (1970), who found that Mexicans stood closest to each other, whites next closest, and blacks farthest apart. Little (1968) requested subjects of various national groups to position dolls to appropriately simulate a variety of social situations. His findings showed that, on the average, Greeks, Americans, Italians, Swedes, and Scots, in that order, assigned increasing distances between communicators.

Little (1968) also investigated the effects of affect and familiarity on the distances between the dolls. He found that "friends are seen as interacting closer together than acquaintances, and acquaintances closer than strangers. In regard to affect, however, although pleasant topics clearly produced the closest placement of the figures, the neutral and unpleasant topic situations were not significantly different" (Little, 1968, p. 5). Although Little's data provided a basis for assessing the effect of status differences on distance, his analyses of the data did not yield such information. He did indicate, however, that "women see interactions of women with authority figures or superiors taking place at a greater distance than men view similar transactions of male figures" (p. 5).

Baxter (1970) also provided some sex difference data. He found that male-female pairs assumed the closest positions relative to each other, next the female-female pairs, and finally the male-male pairs, who were the most distant. For his age variable, Baxter found that children assumed the closest positions relative to one another, then adolescents, and finally adults, who interacted from the farthest distances.

Variations in distance within the culturally acceptable limits were related to liking of the addressee in a number of findings. Sommer (1967, 1969) reviewed some of these studies. Leipold (1963) used an encoding method in which, prior to an interview, subjects were told by a confederate of the experimenter whether to expect a positive or a negative evaluation. Subjects who expected a negative evaluation selected chairs that were farther away from the experimenter during the interview than did those who expected a positive evaluation. Little (1965), using line drawings, silhouettes, and live actresses, asked subjects to select (encode) appropriate distances between them to convey various attitudes. His subjects selected shorter distances to depict intimate relationships between communicators.

Rosenfeld (1965) instructed his subjects to role-play (encode) an approval-seeking in contrast to an approval-avoiding attitude toward another "subject" (a confederate in the experiment). He found that under the approval-seeking instructions, subjects sat closer to the confederate than they did under the approval-avoiding instructions. Golding (1967) used semantic differential ratings of line drawings involving human figures and found that shorter distances were interpreted (decoded) as accepting and responsive, whereas the reverse interpretation was made for greater distances.

In sum, the findings from several studies corroborated one another: communicator-addressee distance correlated with the degree of negative attitude (dislike) communicated to, and inferred by, the addressee. Baxter's (1970) data, which showed that female-female pairs were closer to each other than were male-male pairs, implied that females characteristically convey more liking to others than do males. In the same way, his data implied that characteristic communications of positive affect decrease with age. Further studies carried out by sociologists and anthropologists have shown that distances that were too close, that is, inappropriate for a given interpersonal situation, elicited negative feelings.

Sommer's (1967) review of status relationships and spatial arrangements suggested that the body orientation of communicators, rather than the distances between them, was a more important variable for the communication of status. Nevertheless, Lott and Sommer (1967) found that people of equal status sat closer to one another than did people of unequal status.

EYE CONTACT

Hall (1963) included eye contact along with distance as an important index of proxemics. In the present context, this suggests that a speaker's eye contact with his listener can serve as a measure of his liking of the listener. A number of findings bear on this assumption. Reece and Whitman (1962) studied the effect of an investigator's warmth and coldness upon a subject's verbal output while the subject free-associated. Warmth of the experimenter was defined as more frequent smiling, the absence of finger tapping movements, more eye contact with the subject, and a greater degree of forward bodily lean toward the subject. They found that the nonverbal variables assumed to indicate warmth or positive attitude did indeed significantly affect the interaction; that is, they were more reinforcing. A subject produced more words when the experimenter nonverbally indicated a more positive attitude toward him. Although Reece and Whitman's findings did not permit an assessment of the individual contribution of greater eye contact on the warmth attributed to the experimenter, other experiments have shown eye contact to be an index of the liking of another person.

Argyle and Kendon (1967) reported an unpublished study by Weisbrod (1965), who studied eye contact patterns in a group. Weisbrod found that a speaker rated those addressees who looked at him more as being instrumental to his goals and valuing him more than did those addressees who looked at him less. She also found that a speaker felt more powerful when he received more eye contact from his addressees. Thus, more eye contact with the speaker conveyed to him a feeling of higher status.

Studies by Exline and his co-workers (Exline, 1963, 1972; Exline and Eldridge, 1967; Exline, Gray, and Schuette, 1965; and Exline and Winters, 1965) and by Nachshon and Wapner (1967) showed that more eye contact of communicators is typically associated with more positive attitudes between them. Exline, Gray, and Schuette (1965) found that female subjects, who tended to be more affiliative than males, had more eye contact with an experimenter than did male subjects. Furthermore, they found that eye contact was less when the experimenter questioned the subjects about potentially embarrassing contents than when he questioned them about innocuous contents. For the sex difference effect, the greater eye contact of the more affiliative females was consistent with their characteristically more positive interpersonal attitudes (Anastasi, 1958; Mehrabian, 1971b). Also, the experimenter who asked relatively innocuous questions was more positive than the one who persistently asked personal and possibly embarrassing questions. Thus, both sets of findings showed that more eye contact was associated with more positive attitudes toward the interviewer.

Exline and Winters (1965) reported that subjects avoided the eyes of an interviewer and disliked him after he had commented unfavorably about their performance. Exline and Eldridge (1967) found that a verbal communication was decoded as more favorable by a subject when it was associated with more eye contact.

Argyle and Dean (1965) found that, for a given degree of liking toward an addressee, eye contact decreased as closeness increased. Fischer reported similar findings: "When three profiles are freely placed, the metric distance between figures facing each other is larger than the distance to the third figure, thus compensating for the latter's lesser perceived social closeness by greater metric closeness" (1968, p. 13). Thus, both eye contact and closeness additively reflected communicator liking for, or intimacy with, the addressee. Increases (or decreases) in eye contact were therefore associated with compensatory decreases (or increases) in closeness when the attitude remained the same.

It is interesting to extrapolate the findings that related eye contact and liking to obtain a hypothesis for the visual behavior of approval-seeking

(Crowne and Marlowe, 1964) or dependent individuals as compared to more independent or dominant persons. To a dependent or approval-seeking individual, other people are almost by definition more important sources of gratification (that is, reinforcers) than they are to an independent person. A dependent person is thus expected to communicate more positive attitudes and greater submissiveness nonverbally (for example, with more eye contact). Efran and Broughton (1966) reported a significant correlation between subjects' scores on the Crowne and Marlowe (1960) measure of approval-seeking tendency and their extent of eye contact with others. However, Efran (1968) failed to replicate that finding in a subsequent study. Additional findings by Exline and Messick (1967) showed that eye contact was used by dependent individuals not only to communicate liking but also to elicit liking when it was not forthcoming. They found that dependent males had more eye contact with a listener who provided them with only a few social reinforcers, whereas dominant males decreased their eye contact with less reinforcing listeners.

Other studies indicated that eye contact was also significantly related to status differences between communicators. Findings by Hearn (1957) implied that eye contact with an addressee was a parabolic function of the status of that addressee, provided distance and other variables were held constant. Thus, eye contact was moderate with a very high-status addressee, at a maximum with a moderately high-status addressee, and at a minimum with a very low-status addressee.

Efran's (1968) study also explored eye contact with moderately high-status versus low-status addressees. He investigated the eye contact of college students, using freshmen as speakers. Each freshman addressed a senior and another freshman simultaneously. Efran found that the higher-status senior received more eye contact than did the lower-status freshman.

Eye contact and physical closeness are both proxemic variables and both exhibit similar relations to attitudes between two persons. Therefore, it should not be surprising to find that cultures having the greatest preference for physical closeness also show a consistently greater preference for more eye contact. The single available finding is by Watson and Graves (1966), who found that Arab students not only preferred closer positions but had more eye contact, touched more, and talked louder than did North American students. In all respects the Arabs engaged in more intense mutual sensory stimulation than did the Americans.

A second aspect of cultural differences in the use of these nonverbal cues is their relation to the degree of social stratification of a given culture—the latter being particularly relevant to the implicit communications of status. It is possible that variations in eye contact as a function of addressee status are more clearly defined in authoritarian than in democratically oriented cultures. Also, in authoritarian cultures body relaxation, such as the sideways lean or reclining angle of a seated communicator, may be a more prominent indicator of addressee status. Finally, well-defined movements (for example, the degree to which a person bows in the Orient) may be even more important in some of these cultures than postural relaxation in communicating status differences.

FORWARD LEAN

James' (1932) study suggested that forward lean conveys a more positive feeling than a reclining position. Reece and Whitman (1962) assumed that a warm experimenter attitude was communicated to the subject if the experimenter leaned forward in his chair, smiled, kept his hands still, and had more eye contact with the subject. The combination of these behaviors was indeed more reinforcing to subjects. However, as has already been noted, their design did not allow one to infer which of these experimenter behaviors were the significant reinforcers in the situation.

BODY ORIENTATION

Body orientation (that is, the degree to which a communicator's shoulders and legs are turned in the direction of, rather than away from, his addressee) can also serve as a measure of his status or of his liking of the addressee. For example, James' (1932) study showed that a more direct orientation is associated with a more positive attitude. Some encoding studies employed body orientation as a dependent measure, that is, feelings toward the addressee were the independent effects. The findings from such studies were more ambiguous than those obtained for distance and eye contact (for example, Argyle and Kendon, 1967). Rosenfeld (1965), for instance, did not find a significant difference in his subjects' body orientation when the subjects were instructed to seek approval (liking) from the addressees compared to when they were told to avoid approval.

The methods of previous studies have invariably involved a covariation between the eye contact and the directness of body orientation of the subjects. Further study of the effects of body orientation requires decoding methods in which the stimuli are prepared to permit separate assessment of the effects of body orientation and eye contact.

ACCESSIBILITY OF THE BODY, OR OPENNESS OF THE ARRANGEMENT OF ARMS AND LEGS

Machotka (1965) asked subjects to rate line drawings displaying different degrees of openness in the arm arrangement of nude female figures. Whereas the figures with closed-arm positions were judged as cold, rejecting, shy, and passive, the figures with moderate or extreme open-arm positions were judged as warm and accepting. Thus, the accessibility of a communicator's posture could also signify liking. Also, it is interesting to note that Machotka's subjects preferred moderate open-arm positions more than either the closed-arm or extreme open-arm positions.

RELAXATION

Schlosberg (1954) considered the dimension of sleep-tension as generally relevant to the expression of emotions. Dittmann, Parloff, and Boomer (1965) had more difficulty selecting pleasant bodily cues than pleasant facial cues for their experiment. As pleasant body positions they chose relaxed postures with little movement; as unpleasant positions, they chose those involving obvious muscle tension or fidgety and nervous activity. In their decoding study, Dittmann, Parloff, and Boomer found that dancers were more attuned to bodily cues than were psychotherapists, and that the latter relied heavily on facial cues in making their judgments. Both psychotherapists and dancers, however, were influenced more by facial than by bodily cues. Thus, bodily relaxation was secondary to facial cues in the communication of affect, making a minimal, but still significant, contribution.

In contrast to its role in conveying pleasantness and liking, bodily relaxation is an important index for the communication of status. Goffman (1961) noted that in psychiatric staff meetings, tension was greater in the lower-status interns than in the higher-status psychiatrists. This implied that a speaker's body relaxation was greater in the presence of a lower-status addressee.

Some Recent Findings on Posture and Position

Several experiments conducted in our laboratory were designed to explore (1) positions and postures associated with the communication of varying degrees of status or liking, and (2) the liking or status levels inferred from these cues. So as not to interrupt the general flow of historical developments in this area of research, only highlights of the findings are described here. Specific methods and results obtained in the individual experiments illustrate some of the problems in experimental design and in methods of data analysis and presentation (Mehrabian, 1967a, 1968a, 1968b, 1969b; Mehrabian and Friar, 1969).

The very complex results of the various experiments on implicit attitude and status communications are best summarized by proposing a two-dimensional scheme to characterize posture and position cues. These essentially independent dimensions are termed *immediacy* and *relaxation*. The immediacy dimension includes touching, distance, forward lean toward the addressee, eye contact, and body orientation, in that order of importance (see Appendix A for specific definitions). Thus, for instance, distance loads more heavily on a general measure of immediacy than does body orientation. Increasing immediacy corresponds to greater degrees of touching, forward lean, eye contact and directness of body orientation, and smaller distances.

The five immediacy cues were grouped together as defining a primary position and posture dimension on the basis of experimental findings as well as conceptual considerations. Distance and forward-lean cues are similar in significance because even when the position of furniture is fixed a person can still decrease or increase his distance from another by assuming either a reclining or a forward-leaning position. Even when he has a choice about where to sit, a communicator can lean forward or recline to emphasize his desire to be closer or farther away from another. Thus, touching, distance, and forward lean are easily related conceptually as variations in the degree of physical proximity between communicator and addressee. Although there are no behavioral data available for touching in relation to liking, some questionnaire data were provided by Jourard (1966) and Jourard and Rubin (1968). Their male and female subjects reported considerably more touching with females than with males. Also, as expected, opposite-sexed pairs reported more touching than did same-sexed pairs. Of these two findings, the first has some implications for the relation between liking and touching. Females are generally more affiliative and convey more positiveness socially (Anastasi, 1958; Mehrabian, 1970b, 1971b). Thus, their tendency to have more tactile contact with others is consistent with the idea that touching is one way to communicate liking. These considerations led us to include touching as an important variable of immediacy. Of the five variables, body orientation has yielded the weakest relationships with liking, and therefore is considered the least important immediacy cue. However, when the effects of body orientation and eye contact were experimentally separated (Mehrabian, 1967a), it was found that females inferred a more positive attitude when the female communicator had a more direct body orientation toward them.

Eye contact and orientation exhibited some relation to both status and liking. Nevertheless, these cues were grouped with the immediacy cues and distinguished from the following relaxation cues because they reflect variations in the extent of a communicator's closeness to, and nonverbal interaction with, his addressee. Thus in all instances more immediacy involves greater physical proximity and/or greater mutual sensory stimulation between the communicator and the addressee.

The grouping of cues within the relaxation dimension is more easily justified (see Appendix A for specific definitions of these cues). Factor analyses of data from two experiments yielded a relaxation factor which was defined by arm-position asymmetry, sideways lean, openness of arm position, leg-position asymmetry, and, in one experiment only, reclining angle (Mehrabian and Williams, 1969). These data showed that openness of arm position was a correlate of arm-position asymmetry and, therefore, of relaxation. Since arm-position asymmetry had the highest loading on the relaxation factor in both experiments, it was subsequently used as the sole measure of arm relaxation.

In some situations it is possible that sideways lean also can serve as a measure of liking. This happens when the lean is toward the addressee. In these instances—when people are seated at an angle to each other—the sideways lean of the communicator can convey some of the positive feelings that are conveyed by facing his addressee and leaning toward him. Thus, for experimental situations that involve communicators in a variety of bodily orientations, it may be important to distinguish between lean toward versus away from the addressee, rather than lean forward versus back, as indicated in Appendix A.

The factor loadings in the experiments reported by Mehrabian and Williams (1969) indicated the following ordering of the relaxation cues that were included in that study: arm-position asymmetry, sideways lean, leg-position asymmetry, and reclining angle. Relying on the data given by Mehrabian (1968a) and Mehrabian and Friar (1969) for the strength of hand and neck relaxation cues relative to status differences, the suggested order of importance for relaxation cues is: arm-position asymmetry, sideways lean, leg-position asymmetry, hand relaxation, neck relaxation, and possibly reclining angle. At this point it is not necessary to speculate further about the importance of these cues in determining relaxation, since the information presently available allows for the experimental exploration of their contribution to the overall judgment of a person's relaxation. In general, however, on both empirical as well as conceptual grounds, we feel reasonably confident in grouping the preceding cues as measures of relaxation.

It is now possible to use this two-dimensional scheme characterizing posture and position cues to summarize the findings for the more common, everyday situations that do not include either a threatening addressee or communicator. Appendix A provides the scoring criteria for relaxation and immediacy. Mehrabian (1969c) suggested a set of weights for the computation of total immediacy and relaxation from specific posture and position variables.

Reanalysis of Mehrabian's (1968a) fourth experiment using these measures of relaxation yielded simple relationships, in contrast to the rather elaborate ones which were previously reported. Mehrabian's (1968a) factorial design included two levels of liking of the addressee (*liked* versus *disliked*), two levels of status relative to the addressee (*high* versus *low*), addressee sex and communicator sex. For the standing communicators of this experiment, analysis of variance of the immediacy measure indicated only one significant effect: communicators were more immediate with liked than disliked addressees. A similar analysis of the relaxation scores yielded two effects: communicators were more relaxed with lower- than with higher-status addressees, and they were also more relaxed with females than with males.

Findings by Mehrabian and Friar (1969) for communicators in a seated position were reanalyzed with a factorial design which included communicator and addressee sex and two levels each of attitude and status. The results of this reanalysis indicated that communicators who were seated assumed a more immediate position to liked than to disliked addressees. Female communicators were generally more immediate to their addressees than male communicators. When the communicator was of lower status than the addressee, there was no significant effect due to addressee sex.

The analysis of the relaxation scores obtained in the Mehrabian and Friar (1969) study showed that a communicator was more relaxed when he was of higher status than his addressee; furthermore, male communicators showed greater relaxation with moderately disliked than with moderately liked addresses; there was no corresponding difference for female communicators. Finally, opposite-sexed communicators were more relaxed with each other than were same-sexed communicators.

A third study which also provided data that was reanalyzed for immediacy and relaxation involved the communication of five degrees of attitude toward an addressee (Mehrabian, 1968b). The results of that study indicated a direct linear relationship between immediacy and liking. Also, relaxation was a decreasing linear function of positive attitude toward an addressee. There was one final interaction effect due to Communicator Sex X Addressee Sex X Liking. The means for this effect showed that, in all instances, relaxation linearly increased with increasing dislike of the addressee, with the exception that male communicators who addressed an extremely disliked male exhibited the lowest level of relaxation; that is, they were tense. This was interpreted as being the result of vigilance elicited by a threatening other.

POSTURE AND POSITION DURING THREAT

The findings from the preceding experiments simply summarized the relationships between immediacy and relaxation on the one hand and communications of liking and status on the other. The social situations that were explored in these experiments represented most of the variations in immediacy and relaxation. However, it should be emphasized that there are certain infrequent social situations involving threat or even bizarre invasions of privacy (that is, high degrees of immediacy with unfamiliar persons) in which the relationships are considerably more complex.

Let us first consider the significance of extremes of relaxation and then proceed to a discussion of the effects of various combinations of tension and immediacy. It has already been noted that for most everyday situations there is a small direct relationship between relaxation and negative attitude. In other words, the more relaxed postures convey a more disrespectful feeling. However, when a person assumes a very tense posture, this also tends to convey a negative feeling, namely fear (Mehrabian, 1968a). Thus, both extreme tension and extreme relaxation indicate more negative feelings than a moderate level of relaxation, since extreme tension shows fear, and extreme relaxation shows disrespect. In general, then, liking is a curvilinear function of relaxation, assuming a maximum value for moderate degrees of relaxation.

Extreme tension occurs when a person feels threatened or when he is threatening. This interpretation was supported by the triple interaction in the Mehrabian (1968b) experiment just discussed which showed that males assumed tense postures when they were in the company of extremely disliked males. The complement of this relationship is that a person who is threatening also tends to assume a tense posture, and his threatening attitude is inferred when postural tension is combined with increased immediacy. In this context, the following finding, as summarized by Ellsworth and Carlsmith, is instructive: "If the topic of conversation is neutral to generally postive, subjects like the interviewer significantly more when she looks them in the eye. . . . But in a conversation which is indirectly but persistently critical of the subject, this relationship is reversed" (Ellsworth and Carlsmith, 1968, p. 18). Thus, increasing immediacy in a threatening relationship (as conveyed by the greater tension which we assume accompanied the experimenter's behavior when she was persistently critical) tends to reverse the significance of these cues.

Evidence for the reversed significance of immediacy cues in a threatening relationship is also offered in several of the experiments reviewed by Exline (1972). When a 100 per cent eye contact condition (that is, a stare) was described to subjects in a questionnaire study, they judged it as considerably more negative than a moderate level of eye contact. Such stares are usually associated with either the invasion of another's privacy or with an effort to humiliate and subdue, both of which correspond to threatening interpersonal attitudes (Exline, 1972). There is corroboration from observations of animals: the direct confrontation of one animal by another with a stare usually leads to a flight reaction on the part of the more submissive animal (Coss, 1970). Indeed, this finding has even been replicated with humans by Strongman and Champness (1968), who found that the less dominant person in a pair was the first to look away.

In sum, there is a special combination of nonverbal cues, tension, and high immediacy, which conveys a threatening attitude. Such an attitude elicits vigilance (tension and increased immediacy) or a flight reaction (tension and nonimmediacy). The choice of one of the latter two reactions is determined by the severity of the threat—a flight being sought when the level of threat is extreme.

More generally, the effects of immediacy and relaxation on inferred liking need to be specified separately for different levels of familiarity and different levels of relative status between communicator and addressee. When a communicator and addressee are of the same status, for instance, variations in relaxation are not expected to have the same effects as when the communicator is of lower status than the addressee. Similarly, these effects are expected to differ when a communicator and addressee are familiar rather than unfamiliar with each other.

Summary

A two-dimensional scheme was proposed to characterize posture and position cues and to summarize their role in the communication of liking and status relations. The first dimension, *immediacy,* subsumes touching, closer position, forward lean, eye contact, and more direct body orientation. The second dimension, *relaxation,* includes those cues that indicate an asymmetrical rather than a symmetrical position of the posture and of the limbs. A person assumes a more immediate position with someone he likes, and greater liking is inferred when the other person is more immediate toward oneself. Higher-status members in a social situation are more relaxed than are lower-status members. Relaxation is also related to liking. We tend to be moderately relaxed with those we like and to assume very relaxed postures with those we dislike or do not respect. Our postures are very tense with persons who are threatening. Finally, females are found to convey more positive feelings than males through their consistent preferences for greater immediacy; further, females convey more submissive attitudes by characteristically assuming less relaxed postures in social situations.

3

Language within Language

Verbal Immediacy

Beyond its use for categorizing posture and position cues, the concept of immediacy broadly describes the extent to which any communication behavior reflects or involves a closer interaction. For the posture and position cues, greater immediacy is the result of increasing physical proximity and/or perceptual availability of the communicator to the addressee. Thus, a face-to-face conversation is more immediate than one via video tape, which in turn is more immediate than a conversation over the telephone. Less immediate still is a communication, such as a letter, involving the written medium only. The basic hypothesis relating immediacy to attitudes predicts that less immediacy is selected by a communicator when he has negative feelings toward his addressee, toward the contents of his communication, or toward the act of communicating those contents (Wiener and Mehrabian, 1968). An employer is using less immediate communication when he expresses discontent to an employee via an intermediary rather than in a face-to-face confrontation. In line with the hypothesis, the employer's choice illustrates his difficulty or discomfort in expressing what he has to say. The "Dear John" letter also exemplifies the preference for a less immediate medium to convey contents that are distressing to express in person.

In this chapter we will deal primarily with verbal immediacy, or those variations which occur within speech itself. The variations to be discussed include linguistic components, such as pronouns, tense, or kinds of symbols (words) used to refer to an object. The linguistic components con-

The first section of this chapter contains revised segments from Chapters 2 and 4 of *Language within Language: Immediacy, a Channel in Verbal Communication,* which I co-authored with Morton Wiener. Copyright (1968) by Appleton-Century-Crofts. Reproduced by permission.

sidered in these analyses include words that designate (1) the object(s) of the communication, (2) a relationship among these objects, (3) an implied or explicit relationship of the speaker to the objects or to their relationships, or (4) a relationship of the speaker to the entire message. The word *object* is used here to refer to persons, inanimate entities, or events, and specific characteristics or attributes of any of these instances.

The following example illustrates some of the components within a statement that are possible sources of immediacy variation. If a speaker is describing a party that he attended, several constructions of the event are possible. For instance, he could say, "I think they enjoyed themselves." By varying one pronoun, it can be specified as to who is enjoying the party: "I think I enjoyed myself," "I think we enjoyed ourselves," "I think you enjoyed yourself (yourselves)." In these variations the speaker either includes or excludes himself from the referent group. Another set of variations results from specifying the different objects of enjoyment: "I think they enjoyed themselves," "I think they enjoyed each other," or "I think they enjoyed the party." There are also variations which specify differences in the speaker's relationship to the objects in the statement, such as "I think I enjoyed their company," "I think they enjoyed my company," "I think we enjoyed each other's company," or "I think I enjoyed the party."

Another verbal component which is amenable to this form of analysis is verb tense. The temporal organization of a statement may vary, as in "I think they enjoy themselves," "I think they were enjoying themselves," "I think they have enjoyed themselves," or "I think they enjoyed themselves."

Variations denoting the speaker's relationship to his message can be seen in the different modifiers he uses. For example, he may ascribe ambiguity to the event ("They acted as if they enjoyed themselves"), or to himself and his particular interpretation of the event ("I think they enjoyed themselves"). On the other hand, he may indicate certainty about the event ("It is obvious that they enjoyed themselves") or within himself ("I am sure they enjoyed themselves"). Each of these examples is a contrast to the simple declarative statement, "They enjoyed themselves."

Instead of attributing all such verbal variations to style or chance, one can consider them a basis for analyzing a communicator's (1) particular experience of an event, (2) relationship to his addressee, or (3) relationship to his message. Wiener and Mehrabian (1968) related immediacy variations to communicator affect on the basis of several complementary considerations. Verbal communications seem to have evolved to denote an "objective" world. Consequently, experiences of affect, evaluation, or preference, which are concomitant with the experience of a complex stimulus, cannot be readily and verbally expressed. That is, in most cultures there are restraints imposed on the communication of affect, evaluation, or preference, particularly when these are negative. If a person experiences affect about an event and does not describe it, then there is an additional component accruing to his experience—the relative uncommunicability of that affect. This unverbalized affect can interfere with the communication process, resulting in ambiguous or idiosyncratic references to internal states. It can also lead to speech disruptions such as the slips, errors, or false starts analyzed by Mahl (1959), or to blocking and hesitation. For example, if someone cannot use the direct form, "Jack makes me anxious," sequencing may be evident in his statements as follows: "I see Jack. . . . I don't feel so good." In this instance both components are present in the communication, but they are not related.

When reflected in speech, the separation of internal-affect and external-object can have instrumental value for a speaker. If, like other behaviors, speech patterns are learned, then it follows that the forms learned for conveying relatively inexpressible affects are more acceptable, likely to be positively received, or less likely to evoke negative response or punishment from others. The separation of affect from the object with which it is associated can thus have value in communications about negative experiences. Separation of events (that is, discrimination of affect from objects, or objects from each other) in speech can take many forms, such as spatial or temporal separation, or separation through exclusion.

In sum, the various forms of separation, nonidentity, or nonimmediacy that occur in speech are expected to be most frequently associated with negative affect. The degree of nonimmediacy in statements about neutral, in contrast to positive, experiences will depend on the possibility for direct expression of positive affect. Such possibility is determined by the kind of addressee (peer or authority) or communication situation (formal or informal setting).

Some of the nonimmediacy forms indicate a nonidentity with, or dissimilarity from, the addressee. There is a considerable amount of evidence showing that more dissimilar persons like each other less, because they are less likely to positively reinforce one another (Byrne, 1969; Mehrabian and Ksionzky, 1971a). The inference of negative affect from verbal statements that show dissimilarity is therefore consistent with well-established findings.

There are still other conceptual bases for relating nonimmediacy in speech to positive, neutral, and negative feelings: the approach-avoidance framework is one example (Dollard and Miller, 1950; Lewin, 1935; Miller, 1964). Briefly, approach-avoidance behaviors are associated with positive-negative affect, evaluation, and preference. A speaker's separation of himself from the object of his message, from his addressee, or from the message itself is an instance of avoidance behavior which is motivated by negative affect toward the object, the addressee, or the message respectively. Several categories of speech nonimmediacy are informally described in the following sections.

SPATIO-TEMPORAL INDICATORS

One set of variations in speech literally describes the relationship between a speaker and the object of his communication in spatial or temporal terms. The use of the demonstratives *this, that, these, those, here,* and *there* denotes specific spatial relations. If the actual spatio-temporal situation (near and/or now, far away and/or long ago) is inconsistent with the demonstrative used to describe it, then the statement is readily interpreted. The use of a demonstrative that is incongruous for the actual event of "long ago and far away" is seen in a statement about the Renaissance which starts "This period of history. . . ." A demonstrative that is incongruous for the event "here and now" is noted in the comment, "I don't understand those people . . ." when the people are in the same room as the speaker. In instances where either set of demonstrative pronouns or adjectives can be used for a given condition, the particular selection is considered significant and interpretable. The following statements exemplify this point: (1) Two people are waiting for a third person to arrive. When they see her, one says, "Here's (there's) Jean"; (2) a person responding to another says, "I know this (the, that) person you are talking about"; (3) "These (those) people need help."

Another set of spatio-temporal variations is evident in certain forms of introductory phrases or terms that are not required by the events described (for example, over and above, on the other hand, elsewhere, in the beginning, before, at that time, such time). Specific examples are: "In the beginning, I was writing" in contrast to "I was writing"; or, "I know of several problems over and above yours" in contrast to "I know of several problems also." The first instance in each example is considered less immediate because it includes a temporal or spatial separation.

Temporal referents in speech are another source of nonimmediacy. Temporal relationships are most often expressed through verb tense. If the context allows some variation in tense usage, the specific tense used is interpretable. For example, consider a person who is no longer a member of a particular political party. Asked about his membership, he may say "I have been a member," "I was a member," or "I had been a member." In this example, the successive instances exhibit increasing temporal nonimmediacy between the speaker and the event that is described. As with spatial variations, increasing temporal nonimmediacy is also interpreted as signifying lack of preference, or negative affect and evaluation. The inclusion of spatio-temporal variations in the analysis of nonimmediacy seems to require little further justification or rationale. These variations in our language are often used explicitly to designate the degree of separation of a person from the object of his communication.

DENOTATIVE SPECIFICITY

Another set of variations, denotative specificity, is a function of the amount of ambiguity in the symbol used to denote a specific referent— the communicated object. A symbol (word) may in the literal sense denote a single object (John Smith) or a class of objects (a person). As the number of possible additional referents (other than the specific object that is being referred to) increases, ambiguity increases and denotative specificity decreases. For instance, parents referring to their son's fiancée might say, "our daughter-to-be," "our son's fiancée," "his finacée," "his lady friend," "his friend," "she," "the person," or "that thing." These examples show decreasing degrees of denotative specificity and are interpreted as expressing decreasing degrees of liking.

Variations in the personal pronouns used to denote a referent are also included under denotative specificity. For example, a person may say, "I smoke because I enjoy it." "We smoke because we enjoy it," "People smoke because they enjoy it," "One smokes because one enjoys it," or "You (meaning *I*) smoke because you enjoy it." In these examples, there is a progressive decrease in denotative specificity for the specific subject who smokes and who enjoys it (that is, *I*). Thus, denotative specificity varies with the different symbols that show the communicator's inclusion or exclusion from the group of people referred to in his statement.

Some additional examples may be helpful. A speaker describing an event in which he participated can say: "I danced," "We danced," "The gang danced," or "There was dancing," with decreasing degrees of inclusion and, therefore, decreasing denotative specificity in denoting *I*. Similarly, in a psychotherapeutic setting, a client who recalls an earlier interchange between himself and the therapist may say, "Remember we said," "Remember you said," or "Remember it was said." In these examples, the decreasing denotative specificity is interpreted as showing decreasing positive or more negative attitudes toward the communication, toward the therapy, or toward the therapist.

Apart from varying the degree of ambiguity of the symbol that is used to designate the referent, the use of an overspecific or overexclusive symbol which refers to only a part of the referent is also significant. Over-exclusive references to the object are seen in the following instances: "I like the print of this book," where *book* is the object; or "John's manners irritate me," where *John* is the object.

Denotative specificity may also be lacking because of the use of negation. We frequently hear, "It wasn't bad" instead of "It was good." Other examples are: "I am not sad about going" in contrast to "I am happy about going"; "The chair is not red" versus "The chair is maroon." Such negation lacks specificity because negating an occurrence, object, or quality fails to unambiguously identify what is in fact present.

SELECTIVE EMPHASIS

Variations of selective emphasis are manifested in the order in which objects are introduced into a communication; the frequency, intensity, or extensity attributed to an event; and over- and underresponsiveness to specific contents within a complex stimulus. "My mother and father" versus "my father and mother" is an example of sequencing. The numerous ways of referring to a married couple exemplify both sequence and emphasis: "Let's go see the Smiths," "Let's go see Mary and John," "Let's go see John and Mary," "Let's go see John," or "Let's go see Mary." In these cases, the interpretation of sequencing is evident, but the selective emphasis requires some explanation. If a couple is referred to as "the Smiths," the unity or nonseparateness of the pair is emphasized. The latter form of reference results from a lack of differential experience with the members of the pair. If the same couple is identified as "John and Mary" or "Mary and John," then the separateness of the members of the pair is made more focal, and different attitudes toward the two are implied.

Sequencing and selective emphasis are also evident in the following description of a complex event with multiple attributes and components: "We had a busy day; we went shopping, to the movies, met people, and had lunch." If a speaker identifies the people who were present at a gathering, the order in which he gives the names can vary. Incidentally, such variations in speech are paralleled in other forms of behavior, as in the order in which people are served at a gathering.

A speaker's affect toward objects can be inferred from the sequential order in which he narrates them when alternative sequences are possible for a given condition. As in the other immediacy interpretations, it is hypothesized that objects experienced more positively, or less negatively, occur earlier in the sequence.

Selective emphasis is also evident in the particular attribute constellation implied by the term used to denote the referent. In referring to a specific psychotherapist, the speaker can say "the psychotherapist," "the therapist," "the doctor," "the ward physician," "the man," or "the headshrinker." In referring to a party he can say "I enjoyed the party," "I enjoyed the dancing," "I enjoyed the food," "I enjoyed the people," "I enjoyed the conversation," or "I enjoyed the place." A colleague can be referred to as "my collaborator," "my colleague," "my associate," "my coworker," "my assistant," "my helper," or "my student." In all of these instances the particular attribute that is emphasized signifies its differential significance for the speaker. When there is a shift from a consensual referent (*party*) to a component of it (*conversation*) the interpretation is as follows: the attributes that are de-emphasized through exclusion are less preferred or are disliked. Alternatively, the denoted attribute constellation is disliked least, or is liked and preferred most (Mehrabian, 1967d). In general, though, inferences of negative affect for the excluded aspects of the referent are more likely to be valid.

AGENT-ACTION-OBJECT RELATIONSHIPS

In our discussion of agent-action-object relationships, the person who initiates the activity will be referred to as the agent and the receiver of the action as the object. For example, in the statement "John is looking at Mary," *John* is the agent and *Mary* is the object. There are at least three loci of possible variations in the agent-action-object relationships within a statement.

One set of variations in this relationship is indicated by the specific words used by the communicator for designating the agent(s) and object(s) for an "objective" event. A quarrel between two people can be reported as follows: "They were fighting," "She was fighting with him," or "He was fighting with her."

A second set of variations occurs when responsibility for an activity is attributed to sources other than the ostensible agent(s), when it is possible to attribute responsibility to the latter. "I should go," "I have to go," "I must go," "I am compelled (or driven) to go" in contrast to "I want to go," "I would like to go," or "I will go" illustrate these variations. The attribution of the action to some part or characteristic of the agent in the "objective" situation is also considered part of this set of variations. "It is my desire to go," "Something in me makes me want to go," "My legs automatically carry me there" in contrast to "I want to go" or "I will go."

A third set of variations arises from the use of the passive rather than the active voice. Note, for example, the difference between "I drove the car" and "The car was driven by me," or between "I went to school with my mother" and "I was taken to school by my mother."

All variations in agent-action-object relationships are interpreted as showing different degrees of positive-negative affect toward the activity involved, the persons in the act, or the addressee. For example, if the speaker says, "I had to go" instead of "I went," affect is inferred about "going," or about having to report "the going" to the specific addressee. When an external agent is introduced, it indicates a greater separation of the communicator from the agent, object, or activity in his statement because the source of involvement is other than the consensual agent (*I*). Consider another example. The speaker describes someone dancing with his girl friend as follows: "He was dancing with her" or "She was dancing with him" instead of "They were dancing." The less interactive agent-object relationships in the first two statements, as compared to "They were dancing," indicate the speaker's negative experience of the activity, of the agent and object in the activity, or of his reporting the event. The emphasis on separation, when separateness is not a quality of the event, is what allows the inference of negative communicator affect.

There is less immediacy when the number of responsible agents indicated in a statement is less than what the context implies. For example, a communication describing a mutual activity can be organized to convey only a unilateral relationship. Such variations are possible whether or not the speaker is one of the agents in the event. Thus, "They (we) are dancing" can be expressed as "She dances with him (me)." With such a unilateral relationship, different degrees of participation of the agents are implied. The following sentences are listed in the order of the implied decreasing mutual interaction: "We (they) danced," "She and I (he) danced," "I (he) danced with her," or "The dancing I (he) did was with her." Whereas in the *we* or *they* example the mutuality is explicit, in the *she and I* or *she and he* example the implied mutuality is somewhat decreased through the separation of the two agents. In "I danced with her," the mutuality is only implicit and the communicator (I) is the ostensible agent. Finally, in "The dancing I (he) did was with her," the mutuality is not only implicit, but there is also a further separation of the activity "dancing" from the agent—the major focus is on the dancing, and the other person's participation is almost incidental. This decrease in reported mutuality can be a function of the speaker's negative affect about dancing, a quality of his dancing, or her dancing. If the 'speaker is not one of the agents, the corresponding change may be a function of the speaker's negative affect about *his dancing, their dancing together,* or *them.*

MODIFIERS

Qualifications of a communication include expressions of the speaker's doubt about his opinion, as in "I think (believe, feel) that you are correct," or of his uncertainty about the event, as in "It could be (it seems to be, it might be) that you are correct." With the use of such qualifications, a speaker implies that others, especially the listener, experience the same event differently.

Objectifications of a communication take the form of introductory phrases such as "It is obvious," "It is evident," or "It is simply true," all of which imply certainty on the part of the speaker. He emphasizes a consensus for his experience by asserting the reality of the event, thereby separating himself from the object of the communication.

In sum, qualification introduces a separation of the speaker from others, including the addressee. In objectification, there is a separation of the speaker from the objects in his message. Both forms decrease immediacy and indicate the speaker's less positive attitude toward the event described, or his reluctance to relay this information to that particular addressee. Either may be a function of the specific communicator-addressee relationship; that is, it may occur with one addressee but not with another. Furthermore, uncertainty as expressed in qualification and certainty as expressed in objectification may also signify different personality characteristics of speakers.

Incidentally, the specific localization of uncertainty within a speaker as to feeling (*I feel*), belief (*It is my opinion*), or thought (*I think*) offers intriguing speculative possibilities for trying to change the commitment of a speaker to his message. Thus, if the content of a message is qualified with "I feel," the most successful approach to a change of attitude may require emotionally oriented arguments and emphases, in contrast to a statement qualified with "I think," where a rational or logical approach might be most effective.

AUTOMATIC PHRASING

Automatic phrasing occurs with the use of words such as *just* or *simply*, phrases such as *you know*, nonsemantic sounds such as *uh*, and pauses that are linguistically unnecessary.

The occurrence of words like *just* or *simply* signifies an attempt by the speaker to minimize his association with, or his responsibility for, the communication or the actions described. Some examples are, "I just borrowed it for a moment or two," "It's only a minor damage," "It's really unimportant," or "It's simply unnecessary." These forms are interpreted as showing negative attitudes toward the objects in the message or the reporting of the events to the addressee.

When a speaker uses phrases and words such as *you know, you understand, right?* or *all right?* he implicitly requests verification from the listener that the latter understands what is said. We assume that, in an immediate communication, the speaker takes for granted the listener's understanding. Thus, phrases like *you know* or *I mean* show that the speaker regards himself as separate or different (nonimmediate) from the listener, and therefore imply negative affect.

Other automatic phrases, sounds, pauses such as *well, uh, that is*, and slips or false starts (Freud, 1938) can reflect inconsistent experiences, ambivalence toward the event being described, or ambivalence toward the description of the event to the particular addressee. For example, in "How did you like the party?" "Well (ah, or uh) (pause) it was fine," uncertainty or ambivalence is conveyed by the use of automatic phrases (*well*) and by the pause. Temporal delay in these instances is considered a prime index of separation or nonimmediacy between a speaker and his message. Whereas Mahl (1959) interpreted speech disruptions as anxiety indicators, aborted starts in speech in our context are yet another case of nonimmediacy and are interpreted within a more general framework.

Nonimmediacy Scoring Criteria

Given the assumptions and the general nonimmediacy hypothesis, it is possible to proceed to one set of criteria for scoring the nonimmediacy in spoken or written messages.[1] The following set of criteria is of limited scope, but should help illustrate the approach to the experimental measurement of nonimmediacy. A more thorough set of criteria, yet to be devised, would include careful scrutiny of the scaling problems and issues.

In the criteria described below, the word *object* refers to an event, person, or object which is the ostensible reason for the communication. To minimize unreliability in scoring, it is desirable that for every statement there be some basis for designating the communicator and the object involved. The communicator is by definition the emitter of the message and is generally referred to in a statement by symbols such as *I* or *me*. The context of a statement usually allows one to unambiguously specify the object of communication. In the examples given below, the symbols for the communicator and the object are italicized, and inferred references to the communicator or the object are provided in brackets.

The examples given below are assigned scores for all relevant categories in addition to the scores for the categories being described. This is done to provide a reasonably comprehensive set of complete examples. The symbols to the right of each example have the following significance:

S = Spatial nonimmediacy
T = Temporal nonimmediacy
Ps = Possibility
U = Unilaterality
Pa = Passivity
Pc = Part of the communicator
Po = Part of the object of communication
Cc = Communicator included within a larger class
Co = Object included within a larger class
0 = A score of zero is assigned to examples that do not include any of
       these nonimmediacy categories.

I. The score S is assigned to a "communication unit" only when demonstrative pronouns such as *that* or *those*, as against *the, this*, or *these*, are used to indicate the spatial relation to the object. ("Communication unit" is defined following the presentation of all the nonimmediacy categories.)

1. This section contains rewritten parts of my article "Attitudes in Relation to the Forms of Communicator-Object Relationship in Spoken Communications," *Journal of Personality*, 34 (1966), 80–93, copyright (1966) Duke University Press. Reproduced by permission.

I don't think too much of that *guy*.	S, U
That illness of *X*'s is affecting [*me*] my work.	S, U, P, P
This is the *suit I* want.	0
I don't like the *music*.	0

II. The score *T* is assigned to a communication unit only when the relationship between the communicator and the object is temporally past or future, rather than ongoing or present.

I used to (will or am going to) see *X*.	T, U
I have (or had) met *X*.	T, U
X and *I* meet regularly.	0
I think *X* likes sports.	U

III. The score *Ps* is assigned to a communication unit only when the relationship between the communicator and the object is stated as a possibility. The possible nature of the relationship is usually communicated with the use of auxiliary verbs such as *can, could, may, might, would,* or *able to,* and of phrases such as *it is possible* or *it could be.*

X and *I* can (could, may, might, are able to) meet.	Ps
It is probable that *I* will see *X*.	T, Ps, U
I will buy the *book*.	T

IV. The score *U* is assigned to a communication unit only when there is an absence of reciprocity between the communicator and the object in the explicit statement of the relationship. This category is not applicable to communications in which the object is other than a person.

I didn't like *her*.	T, U
I didn't like the *book*.	T
X is my [*me*] friend.	U
X and *I* used to be friends.	T
I disagree with *X*.	U
X and *I* liked (or saw) Y.	T, U
We [*X* and *I*] are in the same class (neighborhood or team).	U
X and *I* are singers (Christians, Democrats, impolite, tall).	U
X and *I* both went fishing.	T, U
X and *I* went fishing together.	T
X is different from *me*.	U
X and *I* are different (or alike).	0
X and *I* have conflicting personalities.	P, P
X and *I* have the same (or different) interests (backgrounds).	P, P

V. The score *Pa* is assigned to a communication unit only when the communicator, the object, or both are stated as being passively forced into the relationship.

X forced *me* to fight him [that is, X].	T, U, Pa
I want to see X.	U
X and I had to meet.	T, Pa

VI. A communication unit that is a statement of the type "A relation B" can be analyzed with respect to the various types of nonimmediacy of the relationship *per se*, as has been done in categories I through V. In a communication, the symbol used to refer to the communicator (A), or the symbol used to refer to the object (B), may have referents that are not identical to the communicator or the object, respectively. Specifically, the referent of A may be a part of the communicator (Part$_c$ = Pc) or it may be a class of people that includes the communicator (Class$_c$ = Cc). Similarly, the referent of B may be a part of the object (Part$_o$ = Po) or it may be a class of entities that includes the object (Class$_o$ = Co). Thus, a communication of the type "A relation B" can also be scored for the types of denotative nonimmediacy between the referent of A and the communicator and the referent of B and the object of communication.

The score *Pc* is assigned to a communication unit only when the symbol for the communicator (A) refers to a part of the communicator. Similarly, the score *Po* is assigned to a communication unit only when the symbol for the object (B) refers to a part of the object. In either case, *part* is used broadly to mean any one of the following: (1) a physical part, such as the communicator's arm; (2) a dispositional quality, such as a characteristic, attribute, or aspect; and (3) some related object or person, such as the communicator's children, car, or friend.

I like the color of this *chair*.	Po
I hate X's guts.	U, Po
I don't like X's way of doing things.	U, Po
X's manners irritate *me*.	U, Po
I saw X's car.	T, U, Po
I like X's children.	U, Po
X broke my [*me*] arm.	T, U, Pc
My [*me*] thoughts are about X.	U, Pc
My [*me*] friend met X.	T, U, Pc
X's and my [*me*] ideas clash.	P, P
X's illness was affecting my [*me*] ability to concentrate.	T, U, P, P
X's and my [*me*] wife met.	T, P, P
I think X is interesting.	U
I watched X mowing the lawn.	T, U
I disapprove of the way X is behaving.	U

The score *Cc* is assigned to a communication unit only when the symbol for the communicator (*A*) refers to a class of people that includes the communicator. Similarly, the score *Co* is assigned to a communication unit only when the symbol for the object (*B*) refers to a class of entities that includes the object of communication.

They [*I*] say *she* is ugly.	U, Cc
Everybody [including *me*] enjoyed reading X.	T, Cc
One [such as *I*] could enjoy seeing movie X.	Ps, Cc
We [Y and *I*] had to meet X.	T, U, Pa, Cc
Someone [such as *I*] should tell X off.	U, Pa, Cc
Our group [including *me*] does not encourage X's weakness.	U, Po, Cc
Let us [you and *I*] consider X's erroneous argument.	U, Po, Cc
You'd [*I*] think X can be more considerate!	U, Ps, Cc
That's a habit of X's that one [*I*] has to get used to.	S, U, Pa, Po, Cc
I don't like people like that [including X].	S, U, Co
I like people [including X] to be dependable.	U, Co
I like X more than Y.	U, Co
I'd rather someone [including X] be honest.	U, Ps, Co
We [Y and *I*] don't think much of them [Z and X].	U, C, C
We [Y and *I*] don't think much of their [Z's and X's] habits.	U, Po, C, C
Y's and my [*me*] interests are different from Z's and X's.	P, P, C, C

VII. The score *D* is assigned to a communication unit only when, despite explicit expectations, the communicator fails to relate himself to, or disassociates himself from, the object of communication. The scoring of *D* excludes the possibility of a "Part" or "Class" score being assigned to a communication unit. The following examples are taken from situations where the communicator is instructed to say something about himself and a specified object.

X is a good kid (is interesting, is pleasant to be with, behaved rudely, or asks too many questions).
I didn't feel well (was upset, or had a raincoat on).

VIII. The final type of communication unit that also requires some kind of designation is one to which none of the above nonimmediacy scores can be assigned. Instances of this type of communication are given by "X and *I* are working together (are alike, go to the movies together, are enemies, enjoy each other's company, have a mutual agreement, fight all the time, or hate each other)." Such communications are assigned the score 0 for "zero nonimmediacy."

It is now possible to proceed to a discussion of the scaling of nonimmediacy score combinations. The assumptions of the model, summarized above, led us to expect that statements about negative objects would receive a larger number of the nonimmediacy scores than would statements about positive objects. In other words, remembering that N equals the number of nonimmediacy scores assigned to a given communication unit, it was expected that the higher N scores would have increasingly higher frequencies in speech about negative objects than in speech about positive objects. This has indeed been found to be the case (Mehrabian, 1966a; 1967b). Therefore it is possible to set the nonimmediacy scale value of a communication unit equal to N. There is one exception, however, within this scheme. The nonimmediacy scale value of a Disassociated (D) score is greater than that of the other categories, being approximately 2. Thus, D, S, T, U receives a total nonimmediacy score of 5.

A major problem in scoring nonimmediacy is what constitutes the communication unit to be scored. One approach is to divide a statement into units by simple sentences and independent clauses (including in the latter any dependent clauses that are part of the independent clause). There are, however, occasional ambiguous instances. The following alternative set of criteria can be used to resolve these ambiguities: a unit is assigned for different types of statements. Type A: A statement makes reference to the subject and the object ("Before I saw $John$," where $John$ is the object). Type B: A statement makes reference to the subject only ("While I was feeling tired," where $John$ is designated as the object). Type C: A statement makes reference to the object only ("When $John$ was wearing a straw hat"). As in the section on scoring criteria, subject and object may refer to part or class of subject or object.

A Type A unit must contain at least one verb that relates the subject to the object. It can be a dependent clause, an independent clause, a simple sentence, or a complex sentence. If a compound verb that expresses more than one relationship between the subject and the object is employed in a Type A unit, each such verbal relationship is considered a separate unit. Thus, "I talked to $Mary$ and went shopping with $Mary$," or "I talked to $Jack$ and we decided to go shopping," or "I called and talked to him" would be two units. Finally, a Type B or Type C unit is minimally a clause, but one which can be extended to a type A unit. Once a Type B or Type C unit is designated, successive occurrences of these types are not considered new units. Thus, "I went to the store; $Jane$ came home," is considered one unit.

As an example, let us consider the following statement about a teacher's relationship to the communicator: "One of the teachers had said, during my first assembly last year, that he had told each student in the group that he wanted to learn from each of us." This statement consists of three communication units: (1) "One of the teachers had said, during my first assembly last year," scored as Cc ("my first assembly" instead of me), Co ("one of the teachers" instead of a specific referent), T and U for tense and unilaterality; (2) "that he had told each student in the group," scored as *Cc* ("each student" instead of *me*), *T* and *U* for tense and unilaterality; (3) "that he wanted to learn from each of us," scored as *Cc* ("us" instead of *me*), and *T* and *U* for tense and unilaterality. For purposes of illustration, the units would be assigned numerical nonimmediacy scores of 4, 3, and 3 respectively. The average nonimmediacy score assigned to the entire statement would be 3.33.

Experimental Evidence for the Immediacy Hypothesis

A variety of encoding and decoding paradigms have been used to explore the relationship of nonimmediacy in speech to dislike of the referents being discussed.[2] In the encoding studies, the subjects' spontaneous verbalizations were scored according to criteria such as those given above. These studies have consistently shown that statements about disliked persons or experiences are more nonimmediate than those about liked persons or experiences (Gottlieb, Wiener and Mehrabian, 1967; Mehrabian, 1964, 1965, 1966a, 1967b; Mehrabian and Wiener, 1966).

On the other hand, studies have also explored untrained subjects' responses to variations in immediacy. In preliminary studies of this problem, Mehrabian (1966b, 1967c) presented subjects with pairs of statements about a person, object, or event. The statements in a pair differed in degree of immediacy, but did not differ in the explicitly stated attitude toward the object (for example, "Bruce is my neighbor" and "Bruce and I live in the same neighborhood"). It was found that subjects interpreted the more immediate statement in each pair as showing a more positive attitude. Since it is unlikely that the variations in immediacy that occur in everyday conversation contain the focal contrasts employed in the above experiments, the findings did not yield sufficient information about the everyday use of immediacy in attitude inference. However, the findings did show that adults infer attitude variations from contrasts in immediacy.

In everyday speech, it seems that the inference of attitudes by untrained persons requires appropriate contextual cues. For example, if a speaker is introduced to his audience in a hurried and sketchy way, members of the audience infer a lack of respect for the speaker's work or the speaker himself. But such an interpretation is less likely if the speaker is late in arriving and the audience is restless from waiting. Knowledge of context (for example, the necessity of a brief introduction) influences a listener's interpretation of implicit aspects of speech (the brevity of the introduction, irrespective of its explicit meaning).

Some investigators have noted the importance of context for under-

2. This section is a rewritten version of my article "The Effect of Context on Judgments of Speaker Attitude," *Journal of Personality*, 36 (1968), 21–32. Tables 1, 2, and 3 from the article are also included. Copyright (1968) by Duke University Press. Reproduced by permission.

standing the implicit communication of feelings or attitudes (Bird-whistell, 1963; studies reviewed by Davitz, 1964, p. 17; Frijda, 1969; Scheflen, 1965). Scheflen argued that "we must remember that no element has meaning out of context. Said in another way, a unit examined out of context has so many possible meanings that there is too much ambiguity for systematic analysis" (p. 28). In other words, context contributes to a listener's interpretation of a message, and therefore the consideration of context can yield more precise predictions of his interpretation.

The neglect of context in studies of implicit attitude communication (note the reviews by Davitz, 1964, or Mahl and Schulze, 1964) is due to the difficulty in specifying contextual factors. In one set of special cases the concept of immediacy can be used as a framework to help specify the relevant contextual factors. Immediacy of context is defined as the degree of directness and intensity of interaction between a speaker and the object of his speech, as observed or inferred by a listener. A speaker may say "Look at this table" while he is standing far from the table. The listener observes the actual distance between the speaker and the table and notes that it is more than the implied distance in the statement. The immediacy hypothesis indicates that immediate speech in a relatively nonimmediate context implies a positive speaker attitude. Conversely, nonimmediate speech in a relatively immediate context can imply a negative speaker attitude (Mehrabian, 1968c).

THE COMBINED EFFECTS OF VERBAL AND CONTEXTUAL IMMEDIACY

The experiment described in this section was designed to explore the interactive effects of speech immediacy and context immediacy on the feelings that are inferred by an untrained observer (Mehrabian, 1968c). In the experiment, statements were accompanied by a description of the context of speech, which either included information about the observable immediacy of the speaker to the object or about the listener's expected degree of speaker-object immediacy. The effects of two degrees of speech immediacy and two degrees of context immediacy on the degree of positive attitude inferred by the subject were considered. It was assumed that contrast cues from the context are necessary for the inference of attitudes, so that subjects cannot systematically interpret speech immediacy when it is congruent with context immediacy. This assumption was restated in the following hypotheses.

H_1: Nonimmediate statements in an immediate context imply a more negative speaker attitude than (a) immediate statements in an immediate context or (b) nonimmediate statements in a nonimmediate context.

H_2: Immediate statements in a nonimmediate context imply a more positive speaker attitude than (a) immediate statements in an immediate context or (b) nonimmediate statements in a nonimmediate context.

Table 3.1.   Definitions of immediacy categories with examples of context and speech immediacy.

Category	Immediate/Nonimmediate Context	Immediate/Nonimmediate Speech
Distance: Spatial distance between communicator and object of communication.	A man standing on the edge of a pool comments to a friend standing beside him.	"Go ahead and jump into this *pool*."
	A man standing on a balcony overlooking a pool comments to a friend standing beside him.	"Go ahead and jump into that *pool*."
Time: Temporal distance between communicator and object.	Question asked of communicator: "Do you think about *X*?"	"*I* think about *X*."
	"Have you been thinking about *X*?"	"*I* used to think about *X*."
Order of Occurrence: Order of interaction with the object in an interaction sequence.	Question asked of communicator: "Did you visit *X* and *Y*?"	"*I visited X and Y*."
	"Did you visit Y and *X*?"	"*I visited Y and X*."
Duration: Duration of interaction or duration (e.g., length) of communication about interaction.	A is asked to write a long letter about *B*.	A writes a long letter about *B*.
	A is asked to write a short letter about *B*.	A writes a short letter about *B*.
Activity-Passivity: Willingness versus an obligatory quality of communicator-object interaction.	*X* stopped to *help someone fix a flat tire.*	*X* says "I stopped to *help someone fix a flat tire.*"
	X had to stop to *help someone fix a flat tire.*	"I had to stop to *help someone fix a flat tire.*"
Mutuality-Unilaterality: Degree of reciprocity of communicator-object interaction.	Question asked of communicator: "Have you and *X* met each other?"	"*X* and *I* met yesterday."
	"Have you met *X*?"	"*I* met *X* yesterday."
Probability: Degree of certainty of communicator-object interaction.	Question: "Do you take *yoga*?"	"*I* take *yoga*."
	"Could you take *yoga*?"	"*I* could take *yoga*."

47

Table 3.1 (cont.)

Category	Immediate/Nonimmediate Context	Immediate/Nonimmediate Speech
Part$_c$—Communicator Participation: The totality versus only a part, aspect or acquaintance of the communicator interacts with the object.	Question asked of communicator: "Are you going to the *store?*" "Is your friend going to the *store?*"	"*I* am going to the *store.*" "My friend is going to the *store.*"
Class$_c$—Communicator Participation: The communicator interacts individually with the object versus being part of a group of people which interacts with the object.	Question asked of communicator: "Did you go to the *beach* last summer?" "Did you people go to the *beach* last summer?"	"*I* went to the *beach* last summer." "We went to the *beach* last summer."
Part$_o$—Object Participation: The totality versus only a part, aspect, or acquaintance of the object interacts with the communicator.	*X* is asked to write a letter and describe *Y's* personality. *X* is asked to write a letter and describe some of *Y's* habits.	In his letter, *X* describes *Y's* personality. In his letter, *X* describes some of *Y's* habits.
Class$_o$—Object Participation: The object interacts individually with the communicator versus being part of a group of people which interacts with the communicator.	*A* and *B* are talking about *C,* and *A* asks, "Do you see *C* near the pool?" "Do you see the people near the pool?"	*B* says, "*I* see *C* near the pool." "*I* see the people near the pool."
Disassociated—Communicator-Object Participation: The presence versus the absence of participation of the communicator (or object) in the interaction.	Question asked of communicator: "How are you and *B* doing at school?" "How are you doing at school?"	"*B* and *I* are doing well at school." "*I* am doing well at school."

Method. The subjects were 46 University of California undergraduates. The experiment involved two replications of a 2 Speech Immediacy × 2 Context Immediacy × 12 Immediacy Categories design, with repeated measures on all factors. Thus, two replications of 48 experimental conditions were administered to each of the subjects.

A 96-page booklet and one page of instructions constituted the set of materials presented to each subject. Each page of the booklet contained a statement with its associated context. Thus, each booklet consisted of a random presentation of two replications of the 48 experimental conditions. Table 3.1 illustrates some of the materials used. In the table, the speaker and the object of his speech (referred to as object) are in italics. The first column contains definitions of 12 immediacy categories that apply to context or speech. The entries in the second column show the context in which the speech occurred. One nonimmediate speech and immediate context condition of the Activity-Passivity category is presented below as it appeared on a page of the booklet:

What is Fred's attitude toward helping someone fix a flat tire (　　　)?
Fred, on his way home, stopped to help someone replace a flat tire. In talking to a friend later, he said, "I had to stop to help someone fix a tire."

The experiment was group administered in one session. For this and all remaining 95 pages of the booklet, subjects recorded their judgments of the attitudes within the parentheses, using a seven-point scale ranging from −3 (dislike very much) to +3 (like very much).

Results. Table 3.2 summarizes the mean inferred attitude scores for the Speech Immediacy × Context Immediacy × Immediacy Category effects. Analysis of variance of the inferred attitude scores indicated the following 0.01 level significant effects.

A greater liking was inferred when the speech immediacy was greater ($F = 456.5$, $df = 1/45$), and when the context was less immediate ($F = 176.8$, $df = 1/45$). There were significant differences in liking inferred from the various immediacy categories ($F = 7.8$, $df = 11/495$). As hypothesized, there was a Speech Immediacy × Context Immediacy interaction ($F = 9.2$, $df = 1/45$). However, the Speech Immediacy × Category ($F = 27.1$, $df = 11/495$) and the Context Immediacy × Category ($F = 13.8$, $df = 11/495$) effects showed that the effects of speech immediacy and context immediacy were different for the various categories. Therefore, separate tests of the hypotheses for each category are reported in Table 3.3; t-test values are reported only when the simple-main effects for a given category level were significant.

Discussion. The summary of the analysis of variance findings presented in Table 3.3 shows that for the following six of the twelve categories investigated, both hypotheses were supported: Order of Occurrence, Duration, Probability, Communicator Participation ($Part_c$), Object Participa-

Table 3.2. Mean inferred attitude scores.

Category	Immediate Speech		Nonimmediate Speech	
	immediate context	nonimmediate context	immediate context	nonimmediate context
Distance	0.73	1.11	0.18	0.76
Time	0.64	0.69	−0.67	0.33
Order of Occurrence	0.73	1.42	−0.68	0.10
Duration	1.19	1.82	−0.65	−0.06
Activity-Passivity	0.84	0.61	−0.43	−0.60
Mutuality-Unilaterality	0.58	0.83	−0.37	0.56
Probability	0.80	1.79	−0.70	−0.31
Communicator Participation ($Part_c$)	0.50	1.06	−1.12	−0.15
Communicator Participation ($Class_c$)	0.35	1.00	−0.11	0.19
Object Participation ($Part_o$)	0.65	0.92	−0.58	0.42
Object Participation ($Class_o$)	0.88	1.93	−1.42	−0.05
Communicator-Object Participation (Disassociated)	1.27	1.88	−1.60	−0.07

tion ($Class_o$) and Communicator-Object Participation (Disassociated). Several of these six categories subsume speech phenomena that trained observers use to infer speaker attitudes. For example, increases in frequency of obsessional qualification (Probability) are interpreted as showing a negative speaker attitude toward the associated contents. Again, inability or unwillingness of a person to speak at any length (Duration) about someone or some topic is interpreted as showing the object's threatening or negative affect-arousing quality for the speaker (for example, repression of anxiety-arousing contents). Similarly, speech phenomena related to the Order of Occurrence category are interpreted to infer attitudes, as exemplified by a client's tendency to delay the discussion of an unpleasant topic. Finally, instances of the Disassociated category, such as tangential responses when requested to speak about negative emotional contents, are frequently observed in the speech of psychotics. In such interactions, when the psychotic person is asked to speak about a given person or content area, he responds without any specific reference to it.

In sum, the six categories of immediacy for which there is a high degree of consensus among untrained listeners subsume speech phenomena that trained listeners like clinicians frequently use in their inference of speaker feelings or attitudes.

The results summarized in Table 3.3 show that four of the remaining categories (Distance, Time, Mutuality-Unilaterality, and $Part_o$) had similar significance patterns. For these categories, H_1 was supported while H_2 was not (except in the case of the $Part_o$ category where H_{2b} was

Table 3.3. t-test values for the effects corresponding to four hypotheses.

Category	Hypothesis 1a: Compares Columns 1 and 3 of Table 3.2	Hypothesis 2b: Compares Columns 2 and 4 of Table 3.2	Hypothesis 2a: Compares Columns 1 and 2 of Table 3.2	Hypothesis 1b: Compares Columns 3 and 4 of Table 3.2
Distance	1.84*	1.17	1.63	2.49†
Time	4.40†	1.21	<1	4.30†
Order of Occurrence	4.73†	4.43†	2.96†	3.34†
Duration	6.17†	6.30†	2.70†	2.53†
Activity-Passivity	4.26†	4.07†	—	—
Mutuality-Unilaterality	3.19†	<1	1.07	3.99†
Probability	5.03†	7.05†	4.25†	1.67*
Communicator Participation ($Part_c$)	5.43†	4.06†	2.40†	4.17†
Communicator Participation ($Class_c$)	1.54	2.72†	2.79†	1.29
Object Participation ($Part_o$)	4.13†	1.68*	1.16	4.30†
Object Participation ($Class_o$)	7.73†	6.65†	4.50†	5.88†
Communicator-Object Participation (Disassociated)	9.73†	6.54†	2.62†	6.57†

*$P < .05$
†$P < .01$

also supported). The significance pattern for the above four categories shows that variations in speech related to these categories are consensually used by untrained subjects to infer negative attitudes but not positive ones. In contrast, the $Class_c$ category yielded a pattern of significance complementary to that obtained with the latter four categories. For the $Class_c$ category, the significance pattern indicates that nonimmediate speech in immediate contexts does not lead to the inference of high negative attitudes (for example, H_2 is supported but H_1 is not). It may be that variations in speech that are subsumed by the $Class_c$ category are consensually used by untrained subjects to infer positive attitudes but not negative ones. For example, while the interchange "Jack, did you visit Jane?" "Yes, we visited Jane" does not lead to the inference of a negative attitude toward Jane, the interchange "Did you people visit Jane?" "Yes, I visited Jane" does lead to the inference of a positive attitude.

For the final category to be considered, Activity-Passivity, the speech immediacy effects were significant for both levels of context immediacy, but neither context immediacy effect was significant (that is, only H_{1a} and H_{2b} were supported). This finding may be due to the fact that speech classified as Passive can be used to infer negative speaker feelings, even in the absence of contrast cues. For example, "I had to go to visit the doctor" leads to the inference of a negative attitude toward the doctor, or the act of visiting the doctor, in the absence of additional information about the context. In these instances, then, the information contained in speech is so salient that the context is not used by the subject. Speech subsumed under other immediacy categories, such as Probability, can also be decoded to infer attitudes in the absence of context. However, inferences about attitudes on the basis of such speech tend to be less consensual than those based on speech subsumed under the Activity-Passivity category.

It is now possible to rank the immediacy categories in terms of the prevalence of their use by the general population. The Activity-Passivity category ranks first; as a group, the six categories of Order of Occurrence, Duration, Probability, $Part_c$, $Class_o$, and Disassociated rank second; and the five categories of Distance, Time, Mutuality-Unilaterality, $Part_o$, and $Class_c$ rank third. The results show that information about context immediacy allows untrained observers to systematically interpret immediacy of speech to infer attitudes. The results also show that some kinds of speech immediacy can be interpreted only when they occur in specific contexts, whereas one kind of immediacy, Activity-Passivity, does not require any contextual information.

Our discussion of some of the verbal variations in immediacy points out the more general application of the concept and the hypothesis that relates it to feelings. It can be used to study not only communication behaviors in a given channel (such as position), but to identify attitude-communicating behaviors across a variety of channels. The concept thus has considerable heuristic value.

The concept of relaxation has similar value. It should be possible, for example, to identify verbal or nonverbal cues (other than postural ones) that also denote variations in relaxation. If this were to be done, an obvious hypothesis would involve the relationship of these cues to status relations. Indeed, we suspect that the speech disturbance phenomena studied by Mahl (1959) and other instances of automatic phrasing illustrate not only nonimmediacy but some degree of tension in the speech of a communicator.

Summary

Verbal immediacy refers to the degree of intensity and directness of interaction between a speaker and the object about which he speaks, as assessed from the message itself. Previous studies indicate that there is more immediacy in statements about liked others than in statements about disliked others. Also, when subjects are presented with pairs of statements differing in degree of immediacy, but neutral in explicit attitudes, it is found that more immediate statements are judged as indicating a more positive speaker feeling. One of the studies described above investigated the contribution of context to the inference of attitude from immediacy (Mehrabian, 1968c). Untrained observers consistently interpreted speech immediacy to infer attitudes when provided with information about the degree of speech immediacy appropriate or expected in a given context. Consistent interpretation of six kinds of speech immediacy was found in all the contexts investigated. However, consistent interpretation of five kinds of speech immediacy was found only for specific types of context, whereas one kind of speech immediacy was consistently interpreted in the absence of contextual cues.

4

Implicit Rhetoric

A basic aspect of human interaction is the ability to influence and persuade others, whether in a one-to-one situation or en masse. Although numerous studies have explored the contribution of various aspects of speech to persuasion, the role of implicit behaviors in these situations has been overlooked. However, the latter has recently become the focal interest of some researchers (Duncan and Rosenthal, 1968; Rosenthal, 1966), advertisers, and campaign managers. If implicit channels can be used to express many of the same feelings we express verbally, it follows that these channels contain numerous possibilities for implicit rhetoric.

The experiments described in this chapter have explored some of the proxemic, postural, facial, movement, and vocal behaviors of a speaker that were expected to relate to his persuasive effort and the degree to which his message was perceived as persuasive by the addressee. The selection of the set of implicit behaviors and personality attributes for the study was based on their relevance to the implied communication of like-dislike, responsiveness, and potency or status.

In particular, the variables relevant to the implicit communication of liking and status were selected because (1) the related concepts of communicator trustworthiness and expertness have been found as correlates of his effectiveness in eliciting attitude change (Cohen, 1964, pp. 23–29; Hovland, Janis, and Kelley, 1953; Insko, 1967, pp. 43–49) and (2) as already noted in Chapters 1 and 2, liking and status have been identified as two primary referents of implicit communication. Indeed, investigations of communicator credibility (that is, his trustworthiness and expertness) have explored the impact of liking on attitude change. There have been

This chapter is a rewritten version, including Tables 1, 2, and 3, of Mehrabian and Williams' "Nonverbal Concomitants of Perceived and Intended Persuasiveness," *Journal of Personality and Social Psychology*, 13 (1969), 37–58, copyright (1969) by the American Psychological Association. Reproduced by permission.

studies of the effects on attitude change due to a speaker's physical attractiveness, height and weight (Baker and Redding, 1961; Mills and Aronson, 1965), race (Aronson and Golden, 1962), liking of the listener (Mills, 1966), and implied belief similarity to the listener (Weiss, 1957). The latter, in turn, has been shown to be a correlate of liking between two persons (Byrne, 1969). Such studies seem to have been motivated by the assumed correlation between speaker-listener liking and the attitude change elicited by the speaker.

A second group of investigations of communicator credibility suggested the relevance of perceived communicator status in determining attitude change. In Aronson and Golden's (1962) study, engineers, who were of higher socioeconomic status, elicited more attitude change than did dishwashers. Rosnow and Robinson (1967, pp. 2–5) suggested the relevance of voice quality—its authoritativeness, rate of speech errors, or halting and hesitant quality—as additional determiners of the attitude change. The latter vocal cues, in addition to other speech or dress attributes such as social class intonations, can also be construed as correlates of speaker status relative to his listener.

In the absence of more directly relevant literature, the significance of speaker credibility, observed in attitude-change studies, was used as a basis to develop the hypotheses and variables of this study. Our focus was on the effects of implicit behaviors related to the communication of liking, some of which have also been found to be related to status communication. In addition, the study included a series of personality measures, such as intelligence, dominance, anxiety, neuroticism, and introversion, that could consistently influence the frequency with which such implicit cues were produced by speakers.

The implicit communication literature provided a series of derivative hypotheses for the relationship between the liking of a listener, the intended persuasiveness of the speaker, and the perceived persuasiveness of the message by the listener.

In the case of posture and position cues, findings by Mehrabian (1968a) showed that smaller distances from the addressee, more eye contact with him, and smaller reclining angles of the speaker conveyed more liking to the addressee. In addition, female speakers oriented their torsos so they were facing their addressees more directly when the addressee was liked than when he was disliked; the reverse was the case for male speakers, but only when intense rather than moderate or neutral feelings were involved (Mehrabian, 1968b). Finally, findings indicated a curvilinear relationship between relaxation and the degree of liking communicated to an addressee (Mehrabian, 1968b). For instance, sideways lean, which is an index of relaxation (see Appendix A), was found to be moderately high for liked, relatively low for neutral, and very high for disliked addresses with the following exception: male speakers, while addressing very disliked males, tended to assume a relatively low sideways-lean angle. Thus, generally moderate values of sideways lean (12 degrees for females and 8.7 degrees for males) conveyed positive attitudes, and very large (15 degree) or small (6 degree) angles communicated neutral or negative attitudes.

In addition to the preceding posture and position cues, several non-verbal and implicit verbal cues have also been found to convey different attitudes toward another. For example, verbal reinforcers such as uh-huh by definition communicate a more positive attitude (Krasner, 1958), as do positive head nods (Matarazzo, Wiens, and Saslow, 1965). Mehrabian (1965) and Wiens, Jackson, Manaugh, and Matarazzo (1969) found support for the hypothesis that lengthier communications are associated with more positive attitudes. Mahl (1959) and Kasl and Mahl (1965) provided evidence that speech disturbance frequency was a correlate of a speaker's level of anxiety or discomfort. The weight of available evidence provides strong support for Mahl's findings (Mahl and Schulze, 1964). Thus, speech-disturbance frequency should be correlated with the negative attitudes of a speaker toward his addressee, toward his own communication, as in the case of deceit, or when the referents of his message are affectively negative.

Finally, a series of findings by Rosenfeld (1966a, 1966b) led to additional hypotheses for movements and facial expressions as well as other qualities of speech. In Rosenfeld's studies, some subjects were instructed to seek approval from their addressees and others were instructed to avoid approval. The behaviors of the subjects in the approval-seeking (AS) and approval-avoiding (AA) conditions were rated on a series of nonverbal, and implicit verbal, measures. The results, as summarized by Rosenfeld, indicated the following:

> At the nonverbal level, AS subjects emitted a significantly higher percentage of smiles and a significantly lower percentage of negative head nods than did the AA subjects. AS women significantly surpassed AA women in percentage of gesticulations. AS men were significantly higher than AA men in percentage of positive head nods. . . .
>
> At the verbal level, AS subjects emitted significantly lengthier speeches and utterances than the AA subjects. The AS subjects were significantly higher than the AA subjects in percentages of recognitions [verbal reinforcers] and significantly lower in percentage of answers . . . . (Rosenfeld, 1966a, p. 600–601)

Rosenfeld also assessed the perceived effectiveness of the various behaviors produced by his communicator-subjects on the basis of correlations between the frequencies of these behaviors and the subsequent approval received from the addressee-subjects. These correlations showed that "smiles, negative head nods, and gesticulations were less effective than they were intended to be, while positive head nods and self-manipulations were more effective than intended" (Rosenfeld, 1966a, p. 603). Since approval seeking involves the communication of more positive attitudes toward the addressee than does approval avoiding, these findings by Rosenfeld, together with others which have also been noted, led to the formulation of the hypothesis that both the degree of intended and the perceived persuasiveness of a message are correlated with the following implicit cues from the speaker: shorter distances to the addressee and more eye contact with him, smaller reclining angles, more direct body orientation of females and more indirect body orientation of males to the addressee, moderate rather than high or low relaxation, more frequent smiling, frequent positive head nodding, infrequent self-manipulations, frequent verbal reinforcers, more gesturing by females, lengthier communications, and smaller speech disturbance rates.

It will be noted that the above hypotheses do not differentiate between implicit communication behaviors that are expected to be associated with intended persuasiveness and those that are expected to enhance perceived persuasiveness. The hypotheses as stated suggest that the two sets of behaviors are correlated—an assumption which is mostly supported by the attitude-communication literature. In any case, the preceding hypotheses primarily served the function of defining relevant dependent variables to be explored in studies of persuasion. The experiments reported below included all the above variables with the exception of verbal reinforcers.

No specific hypotheses were elaborated to relate communicated status to perceived and intended persuasiveness. This is because communicators and addressees in the following experiments were peers. Thus, although a higher or lower status might have been implicitly conveyed to a listener, its effects seemed unclear because actual peer status was known to both speaker and listener. Since the dependent variables noted previously were found to communicate variations in status, it was hoped that the findings would provide some information about the relation of communicated status to intended and perceived persuasiveness.

In the first two experiments below, encoding methods were used in which the behaviors of subjects were recorded and subsequently analyzed for possible differential occurrence as a function of persuasive effort. The communications that were obtained were next judged for their convincing quality, thus allowing an assessment of the contribution of various implicit cues to the judged persuasive impact of messages. In a final experiment, prepared communications in which the implicit behaviors of communicators were systematically varied were rated by subjects as to their convincingness. Thus the experiments were designed to yield information about the co-occurrence of implicit behaviors with verbal ones when a communicator attempts to be persuasive and the actual judged effectiveness of some of these cues in enhancing the persuasiveness of communication.

Encoding Experiment I

The first experiment employed an encoding as well as a role-playing method. There were three degrees of intended persuasiveness: (1) a high degree of intended persuasiveness, in which the persuasive intent of the speaker was probably obvious to the listener; (2) a moderate degree, in which the persuasive intent of the speaker was probably not obvious to the listener; and (3) communications that involved no persuasive intent at all. A second and independent factor in the experiment was the degree to which subjects agreed with the statements that they were communicating to their addressees. The sex of the subjects was a third independent factor. The sex of the listener was always the same as that of the subject.

METHOD

Thirty-six male and 36 female undergraduates were paid to participate as subjects in the study. When a subject arrived to take part in the experiment, he was given the following instructions:

> In this experiment we would like you first to read each of the numbered statements in the accompanying set of stapled pages. When you finish a given statement (e.g., Statement 3 on "Free Parking Permits"), indicate the degree of your agreement or disagreement with that statement in the answer section below.

At this point a scale ranging from +3 (*I agree strongly with the statement*) to −3 (*I disagree strongly with the statement*) was inserted, along with eight spaces for recording responses.

Each subject was also provided with eight 300-word statements which were designed to elicit varying degrees of agreement and disagreement from the undergraduates. For example, one statement was in favor of lowering the voting age to 18, another favored free parking permits for university students, and a third favored a free week for preparation before examinations.

After a subject had responded to this first portion of the instructions, three statements were selected, one with which he agreed, another to which he was neutral, and a third with which he disagreed. The subject was then given these three statements along with the following instructions.

> Now we can give you some more information about the experiment. We are concerned with *exploring the ways in which people behave when they are being persuasive*—that is, with how people act when they are trying to convince another of something. In order to study this, we are asking you to present three communications based on three of the statements which you read. The directions for these presentations are given on the next three pages.
>
> Prior to your presentation of the first communication, you will have 10

minutes to read the statement carefully and to prepare what you are going
to say and *how* you are going to say it. Feel completely free to modify the
statement in any way you wish, but keep in mind the instructions which you
received for your first communication. It is also important that you know
what you are going to say well enough so that you can freely deliver your
communication in the manner of your choice. This is necessary to approximate the real-life situations which these communications simulate. A poli-
tician always knows what his pitch will be, and a job applicant generally
prepares what he will say well in advance of his confrontation with his
prospective employer.

When you are inside the experimental room and are talking to the experimenter, he will not be allowed to talk to you; however he will be attentive to what you're saying. We must do this in order to have a controlled
experiment. Following your first communication, you will again be given 10
minutes to prepare the second communication. Later, you will have another
10 minutes to prepare the last one.

The specific instructions for the three persuasive conditions, ordered
in terms of increasing intended persuasiveness, were as follows:

(*a*) You are to present statement number ___ as follows. You are to communicate the contents of this statement to your listener in neither a persuasive nor an unpersuasive way, but in a neutral manner. In other words,
you will neither try to be convincing nor unconvincing to your listener.

In this situation you are asked to present a factual and seemingly un-
biased communication. Imagine a situation such as a courtroom, in which
you know that if there is any apparent bias, distortion, or emotional involvement, your presentation will be discarded. In this situation you must present
only the information and nothing else.

(*b*) You are to present statement number ___ as follows. You are to communicate the contents of this statement to your listener in a moderately
persuasive manner. However, you are to do so in a subtle way so that your
persuasive intent is not obvious to your listener. Thus, your approach must
be subtle and yet it must still be effective.

For this situation, imagine a salesman who has a product he wants to sell.
He knows that if he appears to be as enthusiastic as he feels, people will
think that he is only concerned with making the sale. You might also imagine
a job interview in which you want the job but must take care not to appear
pushy. These, then, are the kinds of attitudes which you are to assume
while communicating in this situation.

(*c*) You are to present statement number ___ as follows. You are to communicate the contents of this statement to your listener in a highly persuasive manner without any effort on your part to disguise your persuasive
intent from your listener. In other words, you will be trying very hard to
convince your listener and will in no way conceal the fact that you are
trying to persuade him.

This condition is one in which you are very interested in convincing the
listener and it is desirable to let him know this. Think of a situation in which

your communication will be judged both on its merits as well as on your degree of enthusiasm. Such a situation might be one in which someone has doubted your convictions and you must demonstrate that you really believe what you are saying, even if it means that you will appear pushy.

There were six possible sequences of the three communications for each agreement condition, and two replications of each of the six possible sequences were used for both the male and the female subjects, thus requiring $6 \times 3 \times 2 \times 2 = 72$ subjects for the experiment.

When the subject was ready to present his first communication, he was led into the experimental room in which he addressed a confederate of the experimenter who had accompanied the subject into the room upon the direction of the experimenter. The behaviors of the subject were recorded from an adjacent room through a one-way mirror with the use of video and audio equipment.

Following the presentation of his first communication, the subject and the confederate were asked to leave. The subject returned to the room where he had prepared his first communication to prepare his second. When he was ready, the confederate and the subject were led back into the observation room, where the subject presented his second communication. Then the subject prepared his third communication as he had the first two and conveyed it to the confederate. Four undergraduate males and four females served as confederates in the experiment.

In a final step of the procedure, subjects responded to the Eysenck and Eysenck (1963) Neuroticism and Extroversion scales, Jackson's (1967) Dominance scale, the Mandler and Sarason (1952) Test Anxiety Questionnaire, and the Shipley (1939) Intelligence Test. Subjects also responded to the question, "How good do you think you are at persuading people?" to which possible responses ranged from zero (*I am not effective at all*) to six (*I am extremely effective*). The names of these scales are largely self-explanatory. For instance, the Neuroticism scale and the Test Anxiety Questionnaire were included to measure the subject's level of psychological maladjustment, and thus to explore the social behaviors of more or less maladjusted individuals in this particular social situation. Since the tasks involved the persuasion of another, it seemed that a short measure of verbal intelligence such as the one provided by Shipley would discriminate among the behaviors of subjects who felt more self-assured due to their higher intelligence in this situation. The Dominance scale was included to explore the nonverbal behaviors of dominant persons, particularly in these situations which would encourage various degrees of dominant feelings.

As the preceding method indicates, the presentation sequence of the three communications was counterbalanced within each agreement and communicator-sex condition.

Scoring Procedures. Three judges independently rated the behavior of each subject from audio and video recordings obtained during the running of the experiment. The judges had no information about what the experimental conditions had been and therefore did not know which condition was being administered to a subject when they rated a given segment of recording. In addition, a fourth judge had directly observed the subjects through a one-way mirror, and rated the degree to which they seemed persuasive along with their distance from, and eye contact with, their addressees.

The dependent measures relating to the implicit behaviors of a communicator are given in Table 4.1. These were scored using the criteria of Appendix A. All movement cues were transformed into rate measures of number of movements per minute.

In addition to the dependent measures relating to a communicator's implicit behaviors, three measures of the perceived persuasiveness of each communication were also obtained. As already noted, the judge who viewed the subject through a one-way mirror rated each communication for persuasiveness. Similarly, three judges who viewed audio and video recordings of each communication rated these as to their persuasiveness. Finally, a group of 20 untrained subjects were shown all the communication segments, which they rated for persuasiveness after reading the following instructions:

> Please use the following scale to indicate the effectiveness of the persuasive efforts of the person in each of the segments of communication which you will watch and listen to. In rating each segment, try to take into account everything the person does in addition to what he or she says. In fact, we have tried to minimize the importance of the words by turning down the audio volume.
>
> 0: Not effective at all
> 1: Very slightly effective
> 2: Slightly effective
> 3: Moderately effective
> 4: Very effective
> 5: Very much effective
> 6: Extremely effective

Instructions and spaces for the recording of responses were inserted at this point.

RESULTS

Each judge typically viewed and heard the data recorded on video and audio tapes three times to rate all the behaviors in a given communication. Interjudge reliabilities are reported in Table 4.1. These reliability coefficients were deemed satisfactory; therefore, all of the variables were retained in further analyses of the data.

The scores obtained from the judges for a given subject were averaged for each of the dependent measures. Then the data obtained for each dependent measure were analyzed using a $2 \times 3 \times 12 \times 3$ factorial design. There were two levels of sex of the subject communicator, three levels of agreement with the message being presented (*disagreement, neutral attitude,* and *agreement*), and three levels of intended persuasiveness (*none, moderate,* and *high*). Twelve subjects were nested under the sex and agreement conditions, and repeated measures were taken over the three intended persuasiveness conditions.

Table 4.1 summarizes the results of the intended persuasiveness factor for each of the 25 dependent measures employed in the experiment. For the dependent variables that were significantly influenced by intended persuasiveness, the three mean values corresponding to the three levels of that factor are also provided in Table 4.1. An examination of these means indicates that, in 11 of the 12 cases that were significant, the relationship of the variable to intended persuasiveness was a monotonic one.

In sum, the analyses of variance yielded the following significant effects for increasing degrees of intended persuasiveness: more eye contact; smaller reclining angles; more head nodding, gesticulation, and facial activity; higher speech rate, speech volume, vocal activity, and unhalting quality of speech; and finally, more perceived persuasiveness as judged by the experimenter viewing through a one-way mirror, experimenters viewing video recordings, and subjects viewing video recordings. Since there were 25 such possible effects due to intended persuasiveness, with significance set at the 0.01 level, the expected value of the number of effects being considered significant on the basis of chance alone was 0.25. The number of actual significant effects equalled 12, and therefore compared favorably with the chance value.

Relations Among Personality Variables and Implicit Behaviors. Intercorrelations among all the dependent variables were obtained initially. It was found that abstraction scores of the Shipley (1939) Intelligence Test and rates of foot and leg movement did not relate significantly to any of the other variables. These three variables were therefore eliminated from the subsequent factor analysis.

The following 0.01 level significant correlations ($df = 214$) were obtained between the various personality measures and the implicit communication cues. The Test Anxiety Questionnaire correlated -0.18 with speech rate and -0.19 with unhalting quality of speech. The Neuroticism scale correlated 0.22 with trunk swivel rate and -0.22 with rocking rate. The Shipley Vocabulary Test correlated -0.18 with facial pleasantness. Finally, Jackson's Dominance scale correlated 0.39 with the subject's subjective estimate of his persuasive ability, -0.21 with head nodding rate, -0.22 with arm-position symmetry, and 0.21 with speech rate.

With significance set at 0.01 level, the expected value of the number of correlations (between the six personality and intelligence scales and the implicit behavior of the communicators) that would be considered significant on the basis of chance alone was less than 1.5. There were actually eight such significant effects.

Perceived Persuasiveness and Implicit Behaviors. The following significant correlations at the 0.01 level were obtained between the three indexes of perceived persuasiveness of a communication and the various implicit cues. Three kinds of judgments of the perceived persuasiveness of communication had been obtained. These were (1) judgments by un-

Table 4.1. *Mean values of implicit behaviors and perceived persuasiveness for three degrees of intended persuasiveness.*

Dependent Variable	Reli-ability	F	MS$_e$	Means for Three Degrees of Intended Persuasiveness		
				None	Moderate	High
Position Cues						
Distance	0.95					
Eye Contact	0.50	8.6	284	40%	44%	51%
Shoulder Orientation	0.96					
Posture cues						
Arm-position Openness	0.93					
Arm-position Symmetry	0.87					
Leg-position Symmetry	0.96					
Reclining Angle	0.95	7.6	121	13.8°	13.4°	7.4°
Sideways Lean	0.63					
Movement Cues (Number/Minute)						
Trunk Swivel	0.98					
Rocking	0.98					
Head Nodding	0.97	5.2	8.3	6.1	6.4	7.5
Gesticulation	0.99	18.5	41	6.9	9.1	13.3
Leg Movement	0.97					
Foot Movement	0.96					
Self-manipulation	0.93					
Facial Cues						
Pleasantness	0.79					
Activity	0.49	9.6	0.35	0.70	0.92	1.13
Verbal Cues						
Duration	0.91					
Rate	0.77	27	0.42	2.16	2.35	2.93
Volume	0.88	29	0.47	1.84	1.98	2.65
Vocal Activity	0.44	38	0.45	1.99	2.40	2.97
Unhalting Quality	0.70	8.1	0.44	1.95	2.14	2.38
Perceived Persuasiveness						
E Viewing through One-way Mirror		33	1.7	2.4	3.2	4.2
Es Viewing Video Recording		41	1.03	2.4	3.1	4.0
Ss Viewing Video Recording		29	0.29	1.6	1.8	2.3

trained subjects who watched the video recordings, (2) an experimenter who watched through a one-way mirror while the subject presented his communication, and (3) a group of experimenters who observed video recordings of the communication. The first judgment correlated 0.41 with the second and 0.38 with the third; the second judgment correlated 0.51 with the third. This indicated significant degrees of agreement among these three indexes of the perceived persuasiveness of a communication.

Each of the following variables correlated significantly with all three measures of perceived persuasiveness. The average correlation of the three indexes with vocal activity was 0.51. There was a 0.46 correlation with speech volume, 0.41 for speech rate, and 0.36 for unhalting quality of speech, 0.38 for facial activity, 0.37 for rate of gesticulation, and 0.29 for percentage of eye contact with the addressee. In addition, rate of self-manipulation exhibited significant inverse correlations with two of the indexes and an average correlation of -0.19 with the three indexes of perceived persuasiveness. With $df = 214$, all of the preceding average correlation values are significant at the 0.01 level. Once again, the latter eight significant correlations compare favorably with the 0.22 expected value for the number of correlations that would be considered significant by chance alone.

In sum, rated in order of importance for their contribution to perceived persuasiveness, the above variables would be listed as follows: more vocal activity, more speech volume, higher speech rate, more facial activity, higher rate of gesticulation, less halting speech, more eye contact with the addressee, and lower rate of self-manipulation.

Factor Analysis of the Measures. All of the dependent measures, as well as measures of personality characteristics of the subjects, were factor analyzed to obtain additional information about their interrelationships. In the following summary of the factor analytic results, the statements are worded to eliminate the necessity of indicating the loading directions. A principal component solution yielded four factors with eigenvalues greater than 2.0. Varimax rotation of these four factors yielded a set of groupings which was easy to interpret. The four factors were as follows:

1. Perceived Persuasiveness factor: the persuasiveness of a communicator from the video recordings of his communications, as judged by untrained subjects; percentage of eye contact of the communicator with his addressee; the judged persuasiveness of a communicator as directly observed through a one-way mirror by one of the experimenters; the persuasiveness of a communicator as judged from video recordings of his communications by a group of trained experimenters; relatively low rates of self-manipulation; and greater degrees of facial activity, speech rate, speech volume, vocal activity, and unhalting speech.

2. Nonimmediacy factor: higher degrees of reclining angle of the communicator while seated, less direct orientation toward the addressee, rela-

tively low rates of head movement, greater distances from the addressee, longer durations of communication, male rather than female communicators, and higher estimates by the communicator of his own persuasive ability. (Dominance scores had their second highest loading on this factor.)

3. Dominance factor: low scores on the Test Anxiety Questionnaire, high scores on the Shipley Vocabulary Test, high scores on the Dominance and Extroversion scales, low scores on the Neuroticism scale, and less facial pleasantness.

4. Relaxation factor: greater degrees of sideways lean, leg-position asymmetry, arm-position asymmetry, arm openness; higher rates of gesticulation and rocking; and lower rates of trunk swivel.

Encoding Experiment II

In the second experiment an encoding method was used to investigate the implicit communications of subjects who were instructed to be persuasive versus those of subjects who were instructed to be informative. When a speaker attempts to be persuasive, his listener's positive or negative reception of the message is a salient cue which may interact with the degree of persuasive intent to determine speaker behaviors. Therefore, although no specific hypotheses were proposed, addressee reception of a message was included in the experiment as an additional factor. In one condition, addressees nonverbally (for example, with posture and orientation) conveyed a positive and receptive attitude to the speaker; in the other condition, the addressees were nonverbally negative or unreceptive. The dependent measures were those listed in Table 4.1.

METHOD

The subjects for this experiment were 72 undergraduates who were paid to participate in the study. When a subject arrived to participate in the experiment, he was given a questionnaire in which he was requested to indicate his preference of various presidential candidates in the 1968 election. He rated each of 15 candidates on a seven-point preference scale, which ranged from +3 (*I would not only vote for this candidate but I would also do precinct work for him to help him get elected*) to −3 (*I not only would not vote for this candidate but I would work to prevent him from being elected*).

After rating the candidates, the subject was requested to present either a persuasive or an informative message. The instructions for the intended informative condition were as follows:

> In this experiment we are concerned with the effects on the listener of persuasive versus informative communications. A persuasive communication is one in which the communicator's goal is to change the attitude of the

listener, whereas in an informative communication, the speaker is concerned only with conveying information to his listener.

In this experiment we have randomly assigned the subjects to two groups. The first group consists of those subjects upon whom we are actually experimenting. They will listen to persuasive or informative communications and we will give them tests to determine how these communications affected their beliefs.

The second group in this study, the group of which you are a member, is helping us to create our experimental situation. In order to present the experimental group with realistic communications, we are having members of your group spontaneously present either persuasive or informative communications. The subject matter for your group is presidential candidates. Your communication will be about the candidate that you rated highest on the attitude survey that you have just completed, that is, _____. You are to help us provide an *Informative* communication to one subject in this experiment.

Your listener does not know about your views, but we are going to tell you about his views. The person you will be talking to *feels neutral or is in slight disagreement* [italicized part handwritten] with your views about the candidate of your choice. We would like you to *present your communication in such a way that your listener will not change his opinion of your candidate* on the candidate attitude questionnaire which you have already taken (and which he will take again).

If after you talk to the subject we question him and find out that he is well informed about your communication and that he has not changed his view of your candidate, you will receive a bonus.

Take about 5 minutes now to prepare an informative presentation concerning this candidate. While presenting your communication, the only thing we will require you to do is to remain seated in the chair we will show you; otherwise you will be free to do anything you want, that is, place the chair where you want it, sit whichever way you want, and do and say what you think is appropriate. Please remember, however, that the subject has been instructed to remain silent while listening to you.

The instructions for the intended persuasive condition were identical to the above except for the following changes:

You are to help us provide a *Persuasive* communication to one subject in this experiment.

. . . We would like you to *present your communication in such a way that your listener will change his opinion of your candidate by two or more points* on the candidate attitude questionnaire which you have already taken (and which he will take again).

If after you talk to the subject, we question him and find out that he is well informed about your communication and that he has changed his views of your candidate by two or more points on the candidate attitude questionnaire, you will receive a bonus. Take about 5 minutes now to prepare a persuasive presentation concerning this candidate.

The subject was given about five minutes to prepare his communication in a room which was adjacent to the experimental room. Near him was a confederate, who was pretending to be reading the instructions also. When the subject was ready, the experimenter asked the subject and the confederate to accompany him to the experimental room, which was 20 by 10 feet in size. There were a few pieces of furniture near the walls, leaving an open area in the center of the room. When the experimenter asked the confederate to take a seat, the latter assumed a pre-arranged position. The experimenter then said to the subject, indicating a swivel chair on rollers, "Please take this chair, move it wherever you want it, and present your talk to him [her]." Unknown to the subject, his verbal and nonverbal behaviors were recorded through a one-way mirror from an adjacent room. Observers also scored the eye contact and distance, and judged the persuasivenes of each subject.

Following the brief two- or three-minute presentation of his message, the subject was taken to another room, where he responded to two questions about his performance. The first question was "How much do you think your presentation changed your listener's opinion?" Responses could range from −3 (*greatly in a direction away from mine*) to +3 (*greatly in a direction toward mine*). The second question was, "How good do you think you are at persuading people?" Responses ranged from zero (*I am not effective at all*) to six (*I am extremely effective*).

Subjects also responded to questionnaires including the Mandler and Sarason (1952) Test Anxiety Questionnaire, Jackson's (1967) Dominance scale, the Shipley (1939) Intelligence Test and the Eysenck and Eysenck (1963) Neuroticism and Extroversion scales.

Six male and six female undergraduates were employed as confederates in the study. These confederates were given the minimal amount of information necessary for their performance. They were coached to sit and move in the "receptive" condition with a forward body lean of about 20 degrees from the vertical, facing the subject. Limb placement was relaxed and slightly asymmetrical, with the hands on the lap or loosely clasped, whichever felt more comfortable. They had eye contact with the subject 90 per cent of the time, with moderately pleasant facial expression and occasional nodding. For the "unreceptive" condition, they were instructed to sit leaning back about 20 degrees from the vertical with body orientation turned about 15 degrees away from the subject. Limb placement was more asymmetrical than in the receptive condition. There was only 50 per cent eye contact with the subject, with neutral-moderate facial pleasantness, and no nodding.

Scoring. The video recordings of the subjects' behavior were scored independently by three judges, who used the criteria of Appendix A. In this study, the two dependent measures, vocal activity and unhalting quality of speech, were not scored. There were three other scores obtained from four additional judges who were undergraduates recruited only for this task. A perceived persuasiveness score was based on "How well do you think the subject persuaded his or her addressee?" Responses ranged from zero (*not effective at all*) to six (*extremely effective*). Judgments of communicator comfort were obtained with the question "How comfortable do you think the subject was while making his or her communication?" Judgments ranged from zero (*extremely uncomfortable*) to six (*extremely comfortable*). Finally, judges responded to the question "For this subject, how important do you think his nonverbal behaviors are in communication relative to his verbal behaviors?" Responses ranged from zero (*not at all*, that is, the verbal portion is the only important one), to six (*extremely important*, that is, the nonverbal portion is of primary importance).

RESULTS

Dependent measures for this experiment were scored from complete recordings of the various communications by three judges. In other words, the judges could both hear and see the communicators on the monitor screen while they scored. Reliability ratings for these measures have already been reported in Table 4.1.

The scores obtained from the judges were averaged for each dependent measure and each subject. These average scores were next analyzed using a $2 \times 2 \times 2 \times 9$ factorial design, in which there were two levels of subject sex, two levels of intended persuasiveness (that is, *none* and *high*), two levels of receptivity of the addressee (*receptive* and *unreceptive*), and nine subjects nested under each of the Subject Sex X Intended Persuasiveness X Receptivity conditions.

The significant effects for intended persuasiveness and its interactions with communicator sex or addressee receptivity are summarized in Table 4.2. For example, intended persuasiveness was the only significant factor in the analysis of variance of eye-contact scores. The last two variables listed in Table 4.2 relate to perceived persuasiveness. The latter, as judged by experimenters who viewed through a one-way mirror, was found to be significantly affected only by the intended persuasiveness factor. A similar result was found for perceived persuasiveness as judged by experimenters who viewed the recordings of the communications.

The results summarized in Table 4.2 indicate the following correlates for increasing degrees of intended persuasiveness of a speaker: more eye contact with the listener; decreasing rate of trunk-swivel movement for female speakers only; increasing rates of self-manipulation, only when the listener was receptive; increases in perceived persuasiveness based on judgments of experimenters who viewed the communicator through a one-way mirror; increasing perceived persuasiveness based on judgments of experimenters who viewed a recording of the communication.

Table 4.2. *Significant effects of intended persuasiveness on implicit communicator behaviors and perceived persuasiveness of his message.*

Effect of:	F	MS_e	Condition Interacting with Intended Persuasiveness	Means for two Degrees of Intended Persuasiveness	
				None	High
Intended Persuasiveness on eye contact	3.8	558		36%	47%
Intended Persuasiveness × Sex on Trunk Swivel Rate	4.8	28	M F	5.30 7.80	6.18 3.20
Intended Persuasiveness × Receptivity on Self-manipulation Rate	11.2	35	Receptive Unreceptive	5.4 6.2	11.6 3.0
Intended Persuasiveness × Receptivity on Speech Rate	4.1	1.2	Receptive Unreceptive	2.4 1.7	1.8 2.1
Intended Persuasiveness on Perceived Persuasiveness for Es viewing through one-way mirror	28	2.5		2.17	4.14
Intended Persuasiveness on Perceived Persuasivness for Es viewing video recording	4.3	1.7		2.12	2.75

With 23 dependent variables, three possible significant effects for each variable, and a significance level of 0.06, the total number of significant effects obtained on the basis of chance alone is less than 4.2. The actual number of significant effects equalled seven. The ratio of the actual number of significant effects to the expected value of such effects by chance alone was not favorable in this case, and therefore these findings will be interpreted cautiously.

Correlational Analyses. All of the dependent measures, and measures of personality characteristics and sex of the subjects were correlated. With $df = 70$, the following 0.05 level significant correlation coefficients were obtained. The Neuroticism scale correlated 0.26 with rate of head nodding. Jackson's Dominance scale correlated 0.44 with the subject's estimate of his own persuasive ability, 0.36 with global judgments of the overall comfort of the speaker, 0.29 with the speech volume of the speaker, and 0.24 with the subject's sex—males obtaining the higher dominance scores. Communicator sex exhibited the following significant relationships with the various indexes of nonverbal behavior: males relative to females assumed more symmetrical leg positions and more reclining positions; they had higher leg- and foot-movement rates and were more comfortable as judged by observers; their facial pleasantness and activity, however, was less than that of females.

Finally, as in the first encoding experiment, the implicit communication cues were each related to two available indexes of perceived persuasiveness. These indexes were based on judgments by experimenters who observed the communicator directly through a one-way mirror as he presented his message, and by a group of experimenters who observed video recordings of the communications. The correlation between the two indexes was 0.67, which indicated significant agreement of judgments based on the two methods. With $df = 70$ and $r_{0.05} = 0.232$, the following variables were found to correlate significantly with both indexes: an average correlation of 0.52 with judgments of the predominance of nonverbal over verbal behaviors of the subject-communicator, an average correlation of 0.51 with the global judgments of the comfort of the subject while communicating, 0.49 with speech volume, 0.34 with the subject's estimated success in having persuaded his listener, 0.33 with speech rate, 0.30 with rate of gesticulation, 0.29 with per cent eye contact with the listener, and 0.28 with Dominance scores. In addition, for the following variables only one significant correlation was obtained with the two perceived persuasiveness ratings. This yielded an average correlation of 0.23 with duration of a communication, 0.22 with facial activity, and 0.21 with the subject's own estimate of his general persuasive ability.

With significance set at the 0.05 level, the expected value of significant average correlations between the various dependent measures and perceived persuasiveness is less than 1.3. There were actually seven significant effects, thus comparing favorably with the chance level.

In sum, excluding the predominance of nonverbal over verbal behavior and the comfort indexes which, in a way, were redundant indexes of perceived persuasiveness, as well as excluding the subject's own estimates of his persuasive ability and his success in persuading the listener, greater degrees of the following variables (listed in order of their importance) were found to relate significantly to perceived persuasiveness: speech volume, speech rate, gesticulation rate, eye contact with the addressee, Dominance score of the communicator, duration of communication, and facial activity.

For comparability with the first encoding experiment, the factor analysis of the set of variables for the second experiment employed a rotation of the first four factors that had eigenvalues greater than 2. Varimax rotation of these four factors yielded the following groupings of the variables.

1. Perceived Persuasiveness factor: This factor was defined by the highest loading from judgments of the video recordings in response to the question "For this subject, how important do you think his nonverbal be-

haviors are in communication relative to his verbal behaviors?" Other variables were perceived persuasiveness of the subject as ascertained from a viewing of video tape recordings, less direct shoulder orientation, facial pleasantness and activity, and higher speech rate and volume.

2. Dominance factor: This factor consisted mostly of personality variables and was defined by higher scores on the Dominance scale, low scores on the Neuroticism scale, high scores on the Extroversion scale, relatively high estimates by the subject of his own persuasive ability, male rather than female subjects, the comfort of the subject while he was communicating as estimated by judges who viewed a video recording of the communication, relatively high rates of leg and foot movement, longer durations of communication, and relatively higher rates of self-manipulation.

3. Relaxation factor: This factor was defined in terms of greater angle of sideways lean of the communicator while seated, greater reclining angles, more arm-position and leg-position asymmetry, more arm openness, higher rocking rates, and lower scores on the Test Anxiety Questionnaire.

4. Intended Persuasiveness factor: This factor was defined by the degree to which observers judged the communication to be convincing and persuasive in quality while viewing the subject through a one-way mirror, more eye contact with the listener, the subject's own estimate of his success in persuading his listener in that particular communication instance, relatively low rates of trunk swivel, and high rates of head and hand movement.

Decoding Experiment

The third experiment was designed to investigate the effects of the nonverbal behaviors that either enhance or detract from the perceived persuasiveness of a communication. A decoding method was employed in the experiment. Video tape recordings of nonverbal communications were presented to subjects who were then requested to judge the degree to which the communication was convincing.

The preceding two experiments showed that intended persuasiveness and perceived persuasiveness of communications were correlated. Further, in both experiments, the postural cues relating to relaxation were not generally found to relate individually to either perceived or intended persuasiveness. Thus, an experimental paradigm was required in which a communicator's *total* relaxation could be manipulated to allow assessment of the proposed hypothesis relating relaxation to perceived persuasiveness.

Both of the preceding experiments had indicated that the dependent variables of asymmetry in the positioning of arms or legs, arm openness, reclining angle, and sideways lean were all relevant measures of relaxation. Therefore, in this experiment a decoding method was employed in which four degrees of postural relaxation of a communicator were video recorded and corresponded to increasing degrees of asymmetry of limb placement, reclining angle, sideways lean, and arm openness. Furthermore, the use of a decoding method allowed the investigation of possible interactive effects of relaxation, eye contact, and distance in determining perceived persuasiveness.

Thus the factors investigated in this experiment were the sex of the communicator-model, the sex of the addressee-subject, two distances between the model and the addressee, two degrees of shoulder orientation toward the addressee, two levels of eye contact with the addressee, and four levels of relaxation.

The dependent measure in the study was the degree to which the addressee-subject found a given communication convincing.

METHOD

Undergraduates were hired to participate as subjects. There were four male and four female model-subjects and 114 male and 114 female subject-decoders.

Thirty-two 30-second video tape recordings were obtained from each of four male and four female communicator-models. Four factors were employed to generate the 32 communications of each model: (1) the distance of the model from the camera—either four or 12 feet, (2) the shoulder orientation of the model toward the camera—either zero or 30 degrees turned away from the camera, (3) eye contact vis-à-vis the camera—either 90 per cent or 50 per cent of the 30-second interval, and (4) postural relaxation of the model, which consisted of four degrees:

1. Slightly tense: This was classified as a symmetrical posture in which the subject was leaning forward in his chair about 10 degrees away from the vertical with a straight back, but without obvious muscle contraction or very obvious tension. His hands, arms, and legs were positioned symmetrically and his feet were placed flat on the floor.

2. Slightly relaxed: The model sat leaning about 10 degrees forward from the vertical, with arms and legs placed slightly forward so that, for example, while both feet were on the ground one foot was slightly more forward than the other. Similarly, hands were on the lap but were not in a symmetrical position; for example, one hand was resting on one knee and the other one was resting on the thigh. There was some degree of curvature in the model's back.

3. Moderately relaxed: The model was leaning back at an angle of about 15 degrees away from the vertical and there was a greater degree of asymmetry in the positioning of the legs and arms; for example, one

leg was extended forward whereas the other was bent at the knee. There was a greater degree of curvature in the model's back as the reclining position was more relaxed than in the second condition.

4. Extremely relaxed: The model was reclining backward at an angle of about 30 degrees and leaning sideways in his chair at an angle of about 20 degrees. His legs and arms exhibited an even greater degree of asymmetry. The model in this condition was instructed to be as loose and relaxed as possible.

Thus the four increasing degrees of relaxation were designed in terms of increasing degrees of reclining angle, asymmetry in the positioning of limbs, and sideways lean.

The models' faces were concealed with the use of a blank cardboard mask with slits for the eyes. They sat in the specified position for 30 seconds and were video recorded in that position. In order to introduce variations in eye contact, models looked in the direction of the camera either 90 per cent or 50 per cent of the 30-second interval, in response to signals from the experimenter. Thus, for one of the 50 per cent eye contact conditions, the models looked in the direction of the camera for five seconds, looked away at an angle of about 20 degrees from the camera for another 10 seconds, looked back toward the camera for 10 additional seconds, and then looked away again for the final five-second interval.

The 32 communications of each of four male and four female models were randomized and recorded on video tape, and a number was assigned to each.

The experiment was administered to the subjects in several group sessions. Each subject was presented with the following written instructions and an answer sheet to record his judgments.

> In this experiment we want to find out what things a speaker can do, besides the things that he says, which may make him more or less convincing to his listener. You will be in the role of the listener in this experiment and will be watching 30-second segments of communications on the TV screen. For each of these segments we would like you to imagine the following situation. You are seated in the same room as the communicator who is on the TV screen, and he is trying to convince you of something; you and the communicator are alone together in this room. We have shut off the sound portion of the recording so that you can attend only to the communicator's way of sitting and his selected position in the room relative to you. For all of the different 30-second segments which you will watch, please remember that your position in the room is the same, whereas the different people who are addressing you may move around in the room and assume different seating postures in speaking to you. These positions and ways of sitting are what we would like you to attend to in your task of trying to decide how convincing each of the communication segments seems to you.
>
> For each segment you are to use the following scale to indicate how con-

vincing you think the communication seems to you.

0: Not convincing at all
1: Very slightly convincing
2: Slightly convincing
3: Moderately convincing
4: Quite convincing
5: Very convincing
6: Extremely convincing.

In each group administration, subjects were presented with a random sequence of video recordings of the eight different communicators but, since only the between-model communications were randomized, the subjects within each of the group sessions received the same sequence of communications of a given model.

RESULTS

The dependent measure in this experiment was the convincingness of the communications as judged by the decoder-subjects and ranged from zero to six. A 2 Subject-Sex × 114 Subjects × 2 Model-Sex × 2 Distance × 2 Orientation × 2 Eye Contact × 4 Relaxation factorial design was employed, where subject-sex was the only between-subject effect. The significance of an effect was assessed at the 0.01 level. These results are summarized in Table 4.3.

It is seen from Table 4.3 that communicator sex interacted with distance to, and eye contact with, the addressee in determining perceived persuasiveness. The cell means show that, for male speakers who were seated at a small distance from their listeners, variations in eye contact were not significant (2.07 for 90 per cent eye contact and 2.09 for 50 per cent eye contact). For male speakers who were seated at a relatively greater distance, 90 per cent eye contact was perceived as less persuasive (1.60) than 50 per cent eye contact (1.74). For females, once again the effects of eye contact at a relatively small distance from the listener were not significant (1.96 for 90 per cent eye contact and 1.93 for 50 per cent eye contact). There was a significant effect (in the opposite direction from that for male speakers) when the female speaker was seated at a relatively greater distance from her listener. In this case, her message was perceived as more persuasive for 90 per cent eye contact (1.75) than it was for 50 per cent eye contact (1.67).

Table 4.3 also indicates a Communicator Sex × Orientation effect. Whereas for female speakers a direct (1.80) shoulder orientation did not significantly differ in its effect from an indirect shoulder orientation (1.82), communications of males were perceived as more persuasive when shoulder orientation was indirect (1.97) than when it was direct (1.78). In other words, only in the case of male speakers did a more

Table 4.3. Significant determiners of perceived persuasiveness.

Source	F	df	MS_e	Communicator sex	Mean Perceived Persuasiveness			
					50%		90%	
Eye Contact × Communicator Sex	53	1/226	0.34	M	1.92		1.84	
				F	1.80		1.86	
					4 ft.		12 ft.	
Distance	145	1/226	2.63	M or F	2.01		1.69	
Distance × Communicator Sex	49	1/226	0.55	M	2.08		1.67	
				F	1.95		1.71	
Distance × Eye Contact × Sex	18	1/226	0.37	M (50% eye contact)	2.09		1.74	
				F (50% eye contact)	1.93		1.67	
				M (90% eye contact)	2.07		1.60	
				F (90% eye contact)	1.96		1.75	
					Direct 0°		Indirect 30°	
Shoulder Orientation	29	1/226	1.06	M or F	1.81		1.90	
Shoulder Orientation × Sex	73	1/226	0.48	M	1.78		1.97	
				F	1.80		1.82	
					slightly tense	slightly relaxed	moderately relaxed	very relaxed
Relaxation	208	3/678	5.04	M or F	2.10	2.46	1.65	1.20
Relaxation × Sex	138	3/678	0.66	M	1.95	2.69	1.64	1.24
				F	2.25	2.23	1.67	1.17

direct shoulder orientation detract from the perceived persuasiveness of their messages.

There were also four second-order interactions between communicator relaxation and each of addressee sex, communicator-sex, distance, and shoulder orientation. Finally, a series of three-way and four-way effects, and one five-way effect, which involved the relaxation factor, were also obtained. Examination of the corresponding cell means indicated that the effects of relaxation on perceived persuasiveness were consistently parabolic so that, with minor variations, the cell means corresponded to the main effect of relaxation shown in Table 4.3. Of these effects, the most interesting and strongest interaction was that of Communicator Sex × Relaxation, which is also reported in Table 4.3. This interaction effectively summarizes the contribution of relaxation to perceived persuasiveness and the remaining effects involving relaxation only suggest minor variations within this general pattern. Whereas the cell means for increasing degrees of communicator relaxation on perceived persuasiveness were 1.95, 2.69, 1.64, and 1.24 for male speakers, the corresponding cell means for female speakers were 2.25, 2.23, 1.67, and 1.17. In other words, a slight degree of tension in the posture of male communicators significantly detracted from perceived persuasiveness, compared to slight relaxation. For females, slight tension and slight relaxation had similar effects, both of which differed significantly from those of moderate and extreme relaxation.

With significance set at the 0.01 level, the total number of significant effects expected by chance alone from the analysis of variance was less than seven. The actual number of significant effects was 24, which compares favorably with the number expected by chance.

In sum, the hypotheses for the effects of distance and relaxation were supported in this decoding experiment. An indirect shoulder orientation enhanced perceived persuasiveness more than a direct shoulder orientation only in the case of male speakers. Further, for both male and female speakers who sat at a small distance from the listener there were no effects due to eye contact. However, for males seated at a large distance from the listener increasing degrees of eye contact were perceived as less persuasive, whereas for females who sat at a large distance from the listener increasing degrees of eye contact were perceived as more persuasive. Thus, in general, the hypothesis for eye contact was not supported in this experiment.

Discussion

In considering the findings of the three Mehrabian and Williams (1969) experiments, it is helpful to distinguish between the kinds of implicit cues that are likely to be associated with increasing persuasive effort and those that enhance the perceived persuasiveness of communications. The first encoding experiment showed that the following implicit behaviors were associated both with the increasing intent to persuade and the perceived persuasiveness of a message: more vocal activity, more speech volume, higher speech rate, more facial activity, higher rate of gesticulation, less halting quality of speech, and more eye contact with the addressee. In addition, it was found that smaller reclining angles and more head nodding were associated with increasing intent to persuade and that a lower rate of self-manipulation was correlated with the perceived persuasiveness of a communication.

Intended persuasiveness was a within-subject effect in the first encoding experiment, but a between-subject effect in the second one. Consequently, a smaller number of significant effects were obtained in the second experiment. Increases in persuasive effort were found to be associated with more eye contact with the listener, lower rates of trunk swivel (for females only), and higher rates of self-manipulation when the listener was receptive. Furthermore, the judged persuasiveness of a communication was found to correlate positively with speech volume, speech rate, gesticulation rate, eye contact with the addressee, length of communication, facial activity, and Dominance scores of a communicator. (It will be recalled that the second experiment did not employ the vocal activity and unhalting speech variables found to relate significantly to perceived persuasiveness in the first encoding experiment.) The findings relating to eye contact in both experiments were consistent with a hypothesis and data presented by Exline and Eldridge (1967).

The last three rows of Table 4.1 and the last two rows of Table 4.2 show that when a speaker attempted to be persuasive he was also judged as being persuasive. Correlational data corroborated these results. In the first experiment, for instance, a considerable number of implicit cues were found to be associated with both intended and perceived persuasiveness. Although the second experiment produced few effects related to intended persuasiveness, the implicit cues that were found to contribute to perceived persuasiveness once again overlapped with those obtained in the first experiment. Thus, these findings were consistent with previous studies that showed that the same implicit cues used to encode a given attitude were used to infer that attitude (for example, Rosenfeld, 1966a and 1966b in the case of movement and verbal cues; Mehrabian, 1969b, in the case of posture and position cues).

One aspect of the method used in the first experiment that may be of some concern was the possible two-dimensional manipulation of intended persuasiveness. Subjects in the "moderate" condition were told to be both moderately persuasive and subtle, whereas subjects in the "high" condition were told to be highly persuasive without attempting to conceal their persuasive efforts. The monotonic quality of 11 out of 12 effects reported in Table 4.1 suggests that one rather than two independent variables were involved; or, more precisely, that the obviousness of persuasive intent and degree of intended persuasiveness are correlated dimensions in terms of their behavioral concomitants.

One by-product of the two encoding experiments was that several postural cues were found to define a relaxation factor. When treated individually, these postural variables yielded only one signficant relationship to intended or perceived persuasiveness. Since the proposed hypotheses related intended or perceived persuasiveness to a speaker's total relaxation rather than to individual relaxation cues, the latter were combined in the third experiment to prepare four degrees of postural relaxation. In addition, the position cues of eye contact, distance, and orientation were also included. The latter two cues (distance and orientation) did not have any significant effect on intended or perceived persuasiveness in the first experiment, and it seemed that the absence of such effects could have been due to interactions with other behavioral cues. The use of a decoding method in the third experiment, then, not only allowed an assessment of the effects of total relaxation but also of the main and interactive effects of eye contact, distance, and orientation in determining perceived persuasiveness. The results showed that, as hypothesized, smaller distances from the listener enhanced perceived persuasiveness; also, relaxation exhibited the expected curvilinear relationship. An indirect orientation toward the listener enhanced perceived persuasiveness more than a direct orientation in the case of male speakers, as hypothesized. However, the hypothesized reverse effect for females was not obtained. Finally, eye contact produced significant effects only at greater distances and in opposite directions for males and females—less eye contact from males and more from females were perceived as more persuasive.

Thus, the findings from the decoding experiment in general supported the hypothesis that postures and positions that convey liking to a listener also contribute to the judged persuasiveness of a communication. The exceptions to this were the absence of a significant effect for the shoulder orientation of females and the result for eye contact obtained for males.

The interaction in the third experiment between relaxation and communicator sex showed that, for male communicators, slightly tense postures were perceived as significantly less persuasive than slightly relaxed postures. This was not the case for females. Such a finding suggests that slight degrees of tension in the posture of males hinted at their discomfort about communicating the particular message. Slight tension in the posture of females did not necessarily communicate such discomfort, but was rather interpreted as a socially appropriate posture for females who were communicating to strangers.

At this point, it is possible to review the evidence bearing on the proposed general hypothesis regarding the direct correlation between intended or perceived persuasiveness and the degree of liking conveyed to the addressee. In the preceding three experiments there were frequent instances of absence of significant findings where such findings had been hypothesized. However, among the obtained significant effects, the majority conformed to the proposed set of derivative hypotheses. The only exception was less eye contact of males being perceived as more persuasive—but only in the third experiment, and in contrast to the findings of the first two experiments.

There were four communication cues employed in the study that yielded significant relationships to intended and perceived persuasiveness and for which no hypotheses had been proposed: speech rate and volume, and vocal and facial activity. These are measures of activity level that are generally independent of positive-negative attitude or the evaluative dimension. More precisely, Osgood, Suci, and Tannenbaum (1957) identified activity and evaluation as two independent dimensions. Their data as well as subsequent work showed a small positive correlation between activity and evaluation (for example, 0.33 in Bentler's 1969 study).

With the information that is presently available to us about these activity cues, it is more appropriate to refer to them as measures of communicator *responsiveness* to his addressee. In other words, the significance of these cues is their reflection of the addressee's salience for the speaker in the communication situation. The strongest effects by far showed that a communicator's responsiveness to his listener was a monotonically increasing function of his intended persuasiveness, and that perceived persuasiveness was correlated with communicator responsiveness. These results, which were unexpected, showed that a communicator's responsiveness was an even more important factor than his positiveness in a persuasion situation. During persuasion, increased responsiveness to the target is only natural, since he is the primary focus of one's preoccupation; however, it is interesting, too, that increased responsiveness also contributed to the perceived persuasive quality of a message. Thus, the exploration of this factor as a determiner of the persuasive impact of a message seems quite crucial in further studies of the role of implicit cues in persuasion.

The results of the factor analyses provided surprisingly consistent support for earlier interpretations of certain postural cues (Mehrabian, 1968a, 1968b). In the first experiment, greater degrees of sideways lean, leg-position asymmetry, arm-position asymmetry, arm openness, higher rates of gesticulation and rocking, and lower rates of trunk swivel loaded on one (Relaxation) factor. The only variable not present which might have been expected was the reclining angle of the speaker. Reclining angle did, however, have its second highest loading on this relaxation factor. Thus, the results for this factor provided corroborative support for earlier interpretations of these postural cues as indexes of relaxation. The results also showed that, for a seated communicator, higher rates of gesticulation and rocking were positive correlates of relaxation and a higher rate of trunk swivel was an index of discomfort or tension.

In comparison, the Relaxation factor obtained in the second encoding experiment included all of the postural cues of the preceding Relaxation factor as well as reclining angle. Finally, lower scores on the Test Anxiety Questionnaire and higher rocking rates were associated with increasing relaxation.

A Dominance factor obtained from the second encoding experiment showed that males were more extroverted and dominant, less neurotic, and had a higher estimate of their own ability to persuade others than did females. Furthermore, judges found dominant and extroverted individuals as being more comfortable in the communication situations. This corroborated the obtained relation of a more dominant social position to greater relaxation in several studies reviewed by Mehrabian (1969b). Finally, the more dominant individuals also produced longer communications and engaged in more self-manipulation. Incidentally, the high rates of leg and foot movement that loaded on this factor were most probably due to the male-female distinction, since findings have shown that males have more leg and foot movements than do females while they talk.

The first and fourth factors obtained in the second experiment were designated as perceived and intended persuasiveness respectively, but, due to the correlation between the latter two dimensions, a complete separation of the two factors was not achieved. Thus, although facial activity, speech rate, and volume loaded on the first factor, eye contact and observers' judgments of persuasiveness loaded on the fourth factor. However, head and hand movements and trunk swivel, which were correlates of intended persuasiveness, were grouped within the fourth factor.

The factor analyses also provided information about the significance of various movement cues. In the first encoding experiment, a significant correlation of trunk swivel rate with scores on the Neuroticism scale was obtained. This suggested that trunk swivel movement was an indicator of discomfort or unwillingness to interact with another person in a highly immediate or proxemic manner. As to the results of the factor analysis, the fourth factor provided further support for this interpretation by showing that high rates of trunk swivel tended to be associated with less relaxed postures. Thus, when the physical setting allowed the speaker to minimize his eye contact and directness of orientation toward the listener via such swivel movements, he used these in a casual way to minimize the immediacy.

In the same experiment, rocking rate correlated inversely with the Neuroticism scale, and thus suggested a lower level of discomfort in the speaker—an interpretation which was further supported by the results of the factor analysis where rocking rates were associated with more relaxed postures (fourth factor). In contrast to trunk swivel, rocking did not diminish the immediacy of interaction, since, while rocking, a speaker could directly orient to, and maintain eye contact with, his listener. These findings provided unexpected yet interesting interpretations for trunk swivel and rocking in communication.

The first encoding experiment also yielded the following two results relating to an additional interpretation for head nodding: the inverse correlation between head-nodding rate and scores on the Dominance scale, and the grouping of the variables within the second (Nonimmediacy) factor. This second factor was somewhat difficult to name, since on the one hand it included nonimmediacy cues (that is, greater reclining angles, less direct orientation, and increasing distances from the listener) and on the other hand some self-confidence cues (higher estimates of one's own persuasive ability, males rather than females, longer communications, and higher Dominance scores). The variables subsumed by this factor can be interrelated conceptually. Findings have shown that a person who considers himself of a higher status than his listener does assume relatively nonimmediate postures and positions to that listener (for example, Mehrabian, 1968a; Mehrabian and Friar, 1969). Lott and Sommer (1967), for instance, showed that a person selects more distant positions to listeners whom he considers more different in status from himself. Thus, the inclusion of head-nodding rate in this second factor, together with its significant inverse correlation with Dominance scores, provided the following interpretation: frequent head nodding, in addition to communicating liking to a listener, implies a less confident or submissive speaker.

Just as in the case of head nodding, rate of smiling seems also to reflect both liking toward the listener and a less confident or subordinate speaker. This additional interpretation is based on the third (Dominance) factor obtained from the first encoding experiment. In this factor, facial pleasantness was associated with less dominant, more neurotic, and more anxious tendencies of an individual. Thus, when greater facial pleasantness or higher rates of smiling occur in somewhat awkward social situations (such as those involved in the method of the first experiment), they indicate greater efforts by a speaker to relieve tension and discomfort by "placating" the listener.

The preceding interpretations of the significance of rates of trunk swivel, rocking, head nodding, and smiling are novel and therefore tentative. Head nodding and smiling were seen as having at least two kinds of significance, whereas trunk swivel and rocking rates were only interpreted as negative and positive correlates of relaxation respectively. It is recognized that additional interpretations of these cues are possible and that the qualities of the social situations in which such behaviors occur could highlight different kinds of significance for the cues. For instance, as already noted, frequent smiling in a socially awkward situation may indicate a less confident feeling in the communicator rather than a liking for the addressee. In other social situations, however, where the communicator and addressee are moderately familiar, frequency of smiling could be more an indicator of liking than of discomfort.

At this point, the results of the encoding and decoding experiments can be compared. In general, for a preliminary study of an area of implicit communication, the use of encoding methods seemed preferable to decoding ones. Given, however, such information about important variables from encoding experiments, decoding methods were employed to study the interactive effects of variables more adequately. In this light, the first encoding experiment seems to have been the most informative. Some of the results of that experiment led to the development of the third experiment, in which the effects of total relaxation in a speaker's posture were explored. Thus, the particular sequence of use of encoding and decoding methods led to the development of a more compact set of stimuli for the decoding experiment than would otherwise have been possible. Further exploration of implicit cues in relation to intended and perceived persuasiveness or attitude change can continue with encoding methods. Once findings from such studies are available, the effects of variables obtained from the encoding studies on perceived persuasiveness can be systematically explored in decoding studies.

A final issue to consider is the effect of the implicit communication of status on perceived or intended persuasiveness. The actual status of a communicator, which may be defined in terms of income level and/or education, is in itself a determiner of perceived persuasiveness. However, inferences of socioeconomic status that an addressee can make (for example, from directly available information, or from more subtle indicators such as clothing or vocabulary) may be discrepant from the status that is implicitly communicated to him. Thus, in considering the role of implicitly communicated status, it seems that the critical variable may be the difference between the speaker's actual status and the one that he implicitly conveys to his listener. If this index is positive, that is, if the implicitly communicated status is higher than the actual status, a detrimental effect on the perceived persuasiveness of the message is expected. In contrast, if the index is small in absolute value, then its effect is neither positive nor negative. If the index is moderately negative, that is, if the speaker implicitly conveys a lower status than the one he actually possesses, it is expected that perceived persuasiveness is enhanced. Finally, if the index is substantially negative, then it is expected that once again the effect will be detrimental. A similar hypothesis would relate intended persuasiveness to the communicated-minus-actual status index.

The data from the Mehrabian and Williams (1969) study provided some information relevant to the latter hypothesis relating perceived and intended persuasiveness to implicitly communicated status. For example, head-nodding rate was interpreted as partly an index of a speaker's less confident or submissive attitude toward his listener, and therefore higher head-nodding rates should have been associated with increased persuasiveness of a speaker. The first encoding experiment showed that higher rates of head nodding were indeed associated with greater persuasive effort. Again, in accordance with the results of the factor analysis from the second encoding experiment, higher rates of self-manipulation may be interpreted as communicating a dominant position of the speaker to his listener. It would thus be expected that high rates of self-manipulation should detract from the perceived persuasiveness of the communication, which was indeed the case in the first encoding experiment.

In both the preceding instances, more head nodding and less self-manipulation conveyed greater liking and less dominance, and were associated with intended or perceived persuasiveness. A more interesting exploration of the role of communicated status could involve situations in which the implicit cues that signify more dislike also signify a more respectful or submissive attitude to the listener (for example, greater distances from the listener). Thus, in attempting to be persuasive, distance cues would be affected in opposite directions. This may partially explain the absence of findings with distance cues in the encoding studies, but more generally suggests a paradigm for assessing the relative strengths of status communication and the communication of liking in determining perceived persuasiveness.

Summary

Our three experiments explored the hypothesis that the degree of liking that is implicitly conveyed to a listener is a direct correlate of the intended persuasiveness of a speaker and the perceived persuasiveness of his message. The implicit attitude-communication literature provided a basis for several derivative hypotheses relating to specific position, posture, facial, movement, and verbal cues. An unexpected and very consistent set of results showed that, when a person attempted to persuade a stranger on some issue, his implicit responsiveness to the target increased monotonically with the extent of his persuasive effort. The relations of responsiveness (that is, facial and vocal activity, speech rate, and volume) to intended and perceived persuasiveness were by far the most powerful effects. Nevertheless, the findings supported the hypotheses that related implicit communications of positive affect to persuasive effort and perceived persuasiveness. The intended persuasiveness of a speaker and the judged or perceived persuasiveness of his message were correlated. The findings also helped to determine the referents of some movement cues and suggested a grouping of a set of postural cues which together defined total bodily relaxation.

5

Nonverbal Betrayal of Feeling

Nonverbal behaviors play an important role in many social situations, particularly when a communicator is either unable or unwilling to express his feelings explicitly. Ekman and Friesen (1969a) provided the following appropriate quotes from the older writings on this topic.

> Some actions ordinarily associated through habit with certain states of mind may be partially repressed through the will, and in such cases the muscles which are least under the separate control of the will are the most liable still to act, causing movements which we recognize as expressive. In certain other cases the checking of one habitual movement requires other slight movements; and these are likewise expressive. (Darwin, 1965, p. 28)

> He that has eyes to see and ears to hear may convince himself that no mortal can keep a secret. If his lips are silent, he chatters with his finger-tips; betrayal oozes out of him at every pore. (Freud, 1959, p. 94).

The concept of repression in psychoanalytic theory, for instance, led to the exploration of nonverbal behaviors as a means of inferring a client's "unacceptable" feelings (Deutsch and Murphy, 1955). Indeed, psychoanalysts' early informal discussions of the consequences of repression or reaction formation seemed to provide the impetus for research on nonverbal behavior. More recent studies of nonverbal behavior have moved in many other directions.

But, in light of all that is now known about the significance of various movements, facial expressions, implicit aspects of speech, and postures

Acknowledgment is given to Academic Press, Inc., for their permission to use, in this chapter, a rewritten version, including Tables 1, 2, and 3, of my paper, "Nonverbal Betrayal of Feeling," *Journal of Experimental Research in Personality*, 5 (1971), 64–73.

and positions, it seemed appropriate to return once again to some of the issues that first instigated the study of implicit behaviors. What behaviors are unwittingly emitted by a person during his conversation that may help to identify his distress, discomfort, or deliberate distortion? It was hoped that exploration of this question would produce findings of broader relevance—to identify behaviors in those social situations in which implicit communication of attitudes is either more appropriate or becomes a necessary concomitant of a speaker's affect. Examples of such commonly unverbalized attitudes include: a clinician's feelings toward a client, an employee's distress or frustration with an employer, a teacher's conversation with the parents of an unruly child, or an unverbalized lovers' quarrel.

To explore these issues, it was necessary to select a method in which subjects would verbally express something other than what they really felt or experienced. Deceitful communications seemed to provide a reasonably satisfactory paradigm for that purpose.

Using such a paradigm, Ekman and Friesen (1969a) directed themselves to the following question: If it is assumed that concealed information is bound to find an outlet, where is it most likely to emerge? We can restate their answer succinctly by using the concept of "channel capacity" (the amount of information a communication medium can transmit per unit time [Cherry, 1966, p. 178]). In this regard, facial cues are rated highest, then hand, and finally the feet/legs. Ekman and Friesen's hypothesis was that the areas of the body with lower channel capacity are more informative about deception. Specifically, then, when a person is deceitful his feet/legs should be the most informative about the affect he conceals, then his hands, and finally his face.

To test their hypothesis, Ekman and Friesen showed silent films of two patients to two groups of naive observers. One group viewed the face and head of the speaker, and the other group viewed only the neck and body. The viewers used an adjective check list to describe the attitudes and feelings of the two patients. For the first patient, who was attempting to conceal that she was upset, a good many adjectives of a negative quality were assigned to both the head and body messages. The results for the second patient, who was withholding information about being confused and anxious, were somewhat clearer: her head messages were primarily positive and her body messages were primarily negative. The latter finding supported the idea that in deception the characteristically more informative sources (facial expressions) are less useful indicators than are the less informative sources (body cues such as arm and leg/foot movements).

If the deception had been experimentally induced, rather than assessed on the basis of clinical observation, there would have been minimal ambiguity in interpreting the results of Ekman and Friesen's (1969a) study.

Needless to say, experimental control conditions (which were lacking in the study) would have been necessary also to separate the effects of deception from the subjects' characteristic styles of implicit communication. In other words, if negative affect cues were expected to be more predominant in one part of the body when a subject was being deceptive it would have been important to show that negative affect cues occurred less frequently in that part of the body when the subject was not being deceptive. In addition, a more rigorous study of this problem would have required a larger number of films and standardized scales for rating positive-negative affect to allow statistical tests of the difference in affect conveyed by body and head cues.

All in all, the data from the two particular patients described by Ekman and Friesen (1969a) did not provide a basis for either accepting or rejecting their hypothesis. At this point in research, it would be more appropriate to examine the behaviors of subjects who are being deceptive and compare this to the behaviors of the same or other (control) subjects who are being truthful. Such a preliminary search would help to identify the nonverbal cues that distinguish the two states. In this context, some early experiments are relevant. Exploration of latency measures in word association tasks (for example, Jung, 1905; Luria, 1930; Marston, 1920) or GSR and blood pressure measures (for example, Chappell, 1929) were motivated by the hypothesis that a deceitful person can be expected to exhibit fear or avoidance reactions which are reflected in subtle physiological cues. Although the findings from these experiments did not unequivocally support the hypothesis, they did provide a guideline to the study of nonverbal cues in deceit: a speaker is expected to exhibit a greater degree of negative affect toward the communication situation while being deceitful than while being truthful.

Given this assumption, the literature on implicit communication provided a basis for developing specific hypotheses for various nonverbal cues associated with deceit. The positive-negative affect indicators in implicit behavior, reviewed in Chapter 4, can be rephrased as hypotheses for deceitful communication: (1) Posture and position: A communicator is less immediate to his addressee when he is deceitful than when he is truthful. (2) Movement: When a communicator is deceitful, he gesticulates and exhibits positive head nods less frequently, and smiles more, than when he is truthful. (3) Various aspects of speech behavior: A deceitful communicator speaks at a slower rate, talks less in terms of number of words, and produces more frequent speech errors. Although these hypotheses suggested a limited set of implicit behaviors as possible indicators of deceit, additional cues were employed in the following experiments for exploratory purposes.

For a series of exploratory experiments such as these, it seemed appropriate to employ a diversity of methods. Also, the different contents which the subjects talked about in the three experiments were all designed to be emotionally arousing.

Experiment I: Implying Truthfulness While Conveying Ideas Consistent or Inconsistent with One's Belief

In the first Mehrabian (1971a) experiment, subjects communicated both deceitfully and truthfully to different addressees. Initially, the subjects were asked for their opinions regarding the legalization of abortion —a heavily debated issue, which was selected to elicit strong negative or positive feelings. Each subject then presented a truthful communication regarding abortion (one which was consistent with his or her views), and also a deceitful communication (one which was inconsistent with his views). To simulate two common conditions of deceit, the effects of a reward-shock factor were also explored. In the reward condition, subjects were promised bonus pay for lying successfully, that is, provided the confederate was unable to detect their deceit; in the shock condition, they were threatened with mild electric shock if the confederate detected their deceit.

METHOD

Fifty-six University of California undergraduates were paid to participate as subjects in the experiment. Each subject first indicated his attitude toward abortion, and then wrote a paragraph explaining his position. Those subjects who expressed extreme views (both for and against) were selected to continue the experiment. Those without extreme views were paid and dismissed at that point, although very few had to be dismissed. Participating subjects then received a detailed set of written instructions explaining what they were to do next.

These instructions presented the experiment as a challenge to the subject's ability to always give the impression of truthfulness, whether actually telling the truth or being deceitful. Subjects received two lists of statements, one of arguments supporting abortion and the other of arguments against it, and some information about John B. Watson. They had ten minutes to study the material, after which they made three presentations, one each to three different judges: (1) a practice communication about John B. Watson, (2) a communication advocating abortion, and (3) a communication against abortion. The practice condition always came first, followed by conditions two and three in random order. Thus, one situation was consistent with the subject's belief on the issue of abortion, whereas the other was contrary to his belief as expressed in the initial phase of the expreiment. He was to present both communications

Table 5.1. Summary of significant findings from analyses of variance in Experiment I.*

Dependent Measure (Independent Effect)	F	MS_e	Means			
Immediacy (Reinforcement × Deceit)	3.4	0.17	Reward	Truth 0.06	↔	Deceit −0.20
			Punishment	0.06	↔	0.08
Relaxation (Reinforcement)	4.7	6.1	Reward = .51			Punishment = −.51
Facial Pleasantness (Reinforcement)	30.4	0.23	Reward = 1.13			Punishment = 1.63
(Sex × Deceit)	4.9	0.18	Male	Truth 1.29	↔	Deceit 1.54
			Female	1.39	↔	1.29
Rocking Rate (Sex × Reinforcement)	3.4	140	Male	Reward 3.2	↔	Punishment 4.5
			Female	8.7	↔	1.7

Foot Movement Rate (Deceit)	4.4	38	Truth = 6.8	Deceit = 4.3
Leg Movement Rate (Reinforcement)	3.7	7.5	Reward = 1.7	Punishment = 0.7
(Deceit × Reinforcement)	5.0	6.1	Reward	Deceit
				Truth 2.34 ↔ 0.98
			Punishment	0.30 ↔ 1.03
Speech Duration (Reinforcement)	5.2	15675	Reward = 181 sec	Punishment = 127 sec
Speech Error Rate (Deceit)	4.1	3.6	Truth = 3.13	Deceit = 3.86

* $P < .10$, $df = 1/52$ for all effects reported in this table. Arrows connect cell means which, based on *t*-tests differ significantly at the 0.05 level. Rate measures are number of movements per 100 sec.

89

in a manner that would convince the judges he was giving his true opinion. Subjects had five additional minutes before each presentation to prepare what they wanted to say. No judge knew any particular subject's real attitude on the issue, nor which condition he was enacting at any time; these opinions had been obtained by another assistant in the experiment, who alone knew the subject's attitudes.

In the reward condition, subjects were told that if they convinced both judges that they were telling the truth they would receive a $2.00 reward from the judge they had fooled. In the punishment condition, subjects were told they would receive an electric shock from any judge who correctly concluded they were not telling the truth. A shock device, which was in the room during this condition, was pointed out to the subjects. The addressee-judge, rather than the experimenter, was the dispenser of reinforcers to maximize his emotion-arousing quality for the subject.

Four observers watched each subject's behaviors during the second and third communication conditions through a one-way mirror. Three of them scored various subsets of the dependent measures, listed in Table 5.1, together with speech, gesticulation, and head-nodding rates; the fourth observer alternately scored various categories for reliability. The relevant subset of scoring criteria given in Appendix A was used. Speech error rate was scored later from audio recordings. Like the judges, none of the observers knew any subject's true attitude toward abortion.

RESULTS

Reliability figures for the scoring of each dependent measure, given in Appendix A, were deemed satisfactory. Therefore, all dependent measures were retained for further analyses. The scores obtained from the judges for a given condition and subject were averaged for each dependent measure. Then each dependent measure was analyzed using a $2 \times 2 \times 14 \times 2$ factorial design. There were two levels of sex of the subject-communicator, two levels of reinforcement (anticipated reward versus punishment), with 14 subjects nested under each of the Sex × Reward conditions, and finally two levels of deceit (deceit versus truth), which involved repeated measures.

Table 5.1 summarizes the results of the analyses of variance. The significant effects for each dependent measure are given in parentheses. In the case of two-way interactions, arrows connect those cell means found to differ significantly. For instance, analysis of variance of immediacy scores showed significance for Reinforcement × Deceit: subjects who were promised reward for successful deceit were more immediate while truthful (0.06) than while deceitful (−0.20). There was no corresponding significant difference for subjects who were told they would be shocked if their deceit were detected correctly.

Experiment II: The Effects of Role-played and Actual Deceit

Our second experiment (Mehrabian, 1971a) explored the effects of the following factors on the nonverbal behavior of a subject: the actual deceitful versus truthful quality of the verbal communication, role-playing of a deceitful versus truthful communication, the sex of the communicator, and the interactions of these with the Extroversion and the Neuroticism scores on the Eysenck Personality Inventory (Eysenck and Eysenck, 1963) and the Mandler and Sarason (1952) Text Anxiety Questionnaire. Subjects first gave their opinions on a variety of social issues, 12 of which involved specific persons and 12 of which involved more abstract issues. The subjects then received instructions to present four types of communications: (A) telling the truth so that the listener is convinced he is hearing the truth, (B) telling the truth so that the listener is convinced he is hearing a lie, (C) lying so as to convince the listener he is hearing the truth, and (D) lying so as to convince the listener he is hearing a lie. The subject presented twelve issues to one judge in an order prearranged by the experimenter; three issues were communicated in each of the four ways.

METHOD

Forty-eight University of California undergraduates served as paid subjects in the experiment. They first received instructions for rating each of 24 issues on a seven-point scale ranging from *strongly against* to *strongly in favor*. The issues included such topics as lowering the voting age to 18, peace demonstrations, wiretapping by the government, mercy killing, capital punishment, barring of prayers in public schools, and the control of firearms. For each subject, 12 issues to which he had responded in an extremely favorable or unfavorable manner were selected. To obtain additional commitment from the subject, he was asked to write about two sentences for each topic to explain his position. The experimenter selected three issues for each of the four conditions that have already been enumerated.

The subject was told that the next part of the experiment was a game involving four conditions. He received detailed instructions explaining the four conditions and how he was to proceed in each one. He also received a list of the 12 issues that had been selected for him on the basis of his responses. Each numbered issue was preceded by the letter A, B, C, or D to indicate which condition the subject was to portray in his presentation of that particular issue. The order of the conditions was counterbalanced over all subjects.

After each presentation, the judge-confederate recorded his opinion as to whether the subject was lying or telling the truth. The subjects had

Table 5.2. Summary of significant findings from analyses of variance in Experiment II.*

Dependent Measure (Independent Effect)	F	MS$_e$	Means		
Immediacy					
(Role-played Deceit)	10.6	0.28	Truth = 0.04	↔	Deceit = −0.04
(Sex × Extroversion)	2.9	1.5			
			Extroversion	↔	Introversion
Male			0.13		−0.41
					↕
Female			0.11		0.17
Relaxation					
(Sex)	4.9	14.3	Male = 0.60		Female = −0.60
Facial Pleasantness					
(Actual Deceit)	7.8	0.065	Truth = 1.04		Deceit = 1.15
(Actual Deceit × Role-played Deceit)	12.0	0.08			
			Actual truth		Actual deceit
Role-played truth			1.02		0.99
					↕
Role-played deceit			1.05	↔	1.31
Gesticulation Rate					
(Sex × Extroversion × Actual Deceit)	4.4	2.2			
			Truth		Deceit
Male					
Extrovert			3.2		3.6
			↕		
Introvert			4.3	↔	3.7
Female					
Extrovert			3.1	↔	2.3
Introvert			2.6	↔	2.7

92

			Actual truth	Actual deceit
Head Nodding Rate (Actual Deceit × Role-played Deceit)	4.7	0.53		
		Role-played truth	1.9 ↕	1.7
		Role-played deceit	1.5	1.8
Speech Duration (Role-played Deceit)	7.2	114.0	Truth = 43 sec	Deceit = 38 sec
Speech Rate (Actual Deceit × Role-played Deceit)	9.2	0.087	Role-played truth	Actual truth 2.10 ↕ ↔ Actual deceit 1.99
			Role-played deceit 1.89 ↕	2.02

*$p < .10$, $df = 1/44$ for all effects reported in this table. Arrows connect cell means which, based on t-tests, differ significantly at the 0.05 level. Rate measures are number of movements per 100 sec.

been told that they would receive one point each time the judge scored them as telling the truth when they presented conditions A or C or judged them as lying during conditions B or D. They were also informed that if, at the end of the 12 presentations, they had earned ten or more points, they would receive a bonus of $3.00. As in Experiment I, the subject began with a sample condition to help him relax and become familiar with the setting. The judge-confederates did not know which condition a subject was enacting at any time; they knew only that the subject would be lying 50 per cent of the time. Two male and two female confederates were used in the experiment. Thus, subjects always addressed confederates of their own sex.

Subjects were told afterwards how accurately the judge had been able to guess their performance in the 12 conditions. Three subjects actually received the $3.00 bonus because they had earned ten or more points. In the last phase of the procedure, subjects responded to the Eysenck Personality Inventory and the Text Anxiety Questionnaire.

Four observers who were located behind a one-way mirror in an adjacent room recorded and scored the behaviors, using the categories and criteria of Experiment I. Speech error rate was not scored in this experiment, but eye shift rate was scored.

RESULTS

Scores for each dependent measure were analyzed using a $2 \times 2 \times 12 \times 2 \times 2$ factorial design. There were two levels of communicator sex, two levels of communicator Anxiety (or alternatively, in a second series of analyses of variance, two levels of communicator Extroversion), with 12 subjects nested under each of the Communicator Sex × Personality variable conditions, and repeated measures taken over each of two levels of deceit (truthful versus deceitful actual communications) and role-played deceit (role-played truthfulness and role-played lying).

In one set of analyses of variance, the Extroversion scale was used to explore possible interactions of one personality variable with deceit in determining implicit behaviors. In a second set of analyses of variance, the personality factor employed (and referred to as Anxiety) was the sum of a subject's z-scores on the Test Anxiety Questionnaire and on the Neuroticism scale. These combined Anxiety and Neuroticism scores were used, since initial separate sets of analyses of variance involving the Anxiety and Neuroticism dimensions yielded similar results. The results of this second experiment are summarized in Table 5.2, using the same format as that for Table 5.1.

Experiment III: Behaviors Under High Motivation to be Deceitful

In the third Mehrabian (1971a) experiment, the subject responded to a number of personality scales prior to his participation. The intent of the experiment was completely disguised from the subject, and the method was designed to maximize the subject's desire to lie without being caught.

METHOD

Forty-one University of California undergraduates served as paid subjects in this experiment. Complete data were obtained only from 19 male and 13 female subjects.

Each subject was first administered the Text Anxiety Questionnaire and the Eysenck Personality Inventory. He was then taken to another room, where a confederate of the experimenter, posing as another subject, was seated and seemed to be studying instructions. The subject was given about five minutes to read the same set of instructions, which explained that the experiment was a study of ESP and described the situation in which he and another subject (the confederate) would participate. The two would sit at opposite ends of a partitioned table and try to communicate by ESP. Each would have a button to press. A buzzer would sound only when both buttons were pressed simultaneously. They would be permitted only brief presses (one second or less) and could press the button only once every 15 seconds. Thus, in an eight-minute session, the maximum number of possible buzzes was 32. Since they could not see each other over the partition, the two subjects were to use ESP channels to achieve the buzzes. Allowing that they could get some by chance, they were told that, if they made the buzzer work at least 15 times, they would be considered to have ESP and would receive bonus pay.

The confederate subject enacted either a "cheat" or a "no-cheat" condition on the basis of a prearranged schedule which he selected himself, and which was unknown both to the experimenters and to those who were recording the subject's behaviors. In the "cheat" condition, after about one minute had elapsed, the confederate-subject got up from his chair, looked around the partition, and without saying anything, signaled to the subject when to press his buzzer. If the subject was willing to accept the signal, they continued in this way and achieved the number of buzzes required for them to receive the cash bonus. In the "no-cheat" condition, the confederate simply held his button down almost continuously during the entire interval, so that again the required number of buzzing sounds was achieved.

Following both conditions, the subject reported that he and his partner had successfully communicated using ESP. Following the "cheat" condition, however, the subject knew he had cheated to get the desired number of buzzing sounds. Nine of the subjects did not accept the confederate's offer to cheat or subsequently confessed to cheating. Thus, their data were excluded from the analyses of results.

At the end of the eight-minute period, an interviewer led the subject to an adjacent room, seated him and asked:

Table 5.3. Summary of significant findings from analyses of variance in Experiment III.*

Dependent Measure (Independent Effect)	F	MS_e	Means			
Relaxation (Extroversion)	3.3	7.5	Extroversion = 1.12		Introversion = −0.64	
Facial Pleasantness (Deceit × Anxiety)	11.2	0.21	High-anxiety	Truth 1.6 ↔	Deceit 1.0	
			Low-anxiety	1.0 ↔	1.5	
(Deceit × Extroversion)	6.0	0.24	Extroversion	Truth 1.1 ↔	Deceit 1.5	
			Introversion	1.5 ↔	1.0	
Trunk Swivel Rate (Deceit × Extroversion)	5.3	15.3	Extroversion	Truth 1.1 ↔	Deceit 4.1	
			Introversion	5.1 ↔	1.6	
Head Nodding Rate (Deceit × Anxiety)	3.2	2.7	High-anxiety	Truth 2.8 ↔	Deceit 0.9	
			Low-anxiety	2.1 ↔	2.4	

				Truth		Deceit
(Deceit × Extroversion)	5.1	2.4	Extroversion	3.0	↔	1.3
			Introversion	1.2	↔	1.9
				Truth		Deceit
Self-manipulation Rate (Deceit × Anxiety)	2.9	0.93	High-anxiety	1.1	↔	0.5
			Low-anxiety	0.3	↔	0.8
Speech Rate (Deceit)	4.4	1.3	Truth = 1.7			Deceit = 2.5
Speech Volume (Anxiety)	2.9	0.68	High-anxiety = 2.2			Low-anxiety = 2.7
Percentage Talk During Total Duration of Interaction (Deceit)	3.5	183	Truth = 89%			Deceit = 80%

*$p < .10$, $df = 1/28$ for all effects reported in this table. Arrows connect cell means which, based on t-tests, differ significantly at the 0.05 level. Rate measures are number of movements per minute.

"Could you tell me how you went about trying to communicate with ESP?" "How did you feel while you were trying to communicate using ESP?" "Do you think the choice of a partner is important in this type of situation?" "Did you follow the instructions?"

At all times during these interactions, the interviewer had a relatively pleasant facial expression, sat leaning forward about 10 degrees in his chair in a moderately relaxed posture (that is, relatively asymmetrical placement of arms and legs) and looked at the subject about 90 per cent of the time.

The interviewer told the confederate whenever a subject confessed to cheating, so that the confederate could readjust his schedule. No knowledge of the conditions was available to the interviewer until all the subjects had been run. In the final stage of the procedure, an experimenter who was not the interviewer met with both the confederate and the subject and carefully debriefed the subject.

During the entire interview period the subject's behavior, position, and speech were video recorded from an adjacent room through a one-way mirror, without the subject's knowledge. In addition, observers rated the subject's eye contact with the experimenter. Subsequently, the video recorded tapes were independently scored by three judges who used the categories and criteria used in Experiment II (but not eye-shift rate), in addition to those given in Table 5.3. None of the observers knew which condition he was rating.

RESULTS

The scores obtained from the judges for a given subject were averaged for each of the dependent measures. Average scores for each dependent measure were next analyzed using a $2 \times 2 \times 8$ factorial design. There were two levels of deceit (*deceitful* versus *truthful communication*), and two levels of Anxiety (or Extroversion, in a second set of analyses), and eight subjects nested under each of the Deceit $\times$ Anxiety (or Extroversion) conditions. The Anxiety factor was the same as in Experiment II. The results of this experiment are summarized in Table 5.3, using the same format as in the preceding tables.

Discussion

The results from all three Mehrabian (1971a) experiments suggest the following tentative generalizations. Significant results for immediacy cues (distance, forward lean, and eye contact) were consistent with the hypothesis and showed that a greater degree of negative feeling is conveyed in nonverbal behaviors when a communicator is being deceitful. In one experiment, which explored frequency of eye shifts toward or away from the addressee, no significant effects were obtained, thus suggesting that amount of eye contact, rather than rate of eye shifts, may be the basis for the popular notion that "shifty eyes" reflect deceit.

Postural relaxation was not hypothesized as relating to deceit; the findings likewise did not indicate any relationship. Among the movement cues, the hypotheses for head nodding and gesticulation were supported in every instance where a significant effect was obtained.

In the first two experiments, communicators exhibited more pleasant facial expressions when they were being deceitful. This finding supports Ekman and Friesen's (1969a) hypothesis that facial cues are less likely to be useful for detecting deceit because there is a greater awareness and control of the messages that the face transmits. The finding is also consistent with the interpretation of Mehrabian and Williams that "Greater facial pleasantness . . . [when it occurs] in somewhat awkward social situations . . . may indicate greater efforts of a communicator to relieve tension and discomfort by placating the addressee" (Mehrabian and Williams, 1969, p. 56). Findings from the third experiment suggested further refinement of that interpretation. Introverted or high-anxious subjects exhibited less facial pleasantness while they were being deceptive, whereas the reverse was true for low-anxious subjects. This experiment did elicit much stronger feelings from the communicators than did the first two. So this finding, together with the high-anxious or introverted communicators' generally lower ability to cope with the difficult interpersonal situations involved, indicates that the anxious (but not the less anxious) communicators in the third experiment were experiencing too much distress to have been able to willfully manipulate the situation by smiling more frequently. Thus, Mehrabian and Williams' (1969) suggested interpretation of smiling may be applicable barring extreme cases of communicator discomfort.

Among the implicit cues associated with the speech of a communicator, speech duration, consistent with the hypothesis, was less when a communicator was deceitful. In the second experiment, both the effects of actual and role-played deceit served to decrease speech rate. In the third experiment, however, speech rate was higher when the communicators lied. Since distress was probably very high in the latter condition, the contradiction can be resolved by assuming that speech rate is high for slight levels of discomfort (such as in the truth condition of Experiment II), is low for moderate levels of discomfort (such as in the deceit conditions of Experiment II), and is high for very high levels of discomfort (such as in the deceit condition of Experiment III). It is important to note here that the preceding statement is not based on the specific values of speech rate obtained in the third experiment. In Experiment III, judgments of speech rate were made subjectively, though reliably, by raters who used a five-point scale, whereas in the second experiment speech rate was measured in terms of number of words per 100 seconds.

Speech error rate, scored only in Experiment I, was greater for communicators while they were deceitful than while they were truthful. This is consistent with the Kasl and Mahl (1965) hypothesis that speech error rate is a correlate of a communicator's discomfort or anxiety. It is also consistent with the proposed hypothesis of the relationship between deceit and negative affect communication.

The findings of the three experiments do show that interactions of communicator anxiety (or more generally, communicator ability to skillfully cope with difficult interpersonal situations) with deceitful-truthful communication can be fruitfully explored as determiners of implicit behaviors in such situations. The relevant hypothesis is that the greater one's skill in interpersonal relations, the less is the negative affect communicated implicitly while being deceitful. Experimenting with children versus adults can provide a basis for testing that hypothesis. Also, experiments involving individual difference measures of interpersonal skills, such as the Phillips (1968) social competence scale, could be used to test the same hypothesis with adults.

The differences in the methods of the three experiments require some comment. Experiments I and II were similar in that both employed the same subject in the deceit and truth conditions. Experiment II, however, was superior because several communications of the subject, instead of only one, were elicited in each of these conditions.

The design of Experiment II is of broader relevance for the use of role-playing paradigms in social psychological experiments. The design allowed the examination of the effects of role-played and actual deceit within the same experiment. Analogous designs could, for instance, explore the effects of role-played and actual dislike of another, prejudicial attitudes, or even cognitive dissonance. In Experiment II there was a Role-played Deceit × Actual Deceit effect for facial pleasantness and speech rate. This effect showed that facial pleasantness and speech rate were affected in the same way by role-playing as by actual deceit. Also, head nodding was less frequent for the deceit conditions in the second experiment; however, this difference was only significant when deceit was role-played. In comparing the results obtained from the second experiment with those from the first and third experiments, it is not clear whether the findings for actual deceit have greater validity than do those for role-playing. That is to say, there are as many corroborating effects in the first and third experiments for findings from the actual deceit-truth conditions as there are for findings from the role-playing conditions. Although this was not the result in our study, the incorporation of a "role-playing" versus "actual" factor within the same experiment can provide fruitful information about systematic differences in these two methods. An experiment by Horowitz and Rothschild (1970) does just this. If the two methods are found to yield equivalent results, then the role-playing paradigm would be the preferred one, since it is easier to use.

Finally, although the method of Experiment II used a within-subject design, thus maximizing the efficiency of the experiment, the method of Experiment III was more representative of actual deceitful situations. The interviewer in Experiment III noted a considerably higher level of emotional arousal in the subjects than had been noted in interviews with the subjects in Experiments I or II. There may be some value, then, in modifying the method of Experiment III to develop a similar paradigm which would also include a within-subject, deceit-truth factor.

In addition to the findings that differentiated deceitful from truthful communications, many others supported earlier interpretations of the significance of various nonverbal cues. In the first experiment, eye contact with a threatening addressee (that is, a judge who could possibly shock the subject) was greater than that with a nonthreatening addressee. This is consistent with Mehrabian's (1968b) finding that male communicators exhibited an unusually greater degree of eye contact with extremely disliked males than with extremely disliked females. Mehrabian noted that, although eye contact decreased as dislike of the addressee increased to a moderate level, this effect was reversed for even greater degrees of dislike, thus indicating vigilance in response to a threatening other. A measure of the communicator's relaxation (body lean sideways while seated) was similarly affected by the threatening quality of an addressee.

> The findings relating to sideways lean and shoulder orientation suggest a consistent pattern of differences for the nonverbal behaviors of male and female communicators, vis-á-vis male addressees who are disliked intensely. Relative to females, male communicators exhibit less body relaxation (as indicated by less sideways lean) and a greater degree of vigilance (as indicated by more direct shoulder orientation and a similar trend approaching significance for eye contact) toward intensely disliked males. Otherwise, for the remaining four degrees of attitude, communication behaviors of males and females exhibit similar patterns. The differences obtained for intensely disliked male addressees can be interpreted by suggesting that these addressees are potentially a greater threat to a male than a female communicator, and therefore elicit a greater degree of body tension and vigilance from the former than from the latter (Mehrabian, 1968b, p. 29).

The first experiment further supported the preceding interpretation and the more general interpretations of such phenomena offered in the final section of Chapter 2—communicators were more relaxed when they anticipated possible reward than when they anticipated possible shock.

In interpreting their movement data, Mehrabian and Williams (1969) suggested that rocking and gesticulation rates while seated are correlated with communicator relaxation. Findings from the first experiment supported the proposed interpretation for rocking movements: rocking movement rates of female communicators, who would be expected to be affected most by the threatening quality of an addressee, were lower with threatening than with nonthreatening addressees. Further, gesticulation rate was positively correlated with relaxation in Experiments I and II.

All of the significant findings relating to head nodding in our three experiments supported Rosenfeld's (1966a) interpretation. In the third experiment, high-anxious subjects nodded less frequently than low-anxious ones while they were being deceitful. In general, lower rates of head nodding were associated with deceitful communication.

Mehrabian and Williams (1969) suggested that leg and foot movements occur more frequently when a communicator is of higher status or is more relaxed than his addressee. In the first experiment, leg and foot movements were more frequent when the communicator was truthful than when he was deceitful, and leg movements were more frequent when a communicator talked to a nonthreatening than to a threatening addressee. In the third experiment only, rates of leg and foot movement correlated directly with postural relaxation.

Length of communication has been suggested as an index of a communicator's positive attitude toward the object of his communications, toward the addressee, or toward the communication act itself (Mehrabian, 1965; Rosenfeld, 1966a). In the first experiment, speech duration was greater with a non-threatening than with a threatening addressee. In the second and third experiments, lengthier communications were obtained with truthful than with deceitful communications. Speech rate and speech error rate have already been discussed. Finally, speech volume has previously been found to indicate a more dominant and self-assured feeling of the communicator (note Experiment II in Chapter 4), and indeed in the third experiment speech volume was higher for the less anxious communicators.

In sum, the findings provided the following additional information about the significance of the various nonverbal cues that were employed. Consistent with previous interpretations, (1) greater degrees of eye contact and less relaxation show vigilance and are expected in situations where the addressee is somewhat threatening; (2) in awkward or formal situations smiling is associated with a communicator's effort to relieve tension and placate his addressee; (3) while seated, rates of rocking, gesticulation, and leg and foot movement indicate a communicator's comfort and relaxation; and (4) speech volume is a correlate of a more dominant and self-assured feeling of a communicator. Thus, wherever significant effects were obtained, the results supported the existing interpretations. Since the empirical evidence for the significance of movement rates of the various body parts is sparse, the findings from the three experiments presented in this chapter are helpful in confirming the earlier tentative suggestions.

It may be appropriate in closing to consider the implications of the findings of this study for psychological maladjustment—a problem which initially highlighted the significance of nonverbal and implicit verbal behaviors. A disturbed person's selective attending to segments of his interpersonal experience, which leads to gross distortions or even to denials of significant components of his experience, is an avoidance reaction accompanied by negative affect. Freudian concepts of repression, reaction formation, or denial describe psychological states that are associated with severe distress. Our findings suggest some value in the selection of the deceitful communication paradigm to study maladjustment, since indeed one hypothesis that received support was that negative affect-indicating nonverbal cues occur more frequently in deceitful than in truthful communications. Such tentative findings may have some value in identifying someone's distress while he communicates about various contents and issues.

Summary

In three experiments, the behaviors of deceitful communicators were explored to study the more general situation in which a person is unwilling or unable to verbally convey his feelings. The hypothesis that received some support was that negative affect-indicating cues occur more frequently in deceitful than in truthful communications. Specifically, when being deceitful communicators nodded and gestured less, exhibited less frequent leg and foot movements, assumed less immediate positions relative to their addressees, talked less, talked slower, had more speech errors, and smiled more. In addition to their relevance for deceit, the findings also provided detailed information about the significance of the various implicit cues employed in the study.

6

Inconsistent Messages and Sarcasm

Now that the significance of individual cues in communication has been reviewed, we will consider more complex communications that involve the simultaneous use of several channels. The basic issue behind the study of multichannel communications is the meaning or function of inconsistent versus consistent (redundant) messages. The concept of inconsistent, or double-bind communication (Haley, 1963; Schuham, 1967; Weakland, 1961) has received considerable attention in the past decade, but only recently has it been formulated as a measurable phenomenon.

Implicit in any discussion of inconsistent communication is a referent. In an inconsistent message, various components denote contradictory referents, whereas information provided by various components of a consistent message is redundant. We have seen that the referent of any message can be described in terms of the liking, potency, and responsiveness which it signifies. Thus, there can be inconsistency in the denotation of a referent on any one of these three dimensions. In most of the studies to be reviewed in this chapter, positive-negative feelings (levels of liking) were the referents of communication. However, the methods and questions are also applicable to the study of communications of potency and responsiveness.

There are several interrelated issues in the study of multichannel communications: (1) How does one combine consistent or inconsistent communications of attitude received in several channels to infer the attitude implied in the entire message? (2) Why do people use inconsistent communications at all? If the joint combination of inconsistent verbal

The first two sections of this chapter contain rewritten segments from Mehrabian and Ferris' "Inference of Attitudes from Nonverbal Communication in Two Channels," *Journal of Consulting Psychology,* 31 (1967), 248–52; and from Mehrabian and Wiener's "Decoding of Inconsistent Communications," *Journal of Personality and Social Psychology,* 6 (1967), 109–14, copyright (1967) by the American Psychological Association. Reproduced by permission.

and nonverbal cues leads to a certain attitude which could also have been conveyed with a consistent message, why is the inconsistent message preferred in some cases? (3) Are inconsistent communications more difficult to decode? Do they involve more inaccuracy or ambiguity? (4) If inconsistent communications *are* more difficult to decode, do they contribute to the development of psychopathology in one who frequently receives them, as "double-bind" theorists have suggested?

Both a communicator's verbalizations (Davitz, 1969) and his implicit behaviors, such as those in Appendix A, express his attitudes. The referents implied by his verbalizations may thus either be consistent or inconsistent with those implied in his nonverbal behaviors. How, then, do the individual channels contribute to the overall attitude conveyed by a complex (multichannel) message? For instance, if a communicator uses two channels, verbal and facial, to indicate his attitude, how is the total expressed attitude a function of the attitudes expressed separately in the two components?

Whereas there have been many studies of implicit attitude or feeling communication in single channels, investigation of feelings or attitudes transmitted in two or more channels simultaneously is just beginning. Gates (1927) found that children were more accurate in their judgments of facial than vocal expressions of feeling. Unfortunately, her method only allowed a tentative conclusion that discrimination of feeling is easier on the basis of facial than of vocal cues. But there was some corroboration of Gates' findings in studies by Levitt (1964) and Zaidel and Mehrabian (1969). In the Levitt (1964) study, communicators were filmed as they attempted to convey six emotions facially and vocally, using neutral verbal materials. The decoding of facial and vocal stimuli in combination was only as accurate as the decoding of facial stimuli alone, and both conditions were more accurate than the decoding of vocal stimuli alone. This finding indicated that in a two-channel, facial-vocal communication of emotion, the facial channel contributes more than the vocal channel to the decoding of the total message. The Zaidel and Mehrabian (1969) findings more directly showed that variations in liking are conveyed more readily with facial than with vocal expressions.

Williams and Sundene (1965) also explored the characteristics of two-channel communications of emotion. They used the semantic differential method (Osgood, Suci, and Tannenbaum, 1957) to obtain judgments of the same emotions communicated facially, vocally, and in facial-vocal combinations. All three modes of communication were found to be recognized in terms of three factors: general evaluation, social control, and activity.

It should be noted that none of the foregoing studies investigated those two-channel communications in which the emotion communicated in the facial expression was inconsistent with that communicated vocally. While experimental studies of multichannel communications from any particular population (for example, children or adults) were lacking, theories about the effects of such communications were proposed. Bateson, Jackson, Haley, and Weakland (1956) proposed a "double-bind" theory of schizophrenia, according to which maladaptive responses of schizophrenics come about because they are the frequent recipients of inconsistent attitude communications. A double-bind communication is defined as involving two or more inconsistent attitude messages which are assumed to elicit incompatible responses from the addressee. For example, a mother asks her son to come over and kiss her while she implicitly communicates indifference for what he is requested to do. It is assumed that the child is left with the dilemma of responding to either the verbal or the implicit component, knowing that response to either one will elicit a rebuff. The recipients of frequent double-bind messages are assumed to learn to respond with their own double-bind messages. In the example considered, the child may respond with, "I can't come because my leg hurts" or "I can't come because Trap is holding me," the hurt leg and Trap (a nonexistent companion) being figments of his imagination.

Whereas it was assumed that double-bind communications lead to the development of maladaptive patterns of interpersonal functioning, Haley (1963) also conceptualized most psychotherapeutic processes as being interpretable within a beneficial double-bind paradigm. His thesis was that applications of the beneficial double bind can serve to successfully eliminate the secondary gain that is associated with a symptom and therefore eliminate the symptom.

The above assumptions can be partially clarified through investigation of the ways in which multichannel attitude communications are decoded.

A Linear Model for the Inference of Attitudes from Multichannel Communications

Mehrabian and Wiener (1967) and Mehrabian and Ferris (1967) investigated the combined effects of consistent or inconsistent verbal-vocal communications and consistent and inconsistent facial-vocal communications of attitude respectively. Both studies involved nine sets of communication stimuli.

In the Mehrabian and Wiener (1967) study, verbal-vocal communications were prepared so that three degrees of positive verbal content were associated with each of three degrees of vocally expressed attitude. Having been judged for amount of liking conveyed, the words *honey, thanks,* and *dear* were selected as instances of positive contents (the judgments of these words had comparable mean values and standard deviations). Similarly, the words *maybe, really,* and *oh* were selected as comparable instances of neutral contents; and the words *don't, brute,* and *terrible* were selected as comparable instances of negative contents.

Two female speakers were employed to read each of the nine selected words in positive, neutral, and negative vocal expressions. For these three conditions, respectively, the speakers spoke the words, regardless of content, to convey liking, high evaluation, or preference; a neutral attitude, that is, neither liking nor disliking; and an attitude of dislike, low evaluation, or lack of preference toward the target person. All possible combinations of two speaker conditions, three vocal conditions, three content conditions, and three instances of each content condition were recorded on tape.

To obtain the independent effects of the vocal and content components of these recordings, and to relate these to the effects of the total vocal-content messages, Mehrabian and Wiener (1967) had three different groups of subjects listen to these recorded messages. One group was asked to judge the degree of liking conveyed by each message, relying only on the meanings of the words used and not on the vocal expression. The second group was asked to judge the degree of liking conveyed by each message, relying only on the vocal component and not on the meanings of the words used. Finally, the third group formed their judgments of liking on the basis of all the information combined in each message.

The results of the Mehrabian and Wiener (1967) study showed that the vocal component in the various messages primarily determined the subjects' judgments of affect from the total messages (content and vocal components combined), and that the content component of inconsistent messages had a negligible contribution to the affect inferred from such statements.

In the Mehrabian and Ferris (1967) study, 25 subjects first rated the amount of liking implied by each of 15 written words. From these judgments, the word *maybe* was selected as an appropriate neutral verbal carrier of vocal communications. Three female speakers were then instructed to vary their voices while saying the word *maybe* to communicate liking, neutrality, and dislike toward an imagined addressee. Each speaker said the word *maybe* twice in the same way while her statements were being audio recorded.

The facial communications of three degrees of attitude were selected in a similar manner. Photographs of three female models were taken as they used facial expressions to communicate liking, neutrality, and dislike toward another person. On the basis of the subjects' judgments of the vocal and facial communications, three vocal communications (that is, positive, neutral, and negative) obtained from each of two speakers and three facial communications obtained from each of two models were selected. The facial attitude communications of a given value (for example, positive) were selected to match the vocal attitude communications of the same value. Standard deviations of judgments, as well as their means, were matched. In other words, for each of the three levels of liking, the independent effects of all vocal communications of like-dislike were comparable to the independent effects of all facial communications of like-dislike.

Thus, in both the Mehrabian and Wiener (1967) and the Mehrabian and Ferris (1967) experiments, the separate effect of each component was independently assessed. It was therefore possible to express the dependent measure, the inferred degree of liking from the total message, in terms of the values of the separate components. As already noted, the results of the Mehrabian and Wiener (1967) study showed that most of the variability in the judgment of total attitude was accounted for by variations contained in the vocal component.

In the Mehrabian and Ferris (1967) study, the combined effect of the facial and vocal components was a weighted sum of their independent effects, since there was no significant interaction between them. The following regression equation summarized the relative contributions of facial and vocal components to interpretations of combined facial-vocal attitude communications:

$$A_{\text{Total}} = 0.60\ A_{\text{Facial}} + 0.40\ A_{\text{Vocal}} \tag{1}$$

A_{Total} represents attitude inferred on a -3 to $+3$ scale from the two-channel communications. A_{Facial} represents attitude communicated in the facial component alone on the same scale. Similarly, A_{Vocal} represents attitude communicated in the vocal component alone. The findings given in Equation 1, together with those from the Mehrabian and Wiener study (1967), suggest that the combined effect of simultaneous verbal, vocal, and facial attitude communications is a weighted sum of their independent effects as follows:

$$A_{\text{Total}} = 0.07\ A_{\text{Verbal}} + 0.38\ A_{\text{Vocal}} + 0.55\ A_{\text{Facial}} \tag{2}$$

where all four attitude variables are measured on the same scale (for example, a scale of liking ranging from -3 to $+3$).

In general, then, it is hypothesized that, when there is inconsistency between verbally and implicitly expressed attitude, the implicit portion will dominate in determining the total message. For instance, when there are inconsistencies between attitudes communicated verbally and posturally, the postural component should dominate in determining the total attitude that is inferred. The results reported earlier for the communication of attitudes via posture and position cues (for example, Chapter 2) make it possible to test this hypothesis. Also, two recent studies (Argyle, Salter, Nicholson, Williams, and Burgess, 1970; Argyle, Alkema, and Gilmour, 1971) provided support for the proposed hypothesis. In one of these, implicit communication cues were found to make a greater contribution than verbal cues to the communication of a more dominant (or potent), or a more positive, attitude.

A note of caution is in order regarding the summary of findings given in Equation 2. The Bugental, Kaswan, and Love (1970), Mehrabian and Wiener (1967), and Lampel and Anderson (1968) studies indicated that attitudes conveyed in various channels interact to determine the total inferred attitude. Therefore, Equation 2 is only a first order approximation. More detailed study of the main and interactive effects of various channels is needed. Such a study might include the preparation of video recorded stimuli involving four channels of communication: verbal, vocal, facial and immediacy of position cues.

For example, three levels of verbal attitude could be combined with each of three levels of vocal, facial, and position cues. To facilitate analysis of the results, the levels of the three attitudes communicated in each channel would be equated so that, for instance, the positive facial cues were equal in value to the positive vocal, positive verbal, and positive position cues. Thus, 81 types of communication stimuli, with replications over different communicators of both sexes, would yield a large set of stimuli for decoding. Addressees could vary in personality characteristics (for example, affiliative tendency) or level and kind of psychopathology. The dependent measures could include not only mean judgments for each of the 81 communication types but also the variability and latency of judgments. By examining the variability of responses to inconsistent communications, one could assess the difficulty in decoding them. Such difficulty could be measured also from the latency of judgments of total attitude and might have some additional implications for double-bind theory. The latter suggests that addressees should take a longer time, or have more disagreement, in judging the total attitude conveyed in inconsistent or ambiguous messages.

Such a study would provide detailed answers to the question of how one combines consistent or inconsistent communications to infer an attitude from an entire message, and whether inconsistent communications involve more inaccuracy or ambiguity, thus making them more difficult to decode. If several replications of the 81 stimuli were to be used, the analysis of variance of the data obtained from each subject (for example, as suggested by Anderson, 1962, 1964) would provide a direct check on the linear model proposed in Equation 2, since it would indicate the extent to which the inferences of total attitude deviate from linearity. It is hypothesized, for instance, that the coefficients in the equations for psychologically maladjusted individuals (weighted sums such as Equation 2) are more varied than are those of normals. This hypothesis is based on the assumption that more maladjusted individuals tend to be more idiosyncratic or nonconsensual in their weighting of each component in a total message—that is, in the ways they make inferences from complex communications.

When are Feelings Communicated Inconsistently?

We have now considered the ways in which consistent and inconsistent communications are decoded.[1] There still remains the question of why a person selects an inconsistent message when he has the choice of using a consistent message to convey the same attitude. Why does he select sarcasm, for instance—a message in which he uses a negative vocal component with positive verbal content (for example, "I really like that!")—to communicate a negative attitude to the addressee? He might also have communicated negative attitude in both the verbal and vocal channels. The question, then, is the significance of consistency or inconsistency *per se*. Could it be that redundancy contributes to intensity? One interesting implication of the linear model summarized in Equation 2 is that the effect of redundancy (that is, consistent attitude communication in two or more channels) is to intensify the attitude communicated in any of the component channels. Thus, pushing a child away while turning away from him communicates a more negative feeling toward the child than only pushing him away or only turning away from him. Similarly, holding and kissing a child communicates a more positive attitude toward him than only holding or only kissing him.

The model in Equation 2 indicates that inconsistent attitude communications can be readily classified into two categories—one in which the total impact is positive and another in which it is negative. Positive inconsistency is evidenced when someone verbally insults another while smiling (a girl says "I don't like you much" to her boyfriend with a smile and loving vocalization). Negative inconsistency might involve an irritated facial expression accompanied by positive vocal and/or verbal expressions (someone yells "Oh that's beautiful! Just great!" when angry). These two categories can in turn be distinguished from consistent attitude communications in which all the components are judged as either positive or negative in quality.

Given these distinctions, the problem can be restated in two parts. When are inconsistent negative attitude communications preferred, with preferences for consistent negative attitude communications of the same degree used as a baseline; and when are inconsistent positive communications preferred, using consistent positive-attitude communications as the base of comparison? Thus, it is important to experimentally and/or statistically control for the attitudinal level of the messages produced by, or given to, subjects in various situations.

In the following four experiments (Mehrabian, 1970e), two channels of communication, verbal and vocal, were employed. The inconsistent

1. Acknowledgment is given to Academic Press, Inc. for their permission to use, in this section, rewritten segments and revised Tables 1, 4, 5, and 6, from my paper, "When are Feelings Communicated Inconsistently?" *Journal of Experimental Research in Personality*, 4 (1970), 198–212.

positive messages involved positive vocal and negative verbal components; the inconsistent negative messages involved negative vocal and positive verbal components. The control stimuli for these two sets of messages consisted of moderately positive verbal and vocal communications on one hand and moderately negative verbal and vocal communications on the other.

All of the following experiments employed the same set of verbal-vocal messages. Several instances of each of the four types of message were recorded on tape. Subjects listened to and indicated preferences for these messages while imagining a variety of social situations.

The four experiments constituted an exploratory search for relationships. In the absence of any evidence bearing directly on the problem, it was possible only to elaborate a general tentative hypothesis: inconsistent messages are less formal or more intimate expressions of attitude than are consistent ones. Further, since reservations about the expression of negative attitude were assumed to determine preferences for inconsistent messages, several of the factors involved the elicitation of negative feelings from the communicator by the addressee.

Thus, the study included negative affect-arousing cues in combination with social situations varying in formality. One group of factors was: (1) liking of the addressee, (2) degree of conflict and irritation between the speaker and addressee, and (3) pleasantness of the addressee's behavior toward the speaker. A second group of factors related to the formality of communication situations: (4) the degree of formality of the communication setting, (5) the status of the speaker relative to the addressee, (6) the presence versus absence of bystanders at the time when the message was directed at the addressee, (7) the ability of the addressee to accept unambiguous expressions of dislike toward himself, and (8) the implicit versus explicit quality of a negative message from the addressee to the speaker.

The two personality variables explored in the study were the speaker's social approval-seeking tendency, as measured by the Crowne and Marlowe (1960) Social Desirability scale, and the speaker's anxiety as measured by the Mandler and Sarason (1952) Test Anxiety Questionnaire. These two variables were selected because persons who scored higher on social approval-seeking tendency and anxiety were expected to have greater difficulty in expressing their negative feelings overtly. (At this point, the reader who wishes to do so can proceed directly to the discussion section without loss of continuity.)

METHOD

Verbal Stimuli Used in All Four Experiments. The audio recorded messages employed in all four Mehrabian (1970e) experiments were prepared as follows. A group of 30 University of California undergraduates were initially presented with written sentences such as "I hate it when you do things like that," or "I really don't care for that," and were asked to indicate, using a −3 to +3 scale, how much positive attitude was conveyed by each statement. From these ratings, the following set of statements was selected to represent four categories of affect for male speakers and male listeners: "I really like that," "Now, that's great," and "That was really very nice of you" for strong positive affect; "That makes me feel terrible," "I hate it when you do things like that," and "That's disgusting" for strong negative affect; "That was clever," "I think that's all right," and "That's okay" for moderate positive affect; and "I really don't care for that," "Don't you think that's ridiculous?" and "How do you ever get the gall to do such things?" for moderate negative affect.

The following set of statements was selected for female speakers and female listeners: "That was really very nice of you," "That's great," and "I really like that" for strong positive affect; "I hate it when you do things like that," "That's disgusting," "That makes me feel terrible," and "Why do you want to be so irritating?" for strong negative affect; "That's okay," "I think that's all right," and "That was clever" for moderate positive affect; and "I really don't care for that," "Don't you think that's ridiculous?" and "How do you ever get enough gall to do such things?" for moderate negative affect.

A second set of 15 male and 15 female undergraduates was then asked to communicate a strong positive content with negative vocal expression, a strong negative content with a positive vocal expression, a moderately positive content with moderately positive vocal expression, and a moderately negative content with moderately negative vocal expression. Informal observation of subjects trying to communicate negative contents with positive vocal expressions indicated that it was difficult and that it required a larger number of trials than for stimuli in the other categories. From these audio recordings, a preliminary selection was made, reducing the stimuli to a more manageable set. This set was subsequently administered to two separate groups of 30 males and 30 females, with the following instructions.

For each of the comments which you will hear, please imagine the following situation. You and another person of the same sex and approximately the same age are together. You do something, and the other person makes a comment. For each of the comments, use the scale below to indicate how much preference, liking, or positive evaluation for your action is shown by the other person's comment.

A scale ranging from +3 (*extreme liking, preference,* and *evaluation*) to −3 (*extreme dislike, lack of preference,* and *low evaluation*) was inserted at this point, and spaces were provided for subjects to rate their judgments of each recorded message.

Analysis of the judgments of attitude from these recordings yielded the final set of inconsistent and consistent messages. There were six messages which had positive contents spoken with negative vocal expression (that is, inconsistent negative) and six with moderately negative contents spoken with moderately negative vocal expression. Each of the latter was equated in overall level of attitude communication to each of the first set of six inconsistent negative messages. Thus, for example, for the statement, "That's great!" spoken with negative vocal expression and rated as −0.60, there was a control negative communication, "How do you ever get the gall to do such things?", which was rated −0.53. Similarly, there was another set of six negative content-positive vocal (that is, inconsistent positive) messages with a corresponding set of six control statements which were moderately positive in content and vocal expression. For example, there was the statement "I hate it when you do things like that" spoken with positive vocal expression and rated as +0.95, and the control statement "I think that's all right" spoken with moderately positive vocal expression and rated as +0.89.

In sum, two sets of 24 statements were obtained, one for male speakers and male listeners, the other for female speakers and female listeners. The 24 messages of male speakers were audio recorded in four random sequences, as were the 24 messages of females.

Experiment I. The factors investigated in the first Mehrabian (1970e) experiment were two levels of attitude toward the addressee, like versus dislike; two degrees of conflict between speaker and addressee, resolved versus unresolved; and the pleasantness of the addressee's behavior which elicited a communication from the speaker, pleasant versus unpleasant. In addition, the Crowne and Marlowe (1960) Social Desirability scale and the Mandler and Sarason (1952) Text Anxiety Questionnaire were administered to the subjects before they listened to the tapes. Thus, two additional factors in the experiment were the high versus low social approval-seeking tendency, and the high versus low anxiety level of the communicator.

Forty-eight male and 48 female University of California undergraduates were paid to participate as subjects in the experiment. In separate group administrations, male and female subjects judged and indicated their preference for each of the 24 messages under the following four within-subject conditions: liked addressee and resolved conflict, liked addressee and unresolved conflict, disliked addressee and resolved conflict, disliked addressee and unresolved conflict. The instructions for each condition were presented to the subject in a four-page booklet (one condition on each page). For instance, in the liked addressee, resolved conflict, and pleasant addressee behavior condition, the following instructions were given to the subjects.

Think of someone of the same sex and about the same age as you whom you know reasonably well and whom you like. Imagine the following situation involving yourself and this person. You have been irritated with this person for some time and have just discussed the source of your irritation with him to your mutual satisfaction. Right now, the two of you are together, and this person is doing something which both of you know is quite pleasant for you.

I am going to play some tape recordings of different statements which you are to imagine yourself as possibly making in this situation. First please try, as best you can, to get into the mood of the above situation so as to be able to indicate what kinds of statements you would prefer to make in the situation and what kinds of statements you would not prefer to make in the situation.

At this point instructions for the recording of responses were provided to the subject. For each statement, he indicated a preference score ranging from zero (*I would have no preference at all for making the statement*) to six (*I would have extremely high preference for making the statement*).

The instructions for the remaining conditions were identical to the preceding, with these exceptions: "Whom you like" was replaced with "whom you dislike" in the negative attitude condition. ". . . you have just discussed the source of your irritation with him to your mutual satisfaction" was replaced with ". . . you have not discussed the source of your irritation" in the unresolved conflict condition. ". . . which both of you know is quite pleasant for you" was replaced with ". . . which both of you know is quite unpleasant for you" in the negative addressee behavior condition.

The sequence of four within-subject conditions in the booklets was counterbalanced over all subjects. After reading each condition (that is, each page of instructions in the booklet), subjects listened to a random presentation of the 24 verbal stimuli and recorded their preferences.

Experiment II. In the second Mehrabian (1970e) experiment, the effects of the following variables on the differential preference for inconsistent versus consistent messages were explored: two degrees of addressee status relative to the speaker, high versus low; two degrees of formality of the communication situation, formal versus informal; and pleasant versus unpleasant addressee behavior. In addition to these variables, the Social Desirability scale and the Test Anxiety Questionnaire were administered to the subjects before they listened to the tapes.

Forty-eight male and 48 female undergraduates participated as paid subjects in the experiment. In several group sessions, each subject received a four-page booklet, each page containing instructions for one of the four within-subject conditions: formal situation and pleasant addressee behavior, formal situation and unpleasant addressee behavior, informal situation and pleasant addressee behavior, informal situation and unpleasant addressee behavior.

Each subject was assigned to either a high or low status of addressee condition and received all possible combinations of the remaining two conditions, formality and pleasantness. The order of presentation to the subjects of these four conditions was counterbalanced, and since there were 24 possible sequences of these four conditions, multiples of 24 subjects were employed.

Instructions for the high social status of addressee, formal condition, and pleasant addressee behavior condition were:

> Think of someone of the same sex as you who has a higher social status than you. (A person of higher social status might be an employer, a teacher, or some other person in a position of authority over you; a person of lower social status might be someone whom you have authority over.) Imagine the following situation involving yourself and this person. You are in a situation with this person where it would be very awkward and socially inappropriate for the two of you to have an argument or disagreement. Right now the two of you are together and this person is doing something which both of you know is quite pleasant for you.
>
> Now I am going to play some tape recordings. . . . [The remaining instructions were as in the preceding experiment.]

The instructions for the remaining seven conditions were identical, with the following exceptions: "Higher social status" was replaced by "lower social status"; "quite pleasant for you" was replaced by "quite unpleasant for you"; finally, "it would be socially appropriate for the two of you to have a disagreement or argument," was the replacement in the informal situation.

Experiment III replicated the second experiment with, however, only 24 male and 24 female subjects.

Experiment IV. In the fourth Mehrabian (1970e) experiment, the effects of the following factors on the differential preference for inconsistent versus consistent communications were explored: the addressee's negative attitude communication, explicit versus implicit, as indicated by the phrase "This person has just expressed a negative and cutting remark toward you in a very open and obvious way" versus ". . . very subtle and sly way"; the level of the addressee's tolerance for criticism, as indicated by "This person is the kind of person who can accept frank and unambiguous expressions of dislike toward himself without getting upset" versus ". . . who cannot accept frank and unambiguous expressions of dislike toward himself without getting terribly upset"; and finally the size of the audience, that is, bystanders who observe the interaction of the speaker and addressee, as indicated by "Imagine the following situation involving yourself and this person with no one else being present" versus ". . . with three of your mutual acquaintances present." Once again, social approval-seeking tendency and anxiety level were two additional factors in the experiment.

Forty-eight male and 48 female undergraduates were paid to participate in this experiment. The procedure was similar to that of the preceding experiments. The instructions for one of the conditions were as follows.

Think of someone of the same sex and same age as you whom you know reasonably well and you neither like nor dislike. Imagine the following situation involving yourself and this person, with no one else being present. This person has just expressed a negative and cutting remark toward you in a very open and obvious way. He is the kind of person who can accept frank and unambiguous expressions of dislike toward himself without getting upset.

Now, I'm going to play some tape recordings. . . . [The instructions continued at this point as in the preceding experiments.]

The instructions for all conditions were identical to those for the preceding experiments except for the changes already noted. Each subject was initially assigned to either the explicit or implicit addressee remark condition and received all four combinations of two degrees of addressee tolerance for criticism and two degrees of audience size. The sequence of the four conditions was counterbalanced over the group of subjects.

RESULTS

Experiment I. In each condition of the first experiment, 24 preference scores were obtained from a subject for each of four categories of verbal stimuli: inconsistent positive, inconsistent negative, and control statements for those categories, consistent positive and consistent negative respectively. The six preference scores obtained from a subject in each of these four categories were summed, thus yielding four composite scores for each category.

The preferences for inconsistent negative messages were analyzed using a multiple regression technique described by Cohen (1968), who detailed the procedures whereby multiple regression can be used as a substitute for the analysis of variance or the analysis of covariance. These procedures allowed the expression of the dependent measure (preference for inconsistent negative messages) as a function of the significant effects from the following set: the covariate (preference for consistent negative messages), the independent effects (pleasantness of addressee behavior, communicator anxiety, liking of the addressee, and conflict between speaker and addressee), and all possible interactions among the independent effects.

Some reasons for the use of multiple regression in the Mehrabian (1970e) study are: (1) a single equation readily summarizes all the effects of a complex factorial design, (2) the coefficients in the equation provide information about the relative magnitudes of the various significant effects, and (3) comparisons of the results from several experiments are facilitated when presented in equation form.

The results from the regression analysis of the preferences for inconsistent negative messages are given in Equation 1 of Table 6.1, where the significance of the F values was assessed at the 0.01 level. Equation 1 of Table 6.1 shows that the covariate (N_c = preference for consistent negative communication) is a significant correlate of the dependent variable (N_i = preference for inconsistent negative communication). The predicted adjusted cell means can be computed from Equation 1 by transferring the term involving the covariate to the left-hand side of the equation.

$$N_i - 1.02N_c = 10.43 + 1.10P - 0.76L \qquad (1b)$$

For instance, to predict the two cell means for the first effect, average values of all variables on the right side of Equation 1b, except those of pleasantness of addressee behavior, P, are first computed. This is simple since, in general, average values of all variables and interaction effects equal zero. Therefore, $N_i - 1.02N_c = 10.43 + 1.10P$. Thus, when addressee behavior is pleasant (that is, $P = 1$) the predicted mean = 11.53, and when addressee behavior is unpleasant (that is, $P = -1$) the predicted mean = 9.33. The corresponding actual means were 11.67 and 9.18 respectively.

The predicted means for the liking of addressee effect are given by ($10.43 - 0.76L$) and equal 9.67 when the addressee is liked ($L = 1$) and 11.19 when he is disliked ($L = -1$). The corresponding actual means were 9.76 and 11.10 respectively.

A second regression analysis was carried out for the preference of inconsistent positive communications, in which the preferences for consistent positive communications served as the covariate. Equation 2 of Table 6.1 summarizes the latter results. In this, as in some other instances (for example, Equations 4 or 6 of Table 6.1), the covariate was not significantly correlated with the dependent variable. The obtained cell means for the single effect of Equation 2 were a preference level of 9.52 for positive inconsistent communications with liked, and a level of 8.01 with disliked, addressees.

It is also helpful to briefly note the absolute preferences for the various communication stimuli over all experimental conditions. The mean preference was 8.77 for inconsistent positive messages, 10.43 for inconsistent negative, 14.00 for consistent positive, and 14.02 for consistent negative messages. It is thus seen that, over all the experimental conditions, preferences for the inconsistent messages were significantly less than those for the consistent ones. Furthermore, preferences for inconsistent positive messages were significantly less than for inconsistent negative ones.

Experiments II and III. In Experiment II, preferences for inconsistent negative messages were analyzed as a function of the covariate (preferences for consistent negative messages), and two levels each of communicator anxiety, relative status of the addressee, formality of the communication setting, and pleasantness of addressee behavior. The regression analyses also tested for all possible interactions among the inde-

Table 6.1. Results of the regression analyses for all experiments.*

Results for Experiment I

$$N_i = 10.43 + 1.02\,N_c + 1.10P - 0.76L \qquad (1)$$
$$P_i = 8.77 + 0.76L \qquad (2)$$

Results for Experiment II

$$N_i = 9.11 + 2.05N_c - 0.93F + 0.78PS \qquad (3)$$
$$P_i = 8.00 - 1.59P - 1.27F \qquad (4)$$

Results for Experiment III

$$N_i = 8.09 + 3.03N_c + 1.84P - 0.96X - 1.28XS \qquad (5)$$
$$P_i = 6.72 - 1.07P + 1.07PS - 1.03XS \qquad (6)$$

Results for Experiment IV

$$N_i = 8.14 + 2.69N_c + 0.44E - 1.04X + 0.54XE \qquad (7)$$
$$P_i = 6.79 + 1.76P_c - 0.49BE + 0.94X - 0.53XB - 0.42XET \qquad (8)$$

Notation

N_i = Preference for inconsistent negative messages.

N_c = Preference for consistent negative messages—a normalized variable.

P_i = Preference for inconsistent positive messages.

P_c = Preference for consistent positive messages—a normalized variable.

Independent Effects	Values in Preceding Equations	
	1.0	−1.0
B = Presence of bystanders	Present	Absent
E = Explicitness of negative message from addressee	Explicit	Implicit
F = Formality of setting	Formal	Informal
L = Liking of addressee	Like	Dislike
P = Pleasantness of addressee behavior	Pleasant	Unpleasant
S = Addressee status	High	Low
T = Addressee tolerance for criticism	High	Low
X = Communicator anxiety	High	Low

---

*Since, for each of the preceding independent effects, there were equal numbers of the two conditions (i.e., equal numbers of conditions assigned values of 1.0 and −1.0), these effects had mean values of zero and standard deviations of unity. As a consequence, and due to the factorial arrangement of the conditions, all the significant effects in the various equations (e.g., F or PS in Equation 3) have mean values of zero and standard deviations of unity. Thus, the coefficients in each equation indicate the relative strengths of the various effects in that equation.

pendent effects. The results are reported in Equation 3 of Table 6.1; the corresponding results from the replication experiment (Experiment III) are given in Equation 5 of Table 6.1. The obtained adjusted cell means for the effects predicted by Equations 3 and 5 are given in Table 6.2. The four adjusted cell means for the PS effect of Equation 3 are predicted from

$$N_i - 2.05N_c = 9.11 + .78PS \qquad (3b)$$

For instance, for a high-status addressee ($S = 1$) who behaved pleasantly ($P = 1$), the predicted adjusted cell mean = $9.11 + 0.78 \times 1 \times 1 = 9.89$, as compared with the actual value of 9.99 given in Table 6.2.

Table 6.2. Significant determiners of the preference for inconsistent negative communications in Experiments II and III.*

Results for Experiment II

1. Formality of setting — Formal: 8.35 — Informal: 9.86
2. Pleasantness of addressee behavior × addressee status

	pleasant behavior		unpleasant behavior
High-status addressee	9.99	↔	7.32
			↕
Low-status addressee	9.20		9.93

Results for Experiment III

1. Pleasantness of addressee behavior — Pleasant: 10.06 — Unpleasant: 6.13
2. Communicator anxiety — High anxious: 7.06 — Low anxious: 9.13
3. Addressee status × communicator anxiety

	high status		low status
High-anxious communicator	5.85	↔	8.26
	↕		
Low-anxious communicator	10.41	↔	7.85

*For all the significant effects of Experiment II, $df = 1/91$, $MS_e = 19.7$, and $p < 0.01$. For Experiment III, $df = 1/43$, $MS_e = 20.9$, and $p < 0.05$. t-tests were used to assess the significance of simple effects, and arrows connect cell means that differed significantly at the 0.05 level.

The results of similar regression analyses for preferences of inconsistent positive communications, with preferences of consistent positive communications serving as the covariate, are given in Equations 4 and 6 of Table 6.1. The corresponding obtained adjusted cell means are given in Table 6.3.

Once again, it is helpful to consider the absolute values of mean preferences for the four message categories. In Experiment II, there was a mean preference of 8.0 for inconsistent positive messages, 9.11 for inconsistent negative, 13.17 for consistent positive, and 12.33 for consistent negative messages.

Experiment IV. Preferences of inconsistent negative messages were analyzed as a function of the covariate (that is, preferences for consistent negative ones) and two levels of each of the following: explicitness of the negative communication from the addressee, communicator anxiety level, addressee tolerance for criticism, and audience size. The results of the regression analysis are given in Equation 7 of Table 6.1; the adjusted cell means are given in Table 6.4.

A similar regression analysis was performed on preferences for inconsistent positive messages, with preferences for consistent positive messages serving as the covariate. The adjusted cell means from this analysis

Table 6.3. Significant determiners of the preference for inconsistent positive communications in Experiments II and III.

Results for Experiment II		
1. Pleasantness of addressee behavior	Pleasant: 6.57	Unpleasant: 9.43
2. Formality of setting	Formal: 6.77	Informal: 9.23

Results for Experiment III

1. Pleasantness of addressee behavior	Pleasant: 5.64		Unpleasant: 7.80
2. Pleasantness of addressee behavior × addressee status	high status addressee		low status addressee
Pleasant addressee behavior	6.12		5.16
			$\updownarrow$
Unpleasant addressee behavior	6.14	$\leftrightarrow$	9.46
3. Addressee status × communicator anxiety	high status addressee		low status addressee
High-anxious communicator	5.71	$\leftrightarrow$	8.95
			$\updownarrow$
Low-anxious communicator	6.54		5.67

*For all the significant effects of Experiment II, $df = 1/91$, $MS_e = 19.7$, and $p < 0.01$. For Experiment III, $df = 1/43$, $MS_e = 13.4$, and $p < 0.05$. t-tests were used to assess the significance of simple effects, and arrows connect cell means that differed significantly at the 0.05 level.

are given in Table 6.5; the corresponding regression results being summarized in Equation 8 of Table 6.1.

In this experiment, there was an absolute mean preference of 6.79 for inconsistent positive messages, 8.14 for inconsistent negative, 11.09 for consistent positive, and 11.10 for consistent negative messages.

Table 6.4. Significant determiners of the preference for inconsistent negative communications in Experiment IV.

1. Explicitness of Negative Addressee Message (Behavior)	Explicit: 8.64		Implicit: 7.64
2. Communicator Anxiety	High: 7.51		Low: 8.78
3. Explicitness of Negative Addressee Message (Behavior) × Communicator Anxiety	explicit		implicit
High anxious communicator	8.53	$\leftrightarrow$	6.49
			$\updownarrow$
Low anxious communicator	8.76		8.80

*For all the significant effects in this table, $df = 1/91$, $MS_e = 8.5$, and $p < 0.01$. t-tests were used to assess the significance of simple effects, and arrows connect cell means that differed significantly at the 0.05 level.

*Table 6.5. Significant determiners of the preference for inconsistent positive communications in Experiment IV.**

1. Communicator Anxiety	High: 7.77		Low: 5.81
2. Explicitness of Negative Addressee Message × Bystander Presence	explicit		implicit
Bystanders present	6.29		6.55
	↕		
Bystanders absent	8.07	↔	6.25
3. Bystander Presence × Communicator Anxiety	present		absent
High-anxious communicator	6.96	↔	8.58
	↕		
Low-anxious communicator	5.88		5.74
4. Explicitness of Negative Addressee Message × Addressee Tolerance for Criticism × Communicator Anxiety	high-tolerance		low tolerance
Explicit			
High-anxious communicator	8.16		7.79
Low-anxious communicator	7.00		5.76
Implicit			
High-anxious communicator	8.41	↔	6.70
	↕		
Low-anxious communicator	4.60		5.88

*For all the significant effects in this table, $df = 1/91$, $MS_e = 10.6$, and $p < 0.01$. *t*-tests were used to assess the significance of simple effects, and arrows connect cell means that differed significantly at the 0.05 level.

DISCUSSION

Each of the four Mehrabian (1970e) experiments showed that consistent communications of attitude were preferred over inconsistent ones, and that, among inconsistent communications, positive ones were preferred less than were negative ones. These findings corroborated informal observations made during the preparation of the stimuli, when subjects had greater difficulty producing the inconsistent messages than the consistent ones. This difficulty was even more pronounced when the inconsistent messages were positive. The implication here is that, due to their less frequent use, inconsistent messages are more difficult to produce and that less frequent use reflects a lower preference for them. Another observation was that inconsistent communications of attitude frequently relied on facial expressions. For instance, when some subjects were instructed to say something negative with positive vocal expression, they actually spoke with a neutral vocal expression but assumed a positive facial expression, so that audio recordings of their statements did not reflect substantial inconsistency. Thus, a more general exploration of preferences for inconsistent messages should include facial as well as verbal and vocal expressions.

The first generalization to emerge from the data was that inconsistent messages were preferred more in less formal situations. The experiments included a series of factors for various aspects of the formality of a communication setting. In some conditions, the situation was simply described as formal versus informal; in others, formality was implied by indicating that the addressee was of a higher rather than a lower status. A third manipulation involved the presence versus absence of bystander observers, the assumption being that the presence of observers in the situation tends to increase formality. A fourth manipulation involved an explicit versus implicit insult from the addressee as a cue to which the communicator responded. Here the expectation was that a situation in which the addressee was explicitly insulting would be more informal than one in which an insult was implicit. A final manipulation involved the addressee's tolerance for criticism, based on the assumption that persons who can tolerate criticism tend to elicit more informal interaction than those who cannot.

Experiment I contained none of these formality factors, but Experiments II and III both contained two such factors: formality of the setting, F, and status of the addressee relative to the communicator, S. The two main effects in Equations 3 and 4 of Table 6.1 indicated that both the positive inconsistent and the negative inconsistent messages were preferred less in more formal situations. The cell mean values for the remaining interaction effects involving the formality and addressee status factors in Equations 3 through 6 are given in Tables 6.2 and 6.3. Of the five relevant significant simple effects in these tables, only the following one was contrary to the general trend. The less anxious communicators of Experiment III preferred inconsistent negative messages more with higher- than with lower-status addressees.

Experiment IV contained three factors relating to the formality of the communication setting. These were the presence of bystanders, the implicit rather than explicit insult from the addressee, and the lower addressee tolerance for criticism. There was only one significant main effect for these factors: Equation 7 in Table 6.1 showed that negative inconsistent messages were preferred more when the insulting behavior of the addressee had been more explicit. The cell means corresponding to the various interactions in Equations 7 and 8 are given in Tables 6.4 and 6.5. In these tables, all the significant simple effects involving the three formality factors showed greater preference for inconsistent messages when the situation was more informal. For instance, the second effect of Table 6.5 showed that inconsistent positive messages were preferred more only when the addressee's insulting behavior had been explicit and when bystanders were absent. In other words, both of the informality cues were required in this case for communicators to have greater preference for the inconsistent positive messages.

In sum, the results relating to various aspects of formality in a communication situation showed very consistent support for the following generalization: inconsistent messages are preferred more in the more informal communication settings.

The remaining results from all four Mehrabian (1970e) experiments constituted a considerable list of quite distinct findings. The integration of most of these findings within a coherent framework was nevertheless possible with a detailed consideration of the task presented to subjects in each experimental condition.

Subjects were to indicate preferences for each of the following four kinds of messages: (1) an inconsistent positive message involving a positive vocal and a negative verbal component, (2) a consistent positive message involving moderately positive verbal and vocal components, (3) an inconsistent negative message involving a negative vocal and positive verbal component, and (4) a consistent negative message involving moderately negative verbal and vocal components. The first two kinds of messages were matched for the degree of preference, liking, or positive evaluation for an action that each indicated. The third and fourth kinds of messages were matched in a similar way. Despite such average matching of the inconsistent and consistent pairs of messages over all experimental conditions, when subjects had to respond evaluatively to the addressee in a specific experimental condition, one or the other of the matched pair of messages was clearly the more appropriate response. For instance, when subjects were faced with a choice between a consistent positive and an inconsistent positive message for an addressee who was behaving in an unpleasant way, the inconsistent positive message, which at least included a negative verbal component referring to an action, was more appropriate. In contrast, given the same messages and an addressee who was behaving in a pleasant way, the consistent positive message, which included a positive verbal component referring to an action, was more appropriate.

In sum, even with the statistical controls, preferences for inconsistent positive messages (relative to preferences for consistent positive ones) were to be correlated with the unpleasantness of addressee behavior. Similarly, preferences for inconsistent negative messages (relative to preferences for consistent negative ones) were to be correlated with the pleasantness of addressee behavior.

A second aspect of the subjects' task was that, for all the messages, the verbal contents referred to the action of the addressee; thus, evaluative attitudes toward the person of the addressee could only be expressed with the implicit portion of the messages. That is, when the liking of the addressee was the determiner of message choice, the implicit portions of the messages carried the burden. In these instances, the stronger implicit components of the inconsistent messages (relative to those of the consistent ones) could serve as a basis for their selection for liked-disliked

124   CHAPTER SIX

addressees. Thus, despite statistical controls, preferences for inconsistent
positive messages (relative to preferences for consistent positive ones)
were to be correlated with the liking of the addressee. Further, preferences for inconsistent negative messages were to be correlated with the
degree of dislike of the addressee.

The statements in the preceding two paragraphs were completely supported. The relevant data for the first interpretation was available from
Experiments I, II, and III. The main effects in Equations 1 and 5 of Table
6.1 indicated that inconsistent negative messages were preferred more
when addressee behaviors were more pleasant. The main effects in Equations 4 and 6 of Table 6.1 indicated that inconsistent positive messages
were preferred less when the addressee behaviors were more pleasant.
Additional interaction effects involving pleasantness of addressee behavior in Equations 3 and 6 of Table 6.1 are readily considered in terms
of the cell means given in Tables 6.2 and 6.3. All the relevant significant
simple effects were consistent with the main effects of pleasantness of
addressee behavior.

The results from Experiment I given in Equations 1 and 2 of Table
6.1 supported the second interpretation relating message preference to
addressee liking. The main effect in Equation 1 indicated that negative
inconsistent messages were preferred less when the addressee was liked
more. The main effect in Equation 2 showed that positive inconsistent
messages were preferred more when the addressee was liked more.

Without exception, then, the significant effects were consistent with
the following general conclusions. (1) The verbal component of an inconsistent message conveys evaluative attitudes toward the action of the
addressee and therefore is the basis for selecting a message when the
addressee behaves in pleasant versus unpleasant ways. (2) The implicit
component of an inconsistent message conveys evaluative attitudes toward
the person of the addressee and therefore is the basis for selecting a message when he is liked versus disliked.

It is now possible to proceed to a discussion of the findings involving
communicators' approval-seeking tendency and anxiety levels. These two
measures were included in the study because it seemed that the more
anxious or the more approval-seeking communicators are less willing to
express dislike, and more willing to express liking, to others. In relation
to this assumption, Zaidel and Mehrabian (1969) found that higher
approval seekers were less able to convey variations in negative affect,
either facially or vocally. Although no special hypotheses had been proposed for these two personality variables, findings from the Mehrabian
(1970e) study allow the statement of a hypothesis. As noted in the preceding paragraph, the implicit component of an inconsistent message
conveys evaluative attitudes toward the person of the addressee. (The
examination of the tasks that were presented to the subjects has already

shown how it was possible for them to use inconsistent messages and convey evaluative attitudes toward the action or the person of the addressee, despite the statistical controls.) Therefore, it is expected that communicator anxiety or approval-seeking tendency is a positive correlate of preferences for positive inconsistent messages and a negative correlate of negative inconsistent messages.

To facilitate the presentation and discussion of results, significant effects involving communicator approval-seeking tendency were not included above. In sharp contrast to the results for communicator anxiety, the results relating to communicator approval-seeking tendency were inconsistent and could not be interpreted. In the case of communicator anxiety, however, without exception, the main effects in Equations 5, 7 and 8 of Table 6.1 and all the significant simple effects in Tables 6.2 through 6.5 indicated that the more anxious subjects had more preference for positive inconsistent messages and less preference for negative inconsistent messages.

The individual difference measures included in this study were selected to reflect a speaker's unwillingness to express negative feelings to others. Since a measure of sensitivity to rejection was not available when this study was designed, measures of communicator anxiety and approval-seeking tendency were used; however, it was felt that a direct measure of sensitivity to rejection (for example, Mehrabian, 1970d) would be more appropriate, since persons possessing this trait would be more hesitant about expressing negative feelings to others.

An overview of the results shows that only a part of the findings relating to formality and informality of communication settings had been anticipated. In addition, several consistent lines of evidence that had not been anticipated emerged from the study. For the verbal-vocal stimuli, the verbal components of the inconsistent messages served to convey evaluative attitudes toward the actions of the addressees. In contrast, the vocal portions of these messages conveyed evaluative attitudes toward the addressees themselves. Thus, positive inconsistent messages (which included positive vocal and negative verbal components) were preferred more when the addressee was liked and when his actions were disliked. In contrast, negative inconsistent messages (which included negative vocal and positive verbal components) were preferred more when the addressee was disliked and when his actions were liked. In this context, it was not surprising to find that the more anxious communicators showed a very consistent preference for positive inconsistent messages and a lack of preference for negative inconsistent messages.

The definition of inconsistent negative messages in this study corresponds closely to the concept of sarcasm, but there does not seem to be a term in English that would correspond to instances of positive inconsistency. Some forms of teasing involve positive inconsistency, such as a girl saying "no" to a boy's sexual advances while she implicitly communicates "I am attracted to you." The findings of the present study provided a tentative basis for identifying the conditions under which both types of inconsistent messages are likely to occur and also those under which one type of message is preferred over the other. It would be of interest to explore the implications of these findings for positive and negative inconsistent communications involving more than just verbal and vocal channels (for example, when the face or posture communicates positive affect and the speech communicates negative affect, or vice versa).

The research cited in the preceding section of this chapter has shown that different implicit communication cues exhibit similar relationships to verbal cues when they accompany the latter. Thus, one extrapolation of the findings of the Mehrabian (1970e) study is that, even when other implicit cues are also involved and contribute to inconsistency, the following generalization still holds: verbal components of inconsistent messages convey evaluative attitudes toward another's actions, whereas the implicit (for example, facial or postural) components convey evaluative attitudes to the person himself. In general, then, positive inconsistent messages should be more likely with liked than with disliked addressees, and when the addressee's actions are unpleasant. In contrast, negative inconsistent messages should be more likely with disliked than with liked addressees and when the addressee's actions are pleasant.

In closing, we should note the humorous aspect of positive inconsistent messages, which was not explored. If humor occurs more in informal situations it would not be unexpected to find that positive inconsistent messages (which were found to be preferred in less formal settings) are also used as a form of humor. One type of experimental paradigm which might explore such humor would involve inconsistent messages referring to incongruous situations. For example, one friend says to another "Dig the suave cat in the combat boots" when they observe a third person who is dressed in a coat and tie but has old Army boots on. Here the amusement in the vocal and facial expressions of the speaker is positive and the contents are, at best, mixed positive and negative. Thus, in addition to being humorous, the message expresses a negative attitude toward the third person's "unacceptable" combination of clothing and shoes.

The Pathology-inducing Quality of Inconsistent Communications

One question posed at the beginning of this chapter was whether the frequent decoding of inconsistent messages of liking contributed to the development of psychopathology.[2] The first section of this chapter showed

2. This section includes rewritten segments from Beakel and Mehrabian's "Inconsistent Communications and Psychopathology," *Journal of Abnormal Psychology*, 74 (1969), 126–30, copyright (1969) by the American Psychological Association. Reproduced by permission.

that inconsistency did not lead to confusion or a double bind when the addressees were adults. Further, the experiments in the second section showed that, in the normal population, inconsistency was a subtle means of differentially communicating attitudes toward the actions of the addressee or the addressee himself.

The experiment to follow explored the occurrence of consistent and inconsistent messages of liking from parents toward their more or less disturbed adolescent children (Beakel and Mehrabian, 1969). According to the double-bind hypothesis, parents of more disturbed children were expected to communicate inconsistent attitudes to their children more frequently than were parents of less disturbed children.

In the experiment, inconsistency was measured in terms of the liking conveyed verbally and posturally. Postural, rather than facial or vocal, cues were selected because of their more subtle quality. In the presence of an "evaluative" therapist it seemed that parents would be less able to censor their communications of liking or dislike via postural cues than to censor or control their facial expressions (Ekman and Friesen, 1969a).

Each family met separately with a clinician, who interviewed the parents in the presence of their children. One child in each family was judged as being moderately or slightly maladjusted. The parents' behaviors were video recorded and analyzed to obtain independent judgments of the degrees of liking communicated via speech and postural cues. These judgments, in turn, yielded the required measures of inconsistency.

METHOD

A sample of 21 families, each of which had a disturbed adolescent member, served as subjects in this experiment. The parents' verbal and postural behaviors were audio and video recorded as each family discussed a problem stemming from the child's disturbance. The participants were unaware that their behaviors were being recorded through a one-way mirror. All family members were seated during the session.

Three clinical psychologists, who were familiar with the problems presented in the entire sample, ranked the 21 adolescents concerned for severity of pathology, without regard to diagnostic classification. A 0.85 Kendall Coefficient of Concordance (Winer, 1962) indicated satisfactory agreement among the three judges. The communication data from the parents of the five adolescents receiving the lowest severity scores and the parents of the five receiving the highest scores were analyzed.

For each parent in both pathology groups, six statements averaging approximately 35 words in length were selected from audio recordings of the discussions. The judge who selected these verbal statements had no knowledge of the level of maladjustment of the adolescent in the family. He was presented only with the audio recordings and instructed to select six statements qualifying best as: (1) complete sentences, (2) involving the parent-speaker addressing the child directly, either by name or by the use of the pronoun *you,* and (3) concerning some aspect of the child's behavior problem or personality. These selection criteria were specified on the assumption that such statements would be most likely to contain variations in liking. While selecting the statements, the judge had no access to the postural and gestural correlates of these messages and therefore could not be influenced by the consistency or inconsistency of the total communications.

The judge next viewed the six video portions corresponding to the selected statements, and chose four in which the parent was maximally visible. These procedures yielded a final set of four audio-video messages for each parent. The total set of 80 communications consisted of four audio-video messages for each of 10 mothers and 10 fathers. These communications were coded and randomized.

A group of four judges rated the liking conveyed by each verbal message on a seven-point scale. Later, they viewed the video recordings and used the same scale to provide the "global judgments" of liking conveyed by postures. The monitor screen was shielded to show only a view of the parent-speaker's body for these judgments.

A second group of judges listened to the audio recordings and imagined the appropriate posture assumed by each parent-speaker. They then described the posture they imagined by selecting one word from each of the following four pairs: open-closed, tense-relaxed, forward-back, and toward-away from. These descriptions provided the "weighted judgments" of liking conveyed by the anticipated posture associated with each statement. They then viewed the video recordings and provided weighted judgments of the actual postures. As in the case of the global judgments of posture, the monitor screen was shielded, affording only a view of the parent-speaker's body.

RESULTS

The measures of (1) "judgment of liking in speech," (2) "global judgment of liking in posture," (3) "weighted judgment of liking in actual posture," and (4) "weighted judgment of liking in anticipated posture" constituted the four primary measures of this study, and were obtained as described above. Two additional composite measures of incongruity were also computed for each of the 80 communications: (5) "global incongruity score," a measure of incongruity based on the absolute difference between judgments of liking from speech (the first measure) and from posture (the second measure), and (6) "weighted incongruity score," the absolute difference between the weighted judgment of liking in the actual posture which accompanied a statement (the third measure) and of the liking in posture anticipated for that statement (the fourth measure).

The scores obtained for a given communication from each of four raters were averaged for each of the above six measures. The correlation matrix for all these averaged dependent variables yielded 0.05 level significant correlations between global judgments of liking in speech and weighted judgments of liking in anticipated posture ($r = 0.36$) and between global and weighted judgments of liking in actual posture ($r = 0.40$).

A 2 Pathology × 2 Parent Sex × 5 Individuals × 4 Communications analysis of variance was performed on each of the following four dependent measures. In this design, Individuals were nested under the Pathology and Sex conditions, and Communications were nested under the Pathology, Sex, and Individuals conditions. The following effects were significant at the 0.05 level.

Analysis of variance of global incongruity scores showed only one significant effect: the mothers were more incongruent than were the fathers ($F = 5.21$, $df = 1/60$, $MS_e = 0.28$). Analysis of variance of weighted incongruity scores showed significance for Pathology Group ($F = 4.12$, $df = 1/60$, $MS_e = 1.53$), and Sex of Parent ($F = 12.06$, $df = 1/60$, $MS_e = 1.53$). The four means from the significant Pathology Group × Sex of Parent interaction effect ($F = 4.12$, $df = 1/60$, $MS_e = 1.53$) were compared using t-tests, and showed that the mothers of the less maladjusted group were more incongruent than were mothers of the more maladjusted group and the fathers of both groups. The other three groups did not differ significantly among each other.

Analysis of variance of judgments of liking that were based on speech showed only one significant effect: parents of the more maladjusted adolescents were less positive than were parents of the less maladjusted adolescents ($F = 7.77$, $df = 1/60$, $MS_e = 0.61$). Analysis of variance of global judgments of liking from posture showed no significant effects.

DISCUSSION

The correlations among the various dependent measures provided validational support for the weighting of postural components used in the study. It will be recalled that only two significant correlations were obtained: one between judgments of liking from speech and weighted judgments of liking in anticipated postures, and another between global and weighted judgments of liking conveyed by actual postures. The second correlation showed that the weighted and global judgments of liking in posture were comparable. The first correlation indicated that the anticipated postures (which were described in terms of their components) conveyed a degree of liking comparable to that assessed from the speech upon which the anticipated postures were based.

The results of the experiment did not support the double-bind hypothesis, the postural-verbal communications of parents of more disturbed adolescents did not show greater incongruity than did those of the parents of less disturbed adolescents. Two different measures of incongruity were employed. For one incongruity measure (based on separate judgments of the verbalizations and postures of the parents), there was no significant difference in the incongruity of communications from parents of the more and less disturbed groups. For a second incongruity measure (based on anticipated postures in comparison to actual postures for a verbalization), the mothers of the less disturbed group of adolescents were found to show a greater amount of incongruity. Thus, the data generally failed to support the hypothesis and, for one measure, provided contradictory evidence for the communication of mothers. These findings, which contradict the double-bind hypothesis, are consistent with the conclusions that Schuham (1967) drew from his review.

Whereas the results of this experiment cannot be interpreted in terms of the double-bind theory, they can be interpreted within an alternative framework by considering the overall positiveness (negativeness) of the communications. The parents of the more disturbed adolescents showed more negative attitudes toward these adolescents (in their verbalizations, but not in their postures) than did parents of the less disturbed adolescents.

The relationship between psychopathology of children and the negative attitude messages of their parents can be explained by either or both of the following. The parents of the more disturbed children may feel more negative because the latter create more problems for them than less disturbed children do for their parents. Alternatively, initially negative attitudes of the parents may have contributed to the psychopathology of the children. In either case, the parents' negative attitudes contribute to the perpetuation of their children's maladjustment. In discussing their findings, Mehrabian and Wiener suggested "it could be argued that unusually frequent negative attitude communicating messages do contribute to severe psychopathological functioning . . . for example, indiscriminate negative reinforcement is not conducive to learning the numerous interpersonal and social skills which are lacking in individuals classed as schizophrenics" (Mehrabian and Wiener, 1967, p. 114). Rogers' (1959) conceptualization of psychopathology also suggests a relationship between the negative attitude communications of parents and the psychopathology of their children. In Rogers' theory, greater psychopathology of a child is associated with greater degrees of "conditional positive regard" of parents toward the child. "Conditional positive regard" refers to the conditional quality of the love or liking of one person for another.

One way to interpret and measure Rogers' concept of conditional versus unconditional positive regard is in terms of the frequency and/or intensity with which one individual expresses negative attitudes toward another. Thus, it is not so much the distinction between attitudes communicated toward a person's actions and attitudes toward that person himself which is the critical variable, as Rogers would suggest. Rather it is a question of the intensity of total negative attitude expressed toward another person.

In sum, the findings of the Beakel and Mehrabian (1969) study show that exploration of the overall quality of positive-negative attitude, rather than inconsistency in attitude communication, is a more useful avenue for investigating the relationship between communication patterns and psychopathology.

Summary

Four questions were posed in this chapter: (1) How does one combine consistent or inconsistent communications received in several channels to infer the attitude implied in the entire message? (2) Why do people use inconsistent communications at all if the same attitude can be conveyed with a consistent message? (3) Are inconsistent messages more difficult to decode? (4) Do inconsistent messages contribute to the development of psychopathology in a person who frequently receives such messages?

Exploration of the first question suggested a first approximation linear model which designates the weight of each component in determining the total attitude. In general, it was found that, when there was inconsistency among components, the implicit cues dominated the verbal cues in determining the total impact. Further, when the various components were consistent with one another, the intensity of the attitude inferred from the total message was enhanced.

To answer the second question, two kinds of inconsistent communication were defined. In inconsistent positive communications; the vocal component indicated a positive and the verbal component a negative attitude, thus yielding an overall positive quality. Inconsistent negative communications contained a negative vocal and a positive verbal component, with an overall negative quality. The experiment dealt with the following questions: when are inconsistent positive communications preferred to consistent positive ones, and when are inconsistent negative communications preferred to consistent negative ones? The findings showed that both positive and negative inconsistent messages were preferred more in less formal situations. Also, the verbal portion of inconsistent messages conveyed attitudes toward the actions of the addressee, whereas the nonverbal portion conveyed attitudes toward the addressee himself.

No specific data were available to provide an adequate answer to the third question. However, a more general review by Mehrabian and Reed (1968) of the literature on communication difficulty (or its converse, accuracy) showed that communication accuracy was enhanced by increases in any or all of the following: the immediacy of communication (that is, the number of communication channels made available to the addressee), the percentage of the total number of channels that a communicator habitually required that were made available to him in a given instance, the decoder's ability to modify the rate of transmission of a message, and feedback to the communicator about how his message was being decoded. Also, communication accuracy correlated directly with the simplicity, redundancy, organization, and objectivity of the message itself.

Finally, for the fourth question, the findings from the Beakel and Mehrabian (1969) experiment are relevant. This experiment explored consistent and inconsistent attitude communications from parents to more and less disturbed adolescents, and showed that parents of the more disturbed adolescents were not more inconsistent toward their children, but were simply more negative.

7

Styles and Abilities in Implicit Communication

At the time when most of the experiments reviewed in the preceding chapters were conducted, a theoretical or empirical basis was lacking to select those personality variables most relevant to the study of implicit attitude communications. However, sufficient findings are now available for the formulation of a general approach to the study of individual differences in this area. If the major referents of implicit messages are positiveness (including liking and preference), potency (including dominance-submissiveness and status), and responsiveness, then individual differences can be viewed as characteristic tendencies or abilities to convey these attitudes.

Some of the most consistent findings about individual differences in implicit communication were related to sex differences. They can be examined within this three-dimensional framework. In general, females were found to express more positive feelings toward others than males; for example, they assumed closer positions to others (Long, Ziller, and Henderson, 1968; Norum, Russo, and Sommer, 1967; and Sommer, 1959). Also, female pairs assumed closer positions to one another than did male pairs (Baxter, 1970). Exline (1963) found that women engaged in more eye contact with one another than did men. People reciprocated the positiveness that they received from females by assuming closer positions to them (for example, Henderson, Long, and Ziller, 1965; Mehrabian, 1968a; Willis, 1966). More generally, based on the factor of implicit positiveness identified in Mehrabian's (1971b) study, females were found to be more positive than males. Since females are more affiliative (Anastasi, 1958), their tendency to be implicitly more postive is consistent with

Acknowledgment is given to Academic Press, Inc., for their permission to include in this chapter rewritten segments and Tables 1 and 2 of Zaidel and Mehrabian's "The Ability to Communicate and Infer Positive and Negative Attitudes Facially and Vocally," *Journal of Experimental Research in Personality*, 3 (1969), 233–41.

the hypothesis that persons who score higher on affiliative tendency are interpersonally more positive (Mehrabian and Ksionzky, 1970).

In addition to their greater positiveness, females also tend to be more submissive in their nonverbal behaviors. For instance, they assumed less relaxed postures than did males in social situations (for example, Mehrabian, 1969b).

Findings are also available on some characteristic tendencies in the implicit communications of more anxious and maladjusted subjects. Such persons were less able to conceal their deception from others or to overtly convey negative feelings to others (Mehrabian, 1970e, 1971a). This submissive attitude of maladjusted persons differed from that shown by females in that it was accompanied by implicit communications of negative affect. For instance, more maladjusted persons were found to assume greater distances from others (Fisher, 1967; Long and Henderson, 1968; Smith, 1954; Weinstein, 1965). These findings are consistent with the expectation that psychologically maladjusted persons, particularly hospitalized ones, are more uneasy and insecure in the presence of others. Thus, they convey both negative and submissive feelings during social interaction.

By far the largest number of findings that related implicit communications to individual differences were obtained by using characteristic preferences of physical distance. Some of these related to interpersonal positiveness, and were already noted in discussing sex differences. Other findings showed that lesser distances were selected when with friendlier persons (Smith, 1953). Extroverts, who have a more positive social orientation than introverts, selected closer positions to others (Leipold, 1963; Patterson and Holmes, 1966; Williams, 1963).

These distance findings supported the idea that an individual's characteristic positive-negative interpersonal orientation (for example, affiliative tendency) is relevant to the exploration of individual differences in implicit communication. This hypothesis was tested in its more general form by Mehrabian (1971b) and Mehrabian and Ksionzky (1972). Their data showed that persons who scored higher on a measure of affiliative tendency (Mehrabian, 1970d, and Appendix B) conveyed more positiveness, both verbally and nonverbally, when they interacted with strangers.

The second major group of individual differences relates to consistent implicit expressions of a more potent or dominant attitude. Some relevant measures in this case are the social prestige or status of a person as measured by occupational level (Kahl, 1964; Roe, 1956), age (at least up to the mid twenties), or personality measures of dominance-submissiveness. Dominant or higher-status persons selected more distant positions to others than did those who felt equal (Lott and Sommer, 1967). Kuethe (1964) found that communicators assumed greater distances from persons against whom they were more prejudiced. Since prejudice is a combination of dislike and an implied status difference, this finding was a function of either or both the attitude or status variables, and was consistent with expectations.

A third set of communicator attributes relates to consistent individual differences in responsiveness to others. Included here are such personality variables as emotional empathy (Mehrabian and Epstein, 1972, and Appendix B) and, for more extreme variations, manic-depressive states or catatonic withdrawal. It is possible that the latter relationships were not explored because the relevant implicit behaviors were referred to as "activity" rather than the more interpersonally oriented concept of responsiveness.

It seems that a conceptualization of the activity cues as indexes of responsiveness can be helpful in identifying relevant personality measures. Along these lines, the measure of empathic tendency in Appendix B was given to a group of 78 subjects who were also requested to characterize themselves and their emotions in general, using the semantic differential scales in Table A.1 of Appendix A. A regression analysis was performed in which empathic tendency was explored as a function of characteristic pleasantness, responsiveness, and dominance. The one effect which was significant at the 0.05 level is summarized as follows:

Empathic tendency $= 0.33$ Characteristic responsiveness.

Both variables in the equation are normalized. Thus, this particular personality measure does indeed uniquely tap individual differences in responsiveness to emotional events and can be useful in future studies of this neglected area.

In addition to the preceding three-dimensional framework for denoting individual differences, another variable is the characteristic preference for more implicit (subtle) means to communicate affect, particularly when it is negative. The explicit communication of feelings, particularly negative ones, is generally discouraged in Western cultures (Riesman, 1950). This, incidentally, may be one reason for the tremendous upsurge of sensitivity and encounter groups in which artificial social situations are devised to permit the expression of feelings (Bach and Wyden, 1968; Malamud and Machover, 1965). More conforming and dependent persons, particularly those who are sensitive to rejection, are expected to abide more by implicit social rules. In our culture, therefore, such persons would find it more desirable to express their negative feelings in subtle ways rather than through such obvious channels as facial expressions or verbal contents. It was this idea which led us to include the Crowne and Marlowe (1960) Social Desirability scale in several of the studies already reported and in the study to follow. A measure of sensitivity to rejection which recently became available (Mehrabian, 1970d, and Appendix B) would seem even more appropriate than the measure of approval-seeking tendency which was employed.

In sum, the ability or preference for communications of liking, domi-nance-submissiveness, or responsiveness can be related to personality attributes or other individual differences (for example, sex, ethnic back-ground). Whereas some data is available to relate individual differences to communications of like-dislike, there is little corresponding data in relation to communications of potency and responsiveness.

The Ability to Communicate and Infer Positive and Negative Feelings

The following study illustrates the difficult methodological problems in the study of individual abilities or preferences in the communication of feelings. This study (Zaidel and Mehrabian, 1969) also illustrates some of the issues that historically have been of primary concern to investiga-tors in this area of research.

Specifically, the study was designed to explore the relationships be-tween encoding and decoding abilities in the facial and vocal channels and a communicator's sex and approval-seeking tendency (Crowne and Marlowe, 1960, 1964). Encoding ability was defined in terms of the dis-criminability of cues emitted by an individual for conveying different ideas or feelings. Decoding, in turn, involved the ability to discriminate among different cues. In this sense, a good encoder emits clearly discrim-inable cues corresponding to different feelings, and a good decoder can discriminate different feelings among a variety of cues.

Several questions were raised. First, are encoding and decoding abilities related? Previous research was equivocal on this point. Knower (1945) and Levy (1964) both reported a significant correlation between the ability to encode and decode vocal communications, but Miller (1966) found a smaller, nonsignificant relationship. All three studies differed from ours in their conceptualization of encoding-decoding ability. The former measured (1) the extent to which judges matched different moods such as "happy" or "angry" to a set of intended expressions by a particu-lar encoder, or (2) the extent to which a particular decoder accurately matched moods and expressions of several communicators. In contrast, communications varied along a continuum of like-dislike or positive-negative evaluation in our study. It is possible that our approach and previous approaches to studying communication skills were the same, but since the experimental tasks were not comparable, the previously mentioned results had only indirect bearing on our experiment. More-over, the results of these investigators were based on the vocal channel only, whereas our study included vocal and facial channels.

A second question raised by the study was the long-standing issue of sex differences. The consensus from previous experiments was that there were no sex differences in the ability to encode or decode moods (Davitz, 1964; Miller, 1966), but the issue was open to further evidence.

The third question concerned channel differences. How do vocal and facial expressions compare as transmitters of liking? Gates (1927) found that children were more accurate in their judgments of facial than of vocal expressions of feeling, which suggested that it was easier to discriminate facial cues. In a study using consistent and inconsistent combinations of pleasant-unpleasant facial and bodily expressions, Dittmann, Parloff, and Boomer (1965) found that judges were affected more by facial cues than by body cues. Mehrabian and Ferris (1967) reported that attitudes that were inferred from combined facial-vocal communications were a weighted sum of the attitudes conveyed in each component, with the facial component receiving 3/2 the weight received by the vocal component. Thus, the relative importance of facial cues, as compared to vocal ones, in decoding attitude might have been due to their relative discriminability. A related question was whether encoding-decoding skills were general or channel-specific. Levitt (1964) used a mood identification task and obtained a significant correlation between encoding ability in the facial and vocal channels. It was therefore expected that the abilities to encode (or decode) variations in attitude facially and vocally would be correlated.

A fourth question concerned the contents of communication. Are there encoding-decoding differences with respect to positive and negative attitude communications? In other words, are people generally better able to express or infer negative (or positive) feelings? It has been mentioned that present-day society tends to discourage the explicit verbalization of negative attitudes (for example, Wiener and Mehrabian, 1968), and that the more implicit nonverbal channels have assumed that function. On this basis, negative attitudes were expected to be more effectively conveyed than positive ones, at least in the implicit channels that were investigated.

The general abilities to convey negative versus positive attitudes also suggested the relevance of personality attributes, such as the tendency to seek social approval. In this context, it is helpful to consider the degree to which the various means of attitude communication are nonobvious. A tentative ordering in terms of increasing obviousness is: verbal nonimmediacy, positive inconsistency (that is, implicitly positive and verbally negative), postural nonimmediacy, negative vocal, negative facial, and negative verbal communications. In this connection, persons who are highly concerned about social approval are expected to have a greater preference for expressing their negative feelings in the less obvious channels. In terms of the preceding tentative list, it is therefore expected that high social approval seekers are more prone to use verbal nonimmediacy and positive inconsistency, and less prone to use negative vocal, facial, or verbal communications.

In sum, the following experiments explored a number of interrelated hypotheses:

(1) Encoding and decoding abilities are correlated, and the ability to encode (or decode) variations of liking facially is correlated with the ability to encode (or decode) variations of liking vocally.

(2) Communications of liking are more effective in the facial than in the vocal channel. That is, a wider range of liking can be encoded into, and decoded from, the facial than the vocal channel.

(3) In both the facial and vocal channels, communications of dislike are more effective than those of liking. In other words, negative attitude communications are more discriminable than a corresponding set of positive ones.

(4) The tendency to seek social approval is negatively correlated with the ability to encode dislike facially or vocally.

These hypotheses were investigated in two related experiments. In the first, high and low approval-seeking subjects of both sexes each encoded and decoded facial and vocal expressions of varying degrees of like-dislike. This experiment provided data bearing on the first hypothesis. In the second experiment, a larger group of high and low approval-seeking subjects of both sexes decoded the facial and vocal communications obtained in the first experiment. Since these subjects were not familiar with the encoding tasks, their decoding responses provided evidence for the second, third, and fourth hypotheses. The larger number of subjects in the second experiment also provided adequate data on sex differences.

EXPERIMENT I: THE RELATION BETWEEN ENCODING AND
DECODING ABILITIES OF THE SAME SUBJECTS

All subjects used in the first Zaidel and Mehrabian (1969) experiment were students at the University of California, Los Angeles. The Crowne and Marlowe (1960) Social Desirability (SD) scale was administered to a pool of 49 male and 42 female subjects. Three males and three females who scored low on the SD scale and three males and three females who scored high on the scale were selected to participate in the study. Among the selected subjects, the SD scores of the males at each SD level did not differ significantly (at the 0.2 level) from those of the females in the corresponding level. The 12 subjects were paid to act as encoders and decoders of facial and vocal communications.

The experiment was conducted individually in two sessions, one week apart. In the first session, the subjects were instructed to audio record the words *maybe* and *really* while expressing five degrees of like and dislike toward an imagined addressee. Similarly, they were to take photographs of themselves while expressing the same five degrees of attitude. For each channel, a subject produced 10 expressions in random order consisting of two each of strong liking, moderate liking, neutral, moderate dislike, and strong dislike. Half of the subjects encoded facial expressions first and half encoded vocal expressions first. In both encoding tasks, subjects were left alone while they recorded their own vocal and facial expressions.

A Nikon single-lens reflex camera fitted with a 135-mm lens was used to record the subjects' facial expressions. A nine-foot Rowi pneumatic extension device for activating the shutter mechanism and a machine drive, which automatically advanced the film to successive frames, enabled the subjects to take their own pictures at a distance of about seven feet from the camera without having to adjust or reset the camera. The subjects' vocal expressions were recorded on an audio recorder.

A group of 12 judges selected the sample communications to be used as anchors in the decoding tasks. They rated 23 audio recorded expressions of the words *maybe* and *really* on a seven-point scale of liking. *Maybe* and *really* had been judged as conveying a neutral attitude in a previous experiment (Mehrabian and Ferris, 1967). The same judges rated 28 photographed facial expressions on the attitude scale. On the basis of the obtained ratings, six vocal and six facial expressions were selected as anchors corresponding to strong liking ($+3$), neutral (0), and strong dislike (-3), with a male and female communicator in each category.

In the second session, the decoding phase, subjects rated a series of audio recorded vocal expressions and photographed facial expressions on a seven-point scale of like-dislike. As part of the instructions, the preceding anchor communications were presented to subjects to illustrate the use of the rating scale and to establish a common scale of judgment. The materials consisted of the 120 vocal and 120 facial communications which had been previously encoded by the same group of 12 subjects. Five buffer items were included at the beginning for practice, but were not included in the data. Subjects were asked to judge each message independently, not relative to other expressions by the same or other communicators. Each subject saw a different random order of the 120 photographs, and heard one of three tapes of randomly ordered, recorded vocal messages. Each photo was shown for about three seconds to approximate the duration of the vocal communications. Half of the subjects decoded facial expressions first, and the other half decoded vocal expressions first. (The reader who wishes to do so can proceed directly to the discussion section without loss of continuity.)

Results. In this experiment, each subject encoded two instances of each of five degrees of liking facially and two instances of each of five degrees of liking vocally. Later, each subject decoded the 20 communications (that is, 10 facial and 10 vocal) of his own and the remaining 11 subjects. Using the method of least squares, an overall slope was computed for the various sets of 10 scores which corresponded to the expressions of five degrees of increasingly positive attitude. For example, there were 10 responses of the first decoder corresponding to the facial communications of the first encoder. These 10 responses consisted of pairs of judgments of the extremely negative, moderately negative, neutral, moderately positive, and extremely positive facial communications of liking by the first encoder. The slope for the five pairs of responses (which could range from −1 to 1) yielded an index of the effectiveness of facial communication between the first encoder and the first decoder.

The 12 slopes of the 12 decoders' judgments of a given communicator's facial expressions yielded a mean slope which was an index of that communicator's ability to encode variations in liking facially. Similarly, the mean slope obtained from the twelve decoders' judgments of a given communicator's vocal messages of liking yielded an index which was that communicator's ability to encode variations in liking vocally. Decoding ability was indexed by the mean of all 12 slopes for a given decoder's judgments of the 12 encoders' facial communications, and by the mean of all 12 slopes for a given decoder's judgments of the 12 encoders' vocal messages.

In sum, there were four indexes for each of the 12 subjects, representing the subjects' ability to encode variations in liking facially (1) and vocally (2), and to decode variations in liking conveyed facially (3) and vocally (4). Correlations among these four indexes were computed. The correlation between (1) and (2) was 0.33; between (3) and (4) was 0.11; between (1) and (3) was −0.23; between (2) and (4) was 0.45; between (1) and (4) was 0.26; and between (2) and (3) was 0.30. With 10 degrees of freedom, none of the above correlations were significant, since the critical r for the 0.05 level of significance equals 0.58. However, the above data did suggest certain trends to explore with larger samples of subjects.

EXPERIMENT II: THE EFFECTS OF CHANNELS, SEX AND PERSONALITY
ON THE ABILITY TO CONVEY POSITIVE-NEGATIVE FEELINGS

Thirty-six male and 36 female University of California undergraduates served as decoder-subjects in the second Zaidel and Mehrabian (1969) experiment. All subjects were administered the Crowne and Marlowe (1960) Social Desirability scale. The members of each sex were subdivided into a high SD (that is, a high tendency to give socially desirable responses) and a low SD group. The materials used in the experiment were the encoded communications of the 12 subjects in Experiment I, which consisted of 120 facial and 120 vocal communications of like-dislike. The procedures for decoding these messages were the same as those used in the first experiment.

Results. Using the method of least squares, slopes were computed for each decoder's judgments of the facial and vocal attitude communications of each encoder. Indexes of the effectiveness of these messages were derived in the following way. A slope was obtained from each decoder's set of six judgments corresponding to a given encoder's facial expressions of neutral, moderately positive, and extremely positive attitude. A second slope was obtained from each decoder's set of six judgments corresponding to a given encoder's facial expressions of extremely negative, moderately negative, and neutral attitude. Finally, an overall slope for the total set of 10 facial communications (that is, ranging from extreme dislike to extreme liking) was obtained for each encoder-decoder combination. An equivalent group of slopes was computed for the judgments of vocal communications of like-dislike. All of these slopes had a possible range of −1 to 1. Various means over all subjects obtained from these slopes provided indexes of the effectiveness of facial and vocal communications and of positive and negative communications within and across the two channels. For each decoder subject, the slopes could be used as indexes of his ability to decode positive and negative attitude communications in the facial and vocal channels. Similarly, for each encoder subject, the slopes indexed his encoding ability for positive and negative attitudes in each channel.

With 12 encoders, 72 decoders, and two channels, there were a total of $12 \times 72 \times 2 = 1728$ slopes computed for each of the three sets of communications of positive, negative, and overall attitude.

The slopes for the entire range of attitude communication, that is, for indexes of overall ability to discriminate variations in attitude ranging from extremely negative to extremely positive, were analyzed in a $2 \times 2 \times 3 \times 2 \times 2 \times 18 \times 2$ factorial design. The third factor, encoder subjects, is nested under the first two factors, encoder SD and encoder sex. The sixth factor, decoder subjects, is nested under the fourth and fifth factors, decoder SD and decoder sex. The seventh factor, which involves repeated measures, is the channel factor. All of the following effects were found to be significant at the 0.01 level: encoder SD, encoder sex, decoder sex, channel, Encoder $SD \times$ Encoder Sex, Decoder $SD \times$ Decoder Sex, Encoder $SD \times$ Channel, Encoder Sex $\times$ Channel, Decoder $SD \times$ Channel, and Encoder $SD \times$ Encoder Sex $\times$ Channel. Only a few of these effects are described below. A more general presentation can be found in Zaidel and Mehrabian (1969).

Examination of the means corresponding to these effects indicated that low SD encoders were better able to convey variations in like-dislike (mean slope of 0.40) than were high SD encoders (0.35). Female encoders were better able to convey variations in like-dislike (0.42) than were male encoders (0.33). Female decoders were more discriminating of communications of like-dislike (0.40) than were male decoders (0.36). Facial communications of like-dislike (0.45) were better discriminated than were vocal communications of like-dislike (0.30).

Separate analyses of the slopes corresponding to the abilities to convey variations in positive and negative attitudes were also carried out. Some of the major findings from these analyses are summarized below.

The mean overall slope for the facial communications of negative attitude (0.60) was significantly greater than that for positive attitude (0.43).

Similarly, for the vocal channel, the mean overall slope for negative attitude communications (0.56) was greater than that for positive ones
(0.33). In other words, for both facial and vocal communications, it was
easier to convey variations in negative, than in positive, attitude.

Whereas high SD encoders were better able to convey variations in
positive attitude (0.40) than low SD encoders (0.36), a greater difference
in the opposite direction was found for communications of negative
attitude, as evidenced by the respective mean slopes of 0.70 for low SD
encoders and 0.45 for high SD encoders. Thus, the difference in the overall ability of low SD encoders to communicate attitudes (0.40) relative
to high SD encoders (0.35) was primarily due to the former group's
better ability to encode variations in negative attitude.

Whereas male encoders were better able to communicate positive
attitudes (0.40) than were female encoders (0.36), a greater difference
in the opposite direction was found for communications of negative attitudes (mean slope of 0.66 for females and 0.50 for males). Thus, the
difference in the overall ability of females to convey the entire range of
attitudes (0.42) relative to that of males (0.33) was primarily due to the
females' better abilities to encode negative attitudes.

Separate analyses of the slopes corresponding to communications of
positive and negative attitudes yielded comparable effects for decoder
sex and channel. Therefore, the results reported for these two factors for
the entire range of attitudes apply equally well to positive and negative
attitude communications.

An additional analysis, comparable to the one done in Experiment I,
was carried out on the present data to obtain encoding ability scores for
each of the 12 encoders, and decoding ability scores for each of the 72
decoders. For example, for each decoder in each channel, a mean slope
that indicated his ability to infer variations in positive attitude was computed; a second slope was computed for his ability to infer variations in
negative attitude, and a third slope for his overall ability to infer variations in attitude. Intercorrelations among the set of six encoding ability
scores of the 12 encoders are presented in Table 7.1. Similarly, intercorrelations among the set of six decoding ability scores of the 72 decoders
are presented in Table 7.2.

Table 7.1. Intercorrelations among encoding ability scores.

	Positive Vocal	Negative Facial	Negative Vocal	Overall Facial	Overall Vocal
Positive Facial	0.26	−0.03	0.45	0.39	0.36
Positive Vocal		−0.08	0.43	0.13	−0.21
Negative Facial			0.32	0.86°	0.22
Negative Vocal				0.51	0.64°
Overall Facial					0.36

°$P < 0.05$.

Table 7.2. Intercorrelations among decoding ability scores.

	Positive Vocal	Negative Facial	Negative Vocal	Overall Facial	Overall Vocal
Positive Facial	0.01	0.29*	0.17	0.65*	0.17
Positive Vocal		0.25*	0.14	0.09	0.38*
Negative Facial			0.31*	0.68*	0.43*
Negative Vocal				0.23*	0.47*
Overall Facial					0.27*

*$P < 0.05$.

The encoding ability intercorrelations presented in Table 7.1 showed only two significant correlations: (1) between the ability to encode variations in negative attitude facially and the ability to encode variations over the entire range of attitudes facially, and (2) between the ability to encode variations in negative attitude vocally and the ability to encode variations over the entire range of attitudes vocally. As the data in Table 7.1 indicated, several other correlations approached significance.

The decoding ability intercorrelations indicated several significant effects. With $df = 70$ and $r_{0.05} = 0.23$, the overall ability to decode attitudes from facial communications correlated with that for vocal ones—a relationship due to the correlation between the abilities to decode negative vocal and facial cues. Also, the abilities to decode positive, negative, or overall variations in attitude from facial communications were intercorrelated. However, only the abilities to decode positive or negative attitudes from vocal messages correlated with the overall ability to decode vocal attitude communications. Finally, although the abilities to decode negative facial and positive vocal communications were correlated, the corresponding correlation for positive facial and negative vocal messages was not significant. In four instances, the absence of a significant correlation involved different channels, and in two instances the absence of a correlation involved opposite attitudes.

Discussion

The results of the Zaidel and Mehrabian (1969) experiments can best be summarized in terms of the hypotheses. The first hypothesis predicted intercorrelations between encoding and decoding abilities in both channels. The nonsignificant correlations obtained in Experiment I did not support this hypothesis, although a positive relationship between the ability to encode and decode vocal communications was suggested by the data. The absence of a significant correlation between encoding and decoding abilities in the facial channel was consistent with Osgood's (1966) data.

Additional correlational data obtained in Experiment II showed, for both the facial and vocal channels, that the ability to encode negative attitude contributed more to general encoding ability than did the ability to encode positive attitude. The second experiment also indicated consistency in decoding abilities.

Thus, the study showed consistency in the ability to decode general (overall) and specific (positive or negative) communication cues, for both the facial and vocal channels. This consistency seemed to be greater within than between channels. Although data relating to encoding abilities were only suggestive of similar consistencies, the small sample of encoders did not permit a conclusive assessment of the possible correlations among various encoding abilities, or of the intercorrelations of the encoding abilities with decoding abilities.

The second hypothesis predicted greater variability in attitudes expressed facially than vocally. Relevant data from Experiment II clearly supported this hypothesis. However, the interactions of the channel factor with such individual differences as sex and approval-seeking tendency indicated that this greater variability in facial cues applied more to certain individuals than to others.

Incidentally, the greater effectiveness of the facial channel for communicating attitudes was consistent with the fact that facial communications are given greater weight than are vocal ones in decoding two-channel messages (Mehrabian and Ferris, 1967). Although the Mehrabian and Ferris study used only female subjects, the Zaidel and Mehrabian (1969) finding of channel differences for both sexes provided support for the application of their suggested linear model to both males and females.

A final point about channel differences concerns a methodological problem. It is difficult to devise a method that would allow a separate assessment of encoding and decoding effectiveness in the facial and vocal channels. In attempting to assess encoding effectiveness, the findings are confounded with the average decoding abilities of subjects for the various channels; in attempting to assess decoding effectiveness, one must ultimately rely upon the decodings of some "expert" or special group of subjects. As a consequence, comparisons of communication effectiveness in various channels necessarily involve a confounding of communicators' encoding and decoding effectiveness in the channels. However, in everyday situations the effectiveness of a given channel for conveying variations in attitude also involves the combined effectiveness of encoding and decoding in that channel. It would seem, then, that our findings relating to channel differences are applicable to everyday communication, since the methodology is representative of the communication process. In contrast to the confounding of encoding and decoding for the overall channel effect, our study did allow for a separate assessment of encoding and decoding abilities of different groups of subjects (that is, sex and SD of groups).

The third hypothesis, which predicted greater variability in negative than in positive attitude communications, was supported. A related finding was that the ability to encode negative attitude accounted for a large proportion of the variance in overall ability to convey attitude, both in the facial and vocal channels. These findings supported the view expressed by Wiener and Mehrabian (1968) that our culture discourages the explicit verbalization of negative feelings, and consequently the implicit communication channels have assumed the function of expressing such attitudes. The finding that females are better encoders of negative attitude than are males is in line with this cultural explanation, since males seem to have greater latitude to express negative feelings explicitly.

In addition to the above suggestions, the finding that overall ability to encode attitude was largely a function of ability to encode negative attitude has implications for other research in implicit communication. Moods used in previous research (for example, Davitz, 1964) included positive, neutral, and negative feelings. Although they were labeled in discrete categories, such as "happy," "flirting," or "angry," such data can be re-examined in terms of positive versus negative moods, both for measures of encoding ability and for possible relationships with the personality measures employed in mood-encoding studies (for example, fear of rejection, affiliation, conformity, hostility, or neuroticism).

The fourth hypothesis dealt with interactions between abilities to convey positive and negative attitudes and the approval-seeking tendency. For both the facial and vocal channels, low approval-seeking encoders communicated a more discriminable set of attitudes than high approval-seeking encoders. As predicted, low social approval seekers were better at conveying variations in negative attitude than were high approval seekers, and the latter were somewhat better at conveying variations in positive attitude. Thus, the superior encoding ability of low approval seekers was primarily due to their superiority in communicating negative attitude. In contrast to encoding ability differences, high and low approval-seeking subjects did not differ in their ability to decode positive or negative attitudes. If it is true that the expression of negative feelings is socially discouraged, then it is understandable that persons who seek social approval and tend to conform to social expectations will also tend to inhibit such expressions.

Although no specific hypotheses regarding sex differences were ventured, the results indicated that females were generally more proficient than males in the implicit communication of feelings. Whereas males were somewhat better encoders of positive attitude, females were considerably better than males at encoding variations in negative attitude. Thus the overall superiority of females in encoding attitudes was largely due to their superiority in conveying negative attitude. The results also indicated that females were better in discriminating variations in attitude communicated by others.

Summary

Since the major referents of implicit communication are positiveness, potency, and responsiveness, then characteristic differences in the tendency or ability to convey these attitudes are most relevant to the study of individual differences. In this context, females were found to characteristically convey more positiveness and submissiveness than males. More anxious and more maladjusted persons conveyed less positiveness and more submissiveness. A personality measure of positive interpersonal orientation, affiliative tendency, correlated with a factor consisting of various implicit indicators of positiveness. A measure of empathic tendency was shown to be a correlate of characteristic emotional responsiveness. In contrast to the availability of data for communications of positiveness, corresponding data for communications of potency and responsiveness were mostly lacking.

The Zaidel and Mehrabian (1969) study was presented in some detail to illustrate the methods and problems that are encountered in the study of individual differences in implicit communication. The experiments in the study explored relationships between encoding and decoding abilities in the facial and vocal channels by males and females who differed in their approval-seeking tendency. It was found that the facial channel was generally more effective than the vocal one for communicating attitudes (that is, like-dislike) and that negative attitudes were more readily conveyed than positive ones. The latter finding supported the view that implicit channels are used to express negative attitudes, because explicit (verbal) expression of negative attitudes is socially discouraged. It was also found that an individual's ability to communicate variations in negative attitude largely accounted for his overall attitude-communicating ability. Low approval seekers were better at encoding variations in negative attitude than were high approval seekers, although there was no corresponding difference between the two groups' abilities to decode positive or negative attitudes. Females were considerably better than males at communicating variations in negative attitude, although males were somewhat better communicators of positive attitude. Finally, it was found that various abilities to decode attitudes were interrelated, although the relationships among various encoding abilities, or their relations to decoding abilities, could not be unambiguously assessed.

8

Categories of Social Behavior

Two recent experiments were designed to explore the relationships among nonverbal and implicit verbal behaviors of two strangers in a waiting situation (Mehrabian, 1971b; Mehrabian and Ksionzky, 1972). In both of these experiments, one of the strangers was an experimental confederate; this was not evident to the other person, the subject in the experiment. Confederates were initially coached in detail regarding where to stand, how to orient, how much eye contact to have with the subjects, the degree of their facial pleasantness and positive vocalization, and the number and length of their verbal utterances. Two different sets of 22 confederates, equally divided as to sex, were trained to participate in each of the experiments. The detailed training of confederates and the use of a large number of confederates was designed to minimize the confounding of results by confederate attributes or physical appearance.

In both experiments, one subject and a confederate of the same sex were led into a "waiting room" while the experimenter ostensibly went to prepare the materials for the experiment. Actually, this two-minute waiting period was the experiment proper. Both the subject's and the confederate's behaviors were audio and video recorded. This method was quite effective in eliciting spontaneous and natural social behaviors from subjects.

Waiting with a Stranger: I

In the Mehrabian (1971b) study[1], the waiting room, 9 by 20 feet in size, was empty except for a table placed in one corner of the room. Thus,

1. Acknowledgment is given to Academic Press, Inc., for their permission to use, in this section, rewritten segments and Tables 1 and 2 from my paper "Verbal and Nonverbal Interaction of Strangers in a Waiting Situation," *Journal of Experimental Research in Personality*, 5 (1971), 127–38.

both the confederate and the subject were standing. A standing, rather than a seated, arrangement was used to make possible the exploration of distances and orientations in relation to other cues. The confederate's behaviors toward the subject were predetermined to be either slightly positive, or negative, as follows.

Confederate slightly negative toward the subject: The confederate entered the waiting room ahead of the subject, took a preassigned position near one corner, and faced diagonally across to the opposite corner of the room. He stood with his legs in a moderately asymmetrical position, with both feet resting flat on the floor. His hands and arms were moderately relaxed—his arms in a slightly asymmetrical position, or held behind his back, or one arm hanging loosely with the other holding that forearm. In general, the confederate's posture was intended to communicate a moderate level of relaxation which seemed natural in the waiting situation. The confederate had been trained to look toward the subject's head 25 per cent of the time, and to do so especially if the subject addressed him. The confederate's facial expressions, which were also scored, obtained a mean rating of 1.5 on a scale ranging from zero (no positive expressions) to four (extremely positive expression). As the confederate entered the waiting room with the subject, he looked at the subject, smiled once, and did not exhibit any negative facial expressions during the waiting period. He never initiated a conversation, nor did he ask any questions, but he always responded if the subject initiated a topic or made a remark. His responses were brief, averaging 1.5 words.

Confederate slightly positive toward the subject: In this condition the confederate's behaviors were identical to those in the slightly negative condition, with the following exceptions. His facial expressions were more positive, having been rated 2.6 on the same zero-to-4 scale. For every three verbal initiations of the subject, the confederate initiated once. In a typical initiation, the subject's question was first answered and then a similar question was asked in return (for example, "I'm majoring in Chemistry, how about you?"). The verbal responses of the confederate were longer than in the preceding condition, averaging 4.5 words.

Each confederate was assigned only one condition, either slightly positive or slightly negative, and served as a partner to approximately 12 subjects. All confederates received the same information, regardless of the condition in which they served. They were told that the experiment was a study of the ways in which strangers interact in a waiting situation, that we were using several confederates to insure generality of results, that to insure comparability in the behaviors of various confederates we needed to train them in great detail, and that more natural behaviors would be elicited from subjects if they remained unaware that their partners were experimental confederates.

In the final portion of the experiment, the subjects were requested to answer questionnaire measures of affiliative tendency, sensitivity to rejection (Mehrabian, 1970d), and achieving tendency (Mehrabian, 1968e, 1968f, 1969a).

Each subject's behavior during the two-minute waiting period was observed and recorded through a one-way mirror. Observers scored eye contact and distance, since these are difficult to score from video recordings. The remaining dependent measures and confederate behaviors were scored subsequently from the audio and video recordings. The entire set of dependent measures from the waiting period are included in Table 8.1. Two observers independently scored first the audio recordings and then the video recordings for movements. Reliability estimates for the dependent measures, provided in Appendix A, justified averaging the pair of scores obtained by the two observers for each dependent measure.

The names of the variables in Table 8.1 are self-explanatory. Rate measures, unless otherwise specified below, were in terms of number of units (movements or statements) per minute. Speech rate, speech volume, and vocal activity (that is, a composite of intensity range and fundamental frequency range) were estimated on scales ranging from zero to four. The positive-negative quality of both the vocal component and the verbal contents was scored on a scale ranging from -2 to $+2$. A statement was defined as a simple sentence or an independent clause; a subject's statements were also subdivided into "declaratives," "questions," and "answers." Verbal reinforcers (for example, *yeah, uh-huh, really?,* or *hmmm*) were scored as a separate category and did not qualify as statements. Speech duration of the subject (or the confederate) was the percentage of the waiting period during which he talked.

Behavioral data from the waiting period were factor analyzed. Varimax rotation of the primary factors yielded the groupings listed in Table 8.1. Variables are listed in order according to the magnitude of their loadings, and direction of loading for each variable on the corresponding factor is also indicated. Each subject's z-scores for the variables of a given factor were summed algebraically to serve as a composite score for that factor. For instance, an "intimacy-close position" score was simply a subject's z-score for "shoulder orientation" minus his z-score for "distance."

To compute an affiliative behavior index, however, it was noted that a number of the variables were simply redundant measures of amount of speech. Therefore, the corresponding index included only "statement rate" as the representative measure for the various related cues:

Affiliative behavior = total number of statements per minute + per cent duration of eye contact with the confederate + head nods per minute + pleasantness of facial expressions + number of verbal reinforcers per minute + positive verbal content + hand and arm gestures per minute + pleasantness of vocal expressions

Table 8.1. Summary of the factors characterizing social interaction in Mehrabian's (1971b) study.

		Direction of Loading on Factor
	Factor I: Affiliative Behavior	
1.	Total number of statements per minute	(+)
2.	Number of declarative statements per minute	(+)
3.	Number of questions per minute	(+)
4.	Percent duration of subject's speech	(+)
5.	Percent duration of confederate's speech	(+)
6.	Percent duration of eye contact with confederate	(+)
7.	Head nods per minute	(+)
8.	Pleasantness of facial expressions	(+)
9.	Number of verbal reinforcers per minute	(+)
10.	Positive verbal content	(+)
11.	Hand and arm gestures per minute	(+)
12.	Pleasantness of vocal expressions	(+)
	Factor II: Responsiveness to (or Salience of) Target	
1.	Vocal activity	(+)
2.	Speech volume	(+)
3.	Speech rate	(+)
	Factor III: Relaxation	
1.	Leg and foot movements per minute	(−)
2.	Rocking movements per minute	(−)
3.	Body lean	(+)
	Factor IV: Intimacy (or Close Position)	
1.	Shoulder orientation away from confederate	(+)
2.	Distance from confederate	(−)
	Factor V: Behavioral Index of Distress	
1.	Per cent duration of walking	(+)

Since the cues for affiliative behavior are of primary interest, the intercorrelations among the variables in this first factor are reported in Table 8.2.

The intercorrelations among the variables subsumed within the first factor and reported in Table 8.2 show that positive affect cues were significantly correlated with various indexes of amount of conversation. Together, the positive affect cues in verbalization (such as verbal reinforcement rate, positive verbal content, and positive vocalization); positive affect cues in nonverbal behavior (eye contact, head nods, pleasant facial expressions, gesticulation), and various indicators of amount of conversation (total number of statements per minute, duration of speech) defined a unitary dimension of social behavior. These intercorrelations provided support for Mehrabian and Ksionzky's (1970) hypothesis that affiliative behavior is not simply the exchange of verbalizations, but rather encompasses a broader realm of social cues which consist of the exchange of

Table 8.2. Correlations among variables defining the affiliative behavior factor*.

	2	3	4	5	6	7	8	9	10	11	12
1. Total Statements per Minute	0.99	0.74	0.87	0.78	0.73	0.62	0.56	0.54	0.54	0.46	0.35
2. Declarative Statements per Minute		0.75	0.86	0.75	0.73	0.61	0.55	0.54	0.53	0.46	0.33
3. Questions per Minute			0.63	0.69	0.66	0.47	0.43	0.62	0.49	0.22	0.32
4. Per cent Speech Duration of Subject				0.79	0.67	0.52	0.52	0.45	0.47	0.51	0.32
5. Per cent Speech Duration of Confederate					0.70	0.55	0.52	0.53	0.51	0.36	0.32
6. Per cent Duration Eye Contact with Confederate						0.52	0.59	0.44	0.41	0.41	0.33
7. Head Nods per Minute							0.41	0.37	0.40	0.22	0.30
8. Pleasantness of Facial Expressions								0.32	0.38	0.30	0.33
9. Verbal Reinforcers per Minute									0.39	0.20	0.29
10. Positive Verbal Content										0.16	0.44
11. Hand and Arm Gestures per Minute											0.19
12. Pleasantness of Vocal Expressions											

*With 254 cases, correlations of 0.17 are significant at the 0.01 level.

positive reinforcers. Their model of affiliative behavior was based on the assumption that affiliation is elicited by positive reinforcement and is discouraged by negative reinforcement. The correlational data of the Mehrabian (1971b) experiment support this basic assumption of the interdependence of affiliation and exchange of positive reinforcers.

One result was contrary to expectations: distance and orientation were not found to be part of the primary affiliative behavior factor. Rather, together they defined a separate factor referred to as "intimacy-close position." This finding was surprising, since shorter distances have consistently been found to be correlates of greater liking. More direct orientation has also been found, though less consistently, to correlate with positive attitudes toward the listener (Mehrabian, 1967a). In the Mehrabian (1971b) experiment the absence of a correlation between affiliative behavior and a shorter distance or a more direct orientation may have been due to the averaging of distances and orientations over the total interaction duration. Earlier experiments have usually been based on the initial choice of distance or orientation. Perhaps the averaging minimized the attitudinal significance of a subject's initial choice of distance from the confederate.

Although the initial distance and orientation may be more indicative of like-dislike of the other, the present "close position" factor could also be indicative of some other aspects of social interaction considered by Sommer (1967, 1969). In several of his experiments, Sommer found a consistent difference in the pattern of seating depending on the activity of the subjects; cooperative situations typically involved a closer position (that is, smaller distance and less direct orientation) relative to competitive ones. Other studies have also shown an inverse relationship between distance and orientation, and have led some investigators to posit a limited tolerance for intimacy: the increasing intimacy due to a shorter distance is compensated for in terms of less direct orientation (Argyle and Dean, 1965; Argyle and Kendon, 1967). The results of the Mehrabian (1971b) experiment showed only a few effects for this intimacy (or close position) factor, but did serve to identify it as a part of social interaction that is distinct from affiliative behavior. In other studies where there are variations in the prior familiarity of subjects, or experimentally determined variations in their mutual interdependence in a task, the intimacy index may be of greater value.

The results of the factor analysis indicated that the measure of highest loading on affiliative behavior was "total number of statements per minute." Thus statement rate (that is, total number of simple sentences or independent clauses uttered per minute) is a more satisfactory measure than speech duration, though it is somewhat more cumbersome to score. When audio recordings of social interaction are available, and a more stable index of affiliative behavior is desired, scores for total statement rate, verbal reinforcer rate, positive verbal content, and positiveness of the vocal component can be standardized and summed. Such an index can serve as a convenient dependent measure for most studies of affiliative behavior. The obtaind intercorrelations of these verbal cues with nonverbal communications of positive affect serve as assurance that such a composite measure, which is based on the verbal interchange, is reasonably representative of general affiliative behavior.

Our earlier consideration of the literature in the implicit communication area led to the postulation of three orthogonal dimensions for characterizing the nonverbal aspects of social interaction: communications of liking (which include all of the nonverbal cues within the first factor), responsiveness to the target (or alternatively, the salience of the target for oneself) and potency or status as conveyed by greater relaxation (Mehrabian, 1970a). The Mehrabian (1971b) results show that, when verbal cues are also considered within the complex of social interaction, the same three factors emerge, and that most of the verbal cues that measure amount of verbal interchange are part of the first factor, liking-affiliation. The second factor, responsiveness, which is correlated only slightly with the communication of liking, reflects the extent to which the subject is reacting to another, whether in a positive or a negative way. In persuasive communication situations, for instance, in which the nonverbal expression of liking may be construed as manipulative and insincere, it has been found that increased attempts at persuasion are associated with increased responsiveness to the listener but with only slight increases in actual positiveness toward him (see Chapter 4).

Postural relaxation has been found to be a correlate of higher status of the speaker relative to his listener. The composition of the relaxation index is somewhat different for standing and seated positions. For seated postures, asymmetry in positioning of the limbs and the degree of reclining or sideways lean are the best indicators; for standing positions, sideways lean of the body again serves as a measure of relaxation, but rocking movements and leg and foot movements while in the same place are also important indicators.

In addition to the above factor analytic results for the interrelationships among the various cues, the Mehrabian (1971b) experiment yielded a number of relationships between the factors characterizing social behavior, the experimental condition, and the personality of the participants. Highlights of these results are briefly summarized here. Subjects reciprocated the positive (or negative) behaviors of experimental confederates; those with higher scores on a measure of affiliative tendency communicated more positive affect and were more in tune to the degree of positiveness they received from a confederate. Two kinds of significance were attached to bodily tension, depending on the degree of positive attitude communicated simultaneously. Tension in the generally more positive high affiliators conveyed respect, but in the slightly negative subjects, who were sensitive to rejection, it conveyed vigilance. There was also more tension during interaction with others of higher status. With same-sexed targets, females affiliated more than males, and were more intimate and submissive. Birth order failed to relate significantly to either affiliative behavior or the questionnaire personality measures of affiliative tendency, sensitivity to rejection or achieving tendency. This lack of significant correlations for birth order was consistent with Rosenfeld's (1966c) results from an extensive study of the problem.

Waiting with a Stranger: II

The Mehrabian and Ksionzky (1972) experiment explored the contribution of a different set of experimental factors to the social interaction of a subject with an experimental confederate. The dependent measures, however, were essentially the same as those in the Mehrabian (1971b) experiment and were similarly scored and factor analyzed. The 22 experimental confederates were initially coached to behave in the slightly positive way described under Experiment I. The confederates were unaware of the experimental condition to which a subject was assigned. The audio and video recordings were scored using the criteria of Appendix A. Two raters independently scored each category; their scores were then averaged. No information about subject's personality scores was available to the raters, since those questionnaires were scored last.

The measures taken during the waiting period were factor analyzed and a principal component solution was obtained. Oblique rotation of the primary factors yielded the groupings of these cues given in Table 8.3. For each factor in Table 8.3, the variables listed start with those having the highest loadings, and move to the variable with the lowest loading on the factor. Table 8.3 also provides the direction of loading of the variables on their corresponding factors.

The results in Tables 8.1 and 8.3 are in general agreement. The fourth factor of Table 8.3 was found to be part of the affiliative behavior factor in Table 8.1. In this study, it emerged as a relatively independent aspect of social behavior and connoted greater dependency and subservience to another. Other data from this experiment and related work by other investigators (for example, Jones, 1964) showed that such a distinction between affiliative and ingratiating behavior is helpful when situational factors force mutual dependency between participants: the cooperative condition of this experiment and, more generally, situations in which one person is less confident of his abilities and/or is in a more subservient role relative to another.

The contribution of arm-position asymmetry to the behavioral index of distress is a by-product of object manipulation, which in the experimental situation involved the use of one hand only (for example, writing or draw-

Table 8.3. *Summary of factors characterizing social interaction in the Mehrabian and Ksionsky (1972) experiment.*

	Direction of Loading on Factor
Factor I: Affiliative Behavior	
1. Total number of statements per minute	(+)
2. Number of declarative statements per minute	(+)
3. Per cent duration of eye contact with confederate	(+)
4. Per cent duration of subject's speech	(+)
5. Per cent duration of confederate's speech	(+)
6. Positive verbal content	(+)
7. Head nods per minute	(+)
8. Hand and arm gestures per minute	(+)
9. Pleasantness of facial expressions	(+)
Factor II: Responsiveness to (or Salience of) Target	
1. Vocal activity	(+)
2. Speech rate	(+)
3. Speech volume	(+)
Factor III: Relaxation	
1. Rocking movements per minute	(−)
2. Leg and foot movements per minute	(−)
3. Body lean	(+)
Factor IV: Ingratiation	
1. Pleasantness of vocal expressions	(+)
2. Negative verbal content	(−)
3. Verbal reinforcers given per minute	(+)
4. Number of questions per minute	(+)
5. Self-manipulations per minute	(+)
Factor V: Behavioral Index of Distress	
1. Per cent duration of walking	(+)
2. Object manipulations per minute	(+)
3. Arm-position asymmetry	(+)
Factor VI: Intimacy (or Close Position)	
1. Shoulder orientation away from confederate	(+)
2. Distance from confederate	(−)
3. Head turns per minute (looking around)	(+)

ing designs on a blackboard—another evasive maneuver). Thus, the first two variables of this factor are sufficient for characterizing distress.

Additional results, which related the dependent measures to the independent effects in the study, showed that the results for affiliative behavior were mostly consistent with a model proposed by Mehrabian (1970b) and Mehrabian and Ksionzky (1970, 1971a, 1971b).

The Measurement, and Additional Determiners, of Affiliative Behavior: the Primary Aspect of Social Behavior

The preceding two experiments presented the results of factor analyses of verbal and nonverbal cues in social situations. Frequently an experimenter cannot afford the extensive effort which is involved in assessing affiliative behavior (or positive affect communication) from nonverbal cues. In such cases, it is possible to readily obtain a subtle measure of affiliative behavior on the basis of implicit verbal cues. This procedure was used in the Mehrabian and Diamond (1971a, 1971b) studies which explored the facilitating and inhibiting effects of various furniture arrangements and two types of objects on social interaction[2].

The dyads in the three experiments of the Mehrabian and Diamond (1971b) study were strangers (neither of whom was an experimental confederate) who thought they were waiting for a "music listening" experiment to start. Actually, the waiting period was the experiment proper. The informal social interactions of each pair were recorded and studied as a function of various furniture arrangements and objects in the waiting room.

The audio recording of each pair's interaction was subsequently scored for the following: (1) total statement rate—the number of simple sentences or independent clauses of each subject per minute, (2) per cent speech duration—the percentage of the five-minute interaction period during which each subject spoke, (3) per cent speech duration for the pair, (4) verbal reinforcer rate—the number of uh-huhs, yeses, or other agreements given to the partner, (5) latency of the initial statement—the duration of silence of each subject before his first statement in the interaction, (6) positive verbal content—rated on a five-point scale, and (7) negative verbal content—also rated on a five-point scale.

Again, data from all three of the Mehrabian and Diamond (1971b) experiments supported the hypothesis of Mehrabian and Ksionzky (1970) that positive communications of attitude and amount of conversation are correlated and define an "affiliative behavior" factor. These data indicated that negative contents in communication are not part of this factor. The representative intercorrelations for the various affiliative cues and negative content scores of one of the three experiments are given in Table 8.4.

Total statement rate; speech duration of a subject, singly or with his partner; frequency of verbal reinforcers; and a separate index of positive verbal content are positively intercorrelated—all of these are negatively correlated with latency of a subject's initial statement.

There are three redundant measures of amount of conversation in Table 8.4: total statement rate, per cent speech duration, and per cent speech duration of the pair. To avoid disproportionate contribution from this source to a composite index of affiliative behavior, the best single measure of amount of conversation, total statement rate, was used in computing the following index, where all the variables were first normalized:

2. This section includes rewritten segments and Table 1 from Mehrabian and Diamond's "The Effects of Furniture Arrangement, Props, and Personality on Social Interaction," *Journal of Personality and Social Psychology*, 20 (1971), 18–30. Copyright (1971) by the American Psychological Association. Reproduced by permission.

Table 8.4. Intercorrelations among implicit verbal cues*.

	2	3	4	5	6	7
1. Total Statement Rate	0.86	0.76	0.56	0.23	−0.42	0.31
2. Per cent Speech Duration of Subject		0.82	0.45	0.27	−0.38	0.26
3. Per cent Speech Duration of Pair			0.58	0.50	−0.46	0.20
4. Positive Verbal Content				0.42	−0.39	0.03
5. Verbal Reinforcer Rate					−0.26	−0.01
6. Latency						−0.19
7. Negative Verbal Content						

*With $df = 286$, correlations in excess of 0.16 are significant at the 0.01 level.

Affiliative behavior = total statement rate + positive verbal content
+ verbal reinforcer rate − latency

In addition to the correlational data of Table 8.4, the Mehrabian and Diamond (1971b) experiments provided confirmation that the proposed measure of affiliative behavior is indeed a direct correlate of an individual's affiliative tendency (R_1) and an inverse correlate of his sensitivity to rejection (R_2). For instance, the following regression equation indicates the contributions of the various main effects to affiliative behavior in the first experiment of the study. All variables are normalized in this equation and (O) represents the sum of the angles which both subjects would have to turn in order to assume a face-to-face position:

$$\text{Affiliative Behavior} = 0.21R_1 - 0.14R_2 + 0.21R_1{}' - 0.16R_2{}' - 0.23\,(O)$$

The primed factors are the partner's scores on the personality measures. These findings indicate that those with higher scores on the affiliative tendency measure (Mehrabian, 1970d) exhibited more affiliative behavior, especially when their partners were also more affiliative. Further, those who had scored high on a sensitivity to rejection measure (Mehrabian, 1970d) exhibited less affiliative behavior and were even less affiliative with partners who were also sensitive to rejection.

Additional findings of incidental interest in the Mehrabian and Diamond (1971b) experiment were as follows. The first two experiments included all possible combinations of four distances and three orientations for the seating of dyads who were left alone to wait in a room. Both experiments showed that the less direct orientations (such as when sitting side by side on a couch) were less conducive to conversation, and were particularly inhibiting for the otherwise more sociable pairs—that is, those in which at least one was a more affiliative person. The first experiment also included measures of relaxation, and indicated a general increase in relaxation with increasing distance between the pairs.

The results of the Mehrabian and Diamond (1971a, 1971b) studies suggest that, just as more immediate positions are assumed to those who are better liked, more immediate positioning of persons in social situations may facilitate the communication of liking.

Summary

In summarizing the work presented in this chapter, it is important to distinguish the present approach from others where nonverbal and implicit verbal behaviors were characterized and grouped on an *a priori* basis. The latter attempts to develop typologies for movement and social interaction are exemplified by the work of Bales (1950), Birdwhistell (1952, 1970), Efron (1941), and more recently by Ekman and Friesen (1969b) and Freedman and Hoffmann (1967). Ekman and Friesen suggested a quite thorough system for categorizing movements and related it to the categories proposed by other investigators. However, more evidence is needed for the referential significance of each category, and there is a need for the empirical justification of the separation or grouping of categories proposed by these investigators.

The contrasting approach taken in the studies described in this chapter relied on available evidence on the significance of various cues in communication. Those cues that had been shown to be of some communicative value and that could be reliably scored were used in large-scale empirical studies. Factor analyses of the data indicated that positiveness (affiliative behavior), responsiveness (activity level), and dominance-submission (relaxation) are primary aspects of social behavior, just as they are important referents of implicit communication. In addition, the three factors of ingratiation, distress, and intimacy (close position), which assumed special significance in only certain kinds of social situations, were identified. The ingratiation factor should be of value in studying the behaviors of dependent persons and in situations where there is mutual dependency among interactants. The distress factor provides a simple measure of a person's discomfort while he is in the presence of another and cannot leave. Finally, the intimacy factor has been shown to distinguish social behaviors in cooperative versus competitive situations.

9

Child Communication

Although it is possible to study adult linguistic and implicit communications separately, such a study is considerably more difficult in the case of children's communications. Verbal behavior is not an autonomous medium for the children during the acquisition of language skills, but is rather closely intertwined with nonverbal behaviors and feelings. There are at least two implications of these developmental antecedents of adult communication. First, the study of children's verbal behavior can be enhanced considerably by examining their nonverbal behavior. For instance, the exploration of the latter may facilitate the description of the grammars implied by their linguistic behavior. Second, the study of children's affect-laden communications can contribute to a better understanding of the affective communications of adults. In this respect, implicit affect communications of adults can be regarded as modified and partly censored versions of more spontaneous expressions by children.

With these possible benefits in mind, our approach to child communication differs in two important respects from that of linguists (for example, Bellugi and Brown, 1964; Braine, 1963; McNeill, 1966; Menyuk, 1969; Nakazima, 1965–66; Slobin, 1967). Our assumptions are that children's linguistic behavior cannot be adequately described without the exploration of their concomitant nonverbal behavior. Further, it is also essential to consider the referents of these communications—in particular the underlying feelings and preferences. Linguistic analysis which aims to describe grammars at various stages of child development is concerned with the mapping of the exhibited regularities and sequences only. Although the formal characteristics of language are accounted for, their relationships to their referents (the problem of semantics) are bypassed.

Our approach is based on a theory of language development proposed by Werner and Kaplan (1963). Their approach to the study of children's communications was based on a more general theoretical framework

159

(Werner, 1957). In their particular cognitive-developmental orientation, which they share with Piaget (1960), a child's development is seen as involving progressive differentiation of the cognitive categories. Specifically, any communication situation is characterized in terms of four major categories: *communication behavior, referent, communicator,* and *addressee.* Two other categories, *immediacy,* and *similarity,* describe the extent of differentiation among these components.

Variation in immediacy between communicator and addressee is illustrated by the communicator and the addressee being in each other's presence, in contrast to the communicator writing to an addressee who is somewhere else. Immediacy variation between communicator and referent is shown in the contrast between a referent that is perceptually available to the communicator and one that is not visible. Pointing, for example, would be inappropriate in the latter situation but could be used in the former, if the addressee were present.

Variation in the similarity of components is illustrated in the phenomena of word-realism, where the word and the referent are believed to be inseparable or identical, that is, the relation between the two is much stronger than that of signification (for example, Vigotsky, 1939). Variation in similarity between communicator and addressee is illustrated at one extreme when a person communicates to himself, such as while thinking. In other instances, the communicator and the addressee are considerably dissimilar, such as communications between an adult and a child compared to those between two adults.

Immediacy and Similarity Among the Four Communication Components

The major hypotheses of this chapter, then, are that, relative to adult communications, children's communications involve more immediate and more similar relationships among the four major components: communicator, addressee, communication behavior, and referent. This difference is a function of ability rather than choice. Even though adult communications may exhibit the same qualities as children's (for example, pointing) they are not necessarily restricted to such forms. For example, in response to "Where's my pen?" an adult is able to point as well as say "It's in the right-hand top drawer of your desk."

Thus, the development of children's communication ability can be viewed as a progressive increase in the nonimmediacy and dissimilarity among the four major components. Whereas a young child is only able to communicate about an object that is spatio-temporally present, later he can do so about objects that are absent. An infant who may be able to communicate only when the addressee is present subsequently learns to do so in the latter's absence. At first a child may not distinguish too clearly

between the referent and the word, since he experiences these as inseparable. Later on, the two components are seen as being separate yet interrelated, in that one refers to the other.

With this overview, we can turn to a detailed examination of the relations between various pairs among the four components, and the important
roles of affect and nonverbal cues.

COMMUNICATOR AND REFERENT

The relation between communicator and referent is characterized by the
extent to which a child's actions, affect, and needs are fused with, and are
indistinguishable from, the referent. At early developmental levels, action
oriented, affective, and conative sets dominate both the encoding and decoding of communications (Escalona, 1945; Lewis, 1936). The early words
or other nonverbal communications of infants typically designate events
that are affectively salient, that is, events that are strongly preferred or
not preferred, novel, and emotionally arousing. Subsequently, verbal and
nonverbal behaviors of the child are determined to a larger degree by the
more consensual aspects of the referents. The work of Osgood, Suci, and
Tannenbaum (1957) and related work summarized in Snider and Osgood
(1969) clearly indicated that, even for adults, the major dimensions or
underlying substrata of most referents are their evaluative and emotion
arousing aspects. This suggests that the emotional sets which dominate
child communication continue to influence the way in which referents
are experienced and selectively communicated by adults. Incidentally,
these notions can be investigated with experiments in which children are
asked to name emotion arousing versus neutral objects. It is hypothesized
that the more affectively salient referents are more likely to elicit responses
of either an idiosyncratic or personalized quality.

The stages of this increasing dissimilarity between a communicator and
the referent of his communication can be outlined as follows. Initially,
the referents are apprehended only in terms of the actions and the feelings
which they arouse. Later the referents are relatively independent of the
communicator but are still attributed with animistic properties largely
determined by affect and preference for the referent. Finally, the referents
are defined mainly in terms of their relations to other objects rather than
to the communicator.

COMMUNICATOR AND COMMUNICATION BEHAVIOR

Earlier forms of communication behavior are difficult to distinguish from
the actions of the communicator upon the referent, such as his gestures
or his postures in dealing with it. In subsequent stages, vocalizations,
which are relatively independent of such actions, become the primary
medium of communication. Thus, there is increasing dissimilarity between the communicator's typical actions relative to the referent and the

behaviors used in communicating about the referent. Furthermore, at earlier stages the communication behavior is determined more by the child's attitudes and feelings toward the referent, and is therefore idiosyncratic or personalized. (Note the analogue of this in a game of charades by adults.)

COMMUNICATION BEHAVIOR AND REFERENT

With higher levels of development, the communication behaviors serve as a vehicle for reference and description rather than being part of, or identical to, the referent, as they tend to be for children (Vigotsky, 1939). This progression begins with a high degree of similarity between the communication behavior and its referent. For instance, the communication behavior may be a copy of one of the referent's aspects, as in the case of onomatopoetic expressions. Later, certain qualities of the referent perceived in one sense modality may be imitated in another, as when phonic properties of language are used to represent sizes, shapes, colors, or forms (note the word *zigzag*). In a still later stage, there is no apparent physical similarity or analogy between the communication behavior and its referent; they are related only on the basis of convention.

The most salient quality of a referent for a communicator is inferred by noting the qualities that are being copied or analogized in his communications. For an infant, the significance or meaning of a referent lies in its concrete perceptual and action-related attributes. Later, this significance is determined more in terms of concepts that relate it to other referents. This change in the way referents are perceived is reflected in the increase of abstract qualities in communication with age (Brown, 1958, pp. 248–49). The difficulty in representing an abstract quality such as "truth" with a concrete-perceptual attribute may be one reason why conventional relations are necessary in adult communication.

COMMUNICATOR AND ADDRESSEE

In the relationship between communicator and addressee, there is a progression from the addressee as a particular person to the addressee as the generalized other. Along with this, the communication behaviors become less personalized and idiosyncratic and more consensual in quality. The more consensual communications have overlapping, though not identical, spheres of connotation (reference) for different users. This overlap is considerably greater for adults than for children.

THE CONTEXTUALIZED QUALITY OF CHILD COMMUNICATION

A by-product of high immediacy and similarity among the four components in child communication is that their communication behaviors in general, and language behaviors in particular, are contextualized. Adequate communication is contingent upon the presence of a particular addressee, referent, and an affective or preferential set. This contextualized quality of language or communication is illustrated in situations where children use certain words in the presence of a parent and not with anyone else, or use a word only when they are feeling a certain way. They may also restrict the use of some words to the presence of a particular addressee plus a certain feeling state. At subsequent levels of development, communication behaviors are less contextualized in quality, and no longer require the presence of particular addressees, referents, or internal sets.

Denotation

The simplest form of representation is denotation. Denotation delineates an object or event from its surroundings, whereas representation characterizes some of its attributes. An infant's initial forms of denotation are contingent upon the presence of the addressee and the referent, and occur in a situation in which both somehow share, or interact via, the referent. Pointing is one of these early forms. In pointing, the action and feeling oriented relation of the dependent communicator (the child) is a dominant aspect of the communication about the object to the addresee (the adult).

The infant's ability to gesturally denote evolves from his existing abilities to reach for or touch various objects. Reaching to grasp an object and placing it in the mouth is a common early mode of relating to the environment (Mehrabian and Williams, 1971). Although reaching to grasp does not exhibit a clear-cut relationship to pointing, reaching to touch does provide some basis for denotation. Touching itself can be conceptualized as having three stages: touching to grasp, touching to explore and, finally, touching to denote in the presence of another person. Other gestures, such as bodily orienting or turning to look, can also serve the same function. In other words, an infant may turn toward an object in the presence of another to indicate "I want it," to indicate some curiosity or interest in the object, or simply to draw attention to it. In attempting to determine whether a certain act of touching or pointing is affectively or conatively determined rather than denotative in intent, it is helpful to consider the infant's possible desire for the object at that time. If it can be independently assessed that the object is desired by the infant, then denotation is not assumed. When there is no desire for the object and, furthermore, demonstrative vocalizations such as "da" occur in conjunction with the touching or pointing, then denotation is inferred.

Like motoric and gestural denotation, vocal denotation also evolves from vocalizations that served a different function originally. Early vocalizations of infants tend to be sounds of appeal, such as crying, that are associated with the infant's affective-conative set. Neither such sounds nor playful babblings (lallation) are related to denotation. However, in contrast to lallation, there are certain sounds which are typically associated with straining movements toward objects. (Note the analogues with reaching to grasp and reaching to touch.) It is these *call sounds* which undergo a change in function and begin to be used for denoting, rather than for reaching toward, or asking for, something.

In the development of both the gestural and vocal forms of denotation, the presence of another person is extremely important and indicates the essential role of an interpersonal context for these precursors of representational behavior.

Gestural Representation

"Re-presenting" something means to present it again, typically in its absence. Whereas early forms of denotation are contingent upon the presence of the referent and the addressee, representation occurs when the referent is absent (that is, nonimmediate) and subsequently even when the addressee is absent. A representation can be a pictorial or verbal copy of some quality of the referent. It can also be an analogue of the referent, or relate to the referent through convention only.

One criterion for distinguishing representational behaviors from nonrepresentational ones is that the actions should not be part of the infant's practical or pragmatic dealings. In other words, there is an inverse relationship between the functional or pragmatic value of a behavior and its referential quality. For example, a child may move his head vigorously sideways back and forth to avoid the food being offered to him—a nonreferential response. Progressively, however, he may use this gesture to indicate displeasure and lack of desire for something, and eventually use the same gesture as a general symbol for negation. Thus, such a sideways motion of the head may be used in conjunction with verbal behaviors, such as naming, to indicate absence. For example, the child may say, "dolly," and shake his head sideways to indicate "Dolly isn't here."

In considering the development of gestural representation, it is first necessary to consider the gestural behaviors available to infants that may be used for gestural representation. These behaviors can then be ordered according to the degree to which they are dissimilar to, or nonimmediate from, the depicted referent, to show a developmental sequence.

IMITATION

The first movements of an infant are either elicited by, or occur in conjunction with, the movements of others, as in the case of rhythmic movements of the body in response to rhythmic sounds or movements of another person (note the data of Condon and Ogston, 1966, for adults). Later, the gesture and the movement that it is imitating become increasingly dissimilar and nonimmediate. Thus, the early reflex-type eye movements of an infant which follow moving objects show very little temporal separation between the behavior and the content, that is, the moving objects. Such early movements are behaviorally distinguished from others that are imitative and occur only with certain sets of contents but not with other similar ones. For example, during the second half of the first year, an infant may sway to movements of some person but not to movements of objects. Later on he may even sway in imitation of moving objects. Finally, the infant uses movements to imitate nonkinetic properties of objects, such as their form or size. This begins at about the end of the second year and occurs mostly during the third year. For example, one of Piaget's daughters opened her mouth to portray the opening of a box (Flavell, 1963). Another child extended his arms sideways and outwards when he saw large objects or persons.

DELAYED IMITATION

Other forms of gestural representation involve delayed imitation. Delayed, in contrast to coactive, imitation reflects a significant development, for it implies an internal model or schema. Information about an object is retained internally to be used later when the child represents it with some behavior. Early examples of such internalized models are concrete behaviors. For example, children who are asked to represent an object in some medium, such as with a drawing, sometimes use gestural imitation as a mediating link in their attempts to translate the perceived object into a drawing. A boy who is asked to copy an orange may puff his cheeks first and then draw a large circle.

One basis for inferring an internal model is when the child shows that he considers certain of his imitations inadequate and corrects them to conform more to what he thinks is a good imitation. Such corrections are possible only if there is some internalized standard or model by which the behaviors are judged. Progressive corrections that are based on a less observable internalized model are illustrated in the following example. An experimenter taps a pencil on a table and stops to wait and see how the child responds. The child first claps his hands. Next, he strikes one hand with the pencil which is held in the other. Finally, he starts scraping the pencil against the table and taps it occasionally as he moves it sideways.

Thus, the two criteria characterizing increasing ability to represent objects gesturally are: (1) the ability to represent the referent when it is nonimmediate, as in delayed imitation, and (2) the ability to represent the referent with a behavior that is dissimilar to the referent, *provided* the subject also possesses the ability to give an adequate gestural copy.

The second criterion needs further comment. Dissimilarity of the gesture from the referent is regarded as an advanced form of representation only when it can be ruled out that the dissimilar gesture is simply an inadequate copy. Thus, if we ask a child to represent an object with a gesture and, due to poor coordination, his product only vaguely resembles the object, it is erroneous to infer a high level of representational ability. In contrast, if we have already ascertained that the child is capable of providing an adequate copy-gesture of the referent but also uses a dissimilar gesture as an alternative representation, then a more advanced state is inferred.

The following test can also be performed to ascertain whether a child responds dissimilarly to an event and a copy of it. If his responses to the two are dissimilar and if he is also willing to use the copy as a substitute for the original under circumscribed conditions, then it is assumed that he is representing. This test hinges upon the assumption that, if the child discriminates the copy from the actual pragmatic action, then he is not accepting erroneously one for the other. Rather, while distinguishing them, he is using one to represent the other.

ANTICIPATION

Besides imitation, anticipatory behavior provides another important source of gestural representations. A dog orients or points in the direction from which food is brought to him whenever he hears a food-signalling buzzer. He might also salivate or make chewing or biting movements in anticipation of the food. Similarly, a child might make chewing movements as he is being offered food, even before the food is placed in his mouth. Such anticipatory behaviors are initially difficult to distinguish from subsequent representational ones, especially in children ranging from 10 to 15 months. One criterion for such a distinction is the extent to which the gesture is inappropriate for the particular context. The less appropriate the behavior, the more is its representational quality. For example, if a child closes his eyes just before he is put to bed, this is less representational than if he closes his eyes at a time when there is no issue or question of going to bed. A second criterion is the dissimilarity of the behavior from the pragmatic action being represented. Lying down and closing the eyes is more similar to sleeping than is standing up and closing the eyes, and thus the latter is more representational than the former.

PLAY

Play situations provide important data about a child's representational ability. Initially, the infant does not distinguish between the playful quality of a situation and the reality with which it is associated. At this stage, then, the child's portrayal is quite idiosyncratic and is not representational in that he cognizes himself *as being* the object(s) in his play. Later the child shows increasing concern to obtain a realistic copy of the play object(s). Thus, an imitation that very vaguely and idiosyncratically resembles a car and that initially was used in play is now considered inadequate. Also, in playful imitation of other people, the child begins to show increasing concern with producing a close approximation of the action of others. This kind of playful imitation is distinguished from the earlier variant in that it includes novel movements that were not part of the child's repertoire.

In Piaget's (1960) terms, the first stage of playful imitation is dominated by assimilation; the representations of the different qualities of the objects are limited by the behaviors available to the child, and are therefore of an idiosyncratic quality. Next, the qualities of the objects being represented primarily determine the imitative behaviors elicited from the child. In other words, the child modifies his behaviors to accommodate to the patterns exhibited by the object and, in the process of doing so, produces novel behaviors.

Finally, at the most advanced level of play, the child not only produces novel behaviors but does so in novel contexts. He uses gestures that are associated with certain objects in pragmatic action, but now in the absence of the objects, or with objects that are not appropriate for pragmatic action. For example, drinking from a glass is represented simply with an empty hand; sleeping with a pillow is represented by putting one hand underneath the cheek to represent the pillow. These "empty" gestures (the object of action being absent) increase in frequency between the ages of 2 and 4.5.

Considering these developments in the ability of children to gesturally denote and represent the qualities of objects, it is surprising, perhaps, that they do not continue to use the gestural medium for representation. A primary reason is the social context in which the child develops. The adults in his environment use the linguistic medium for communication and insist on teaching him to do the same. This differential treatment of verbal behavior accounts for the de-emphasis of gestures in communicating specific events, objects, or abstract ideas. In conjunction with this, another deterrent is that the child's social milieu does not provide an adequate source of conventional gestures for communicating complex or intricate referents. As a consequence, he has as much difficulty in using gestures as does an adult participating in a game of charades. Nevertheless, as we have seen, gestures and movements continue to convey preferences and affect during adult life.

Verbal Denotation and Representation

As in the case of the development of the gestural medium, verbal denotation and representation will be considered in terms of increasing dissimilarity and nonimmediacy of communication behaviors and referents. Before proceeding to the details, it is important to emphasize that the representational activity of a child is not an isolated phenomenon. It is associated with expressions of his feelings, needs, and preferences and, later, with the sharing of his curiosity and discoveries with the adults around him. Thus verbal communications are also contextualized. They are bound to specific addresses and situations and involve certain feelings toward these. In contrast, adult communication is relatively free from such bounds.

INCREASING DISSIMILARITY OF COMMUNICATION BEHAVIOR AND REFERENT

There are three degrees of dissimilarity between a linguistic communication and its referent: onomatopoeia, physiognomic representation, and conventional forms.

Onomatopoetic and Physiognomic Forms. The use of onomatopoetic forms is contingent upon the child having in his repertoire the sounds used in such expressions. These sounds are acquired during the early stages of development when a child imitates the distinctive sounds in his environment that arouse his feelings and interest. Examples are those of animals, toys, cars, or planes. He may produce the sound of an object that he wishes to receive, for example, saying "choo-choo, choo-choo" to indicate that he wants his train. Subsequently, the same sounds may accompany an orientation or pointing toward the objects that evoke the sounds. In this way, the sounds take on the new function of drawing the attention of another person to an object. The familiar example of "bow-wow" for "dog," which may later be generalized to refer to other animals, illustrates the onomatopoetic form of representation. Onomatopoetic forms are selective verbal analogues of certain sonic properties of objects rather than simple imitations. This is because they typically include the phonemes available in the particular language of the child's parents and lack the phonemes not found in that language (Brown, 1958).

It is possible that this correspondence of the phonetic content of the child's vocalizations with that of the adult culture arises from the imitation of onomatopoetic sounds produced by adults. Whether onomatopoetic forms are spontaneously emitted by a child or imitated from his parents, the important issue is the ease with which a child learns onomatopoetic designations or representations in contrast to conventional ones. This question can be investigated with autistic children, who are frequently taught verbal designations for objects in laboratory settings. Differences in the rate of learning of onomatopoetic versus conventional forms of reference, or more generally, of verbal forms with increasing degrees of dissimilarity to the object being portrayed, can be explored in controlled experiments.

Physiognomic representation, in contrast to onomatopoeia, involves the imitation of the nonsonic qualities of objects (Jespersen, 1922; Newman, 1933). For example, children use variations of sound duration to represent variations in length, and they use "grave" versus "acute" vowels to indicate large versus small size or close versus distant objects.

The vocal expressions that are frequently overlooked in the analysis of child grammars are quite relevant in the representation of the nonsonic properties of objects. For example, the same word may be spoken at a very high pitch to represent lightness or coldness, or at a low pitch to represent a heavy or warm quality.

An infant can be trained to use his own spontaneous vocalizations for representational purposes using available methods from other areas (Holt, 1931; Mowrer, 1950). Suppose a baby produces a sound in the presence of an object simply as an imitation rather than to denote the object. Both the form of the sound and its reference to a particular object can be stabilized by imitating the infant's vocalization. If he imitates these imitations of him, his behavior can be reinforced. Specifically, his attention is drawn to the object by pointing or orienting and his imitative behavior is reinforced. An effective reinforcement is to use the child's vocalization in the presence of the object as a signal for the adult to perform a service for him, such as bringing him the object. These procedures can also be used in training autistic children to speak.

Conventional References. Conventional forms of representation develop in part from the generalization of onomatopoetic or physiognomic sounds to represent more varied referents. For example, an onomatopoetic sound initially attached to a particular object may be subsequently generalized to refer to other similar objects (for example, "bebau" originally for dog, then for animals in general). Thus, the analogy between the verbal form and the represented object becomes less important.

Other conventional terms develop through modification of the idiosyncratic expressions. There are four categories of such modification. First, syntactic restrictions are imposed upon the onomatopoetic or physiognomic expressions. Thus, although the original physiognomic term may refer to an object (that is, may be a noun), it may be used subsequently in a variety of other forms, such as verbs or adjectives, and be appropriately modified in accordance with syntactic requirements. Second, composite forms may develop in which one part is a conventional word and the other is an idiosyncratic one, each referring to a different aspect of the referent. Third, composite forms may evolve in which both the conventional and the idiosyncratic terms refer to the same object, such as "bow-wow, dog." Fourth, the child may produce the idiosyncratic term in response to the adult's demand for a conventional one, such as when a child says, "bow-wow" in reply to "Johnny, say *dog*." A child may use the onomatopoetic expression with a familiar addressee, but use the conventional form with an unfamiliar person. Also, when the child is anxious or whenever strong feelings are involved, there is often a temporary return to the idiosyncratic term although he uses the conventional one in most situations.

These transitional forms of verbalization illustrate the increasing internalization of the syntax of the language, and greater awareness of the significance of the conventional forms through uses of these forms in conjunction with the personalized one.

In constructing tests of early linguistic ability (Mehrabian and Williams, 1971) one measure could be based on the elicitation of these four forms of modification. Instructions such as, "Do you have another name for this?" or "What else can you call this?" can be used when either a personalized or a conventional term has been given by the child. Incidentally, these forms also occur in psychopathology where there is a corresponding deterioration of the linguistic function.

In shifting from the use of personalized forms to conventional forms, the child continues to maintain his particular idiosyncratic sphere of associations. However, with increasing use of the conventional terms and with differential reinforcement of such usage by the adults around him, he begins to change his sphere of connotations to correspond more to those of his social environment.

It is during these transitional stages that the child implicitly recognizes two sets of facts about verbal symbols. First, the objects of his world each have a name, and if there is a name there is a corresponding object to be found. This recognition, although not explicit, is manifest in the following discontinuous change in the behavior of the child. There is a sudden interest in names, as shown in his unceasing requests for the names of things around him. This sharp increase in interest has also been observed with deaf and mute children (Keller, 1903, p. 315). Second, the child becomes aware that words can be used to directly affect the actions of others. For instance, as he shows an interest in the names of objects, the child also tends to call people by name repeatedly. He calls somebody's name, the person turns around and orients toward him. However, the child doesn't seem to have anything more to say or want, so the person turns back to his activity, and the child calls his name again.

This sudden interest in words and the realization of their power can be drawn upon in the training of language skills in either normal or retarded children. The child can be prompted to use verbal commands to which the parent or experimenter responds, such as "Give me the book," "Raise your hand," "Put the book on the table." The actions of the adults in these situations are very highly reinforcing to the child, and tend to perpetuate his verbal behavior.

INCREASING NONIMMEDIACY OF COMMUNICATION BEHAVIOR AND REFERENT

So far we have considered variations in the degree to which the verbal behavior of the child becomes progressively dissimilar from its referents. Another aspect of the development of language skills is the increasing ability to represent nonimmediate objects. As already noted, early vocalizations, which involve the desire for an object, are restricted to situations where that object and the person who can bring it to the infant are present. Subsequently, the object is named to denote it rather than to ask for it, but only when a certain addressee is present. Finally, a name is used for an object that is not in the visual field of the infant.

The early single-component utterances, then, typically refer to a multiplicity of interrelated objects and actions (Lombroso, 1909). Thus, the word "ma" spoken by the infant may refer to the entire feeding activity, including the mother, the milk bottle, and the pleasurable sensations associated with feeding and with being helped. Subsequently the same word is used when the bottle is present and the drinking of milk is anticipated. At a later stage it refers only to the bottle even when drinking is not anticipated. Thus, a name which arose from the sum total of the child's activity vis-à-vis a particular object is subsequently used to designate a particular part of the complex occurrence (for example, the object, the action, or possibly the feeling component).

Thus, a child relates to referents in terms of his actions and feelings associated with them. In support of this, it is noted that objects that seem quite different to an adult are often given the same name by an infant when his actions or feelings associated with those objects are similar. In contrast, those objects that are the same from an adult point of view can be named differently by the infant because his actions toward them are different (Stern and Stern, 1920). A related phenomenon is that a child who can already speak can be taught to use arbitrary names consistently as long as he is allowed to construct a play situation relating to the objects being named. For example, he can be taught to call a spoon "papa" and a fork "mama" in a play situation. Outside this play situation, however, he is not capable of consistently using the arbitrary name for the object (Brown, 1958).

It is interesting to note that the association of names with specific contexts has also been observed in some cases of aphasia. The patient understands language when it is appropriate to the actions he performs but not when it is irrelevant to his actions. Thus, he is able to understand the verbal directions relating to a series of tasks he is performing, but fails to comprehend them when he is not performing the tasks (Hanfmann, Rickers-Ovsiankina, and Goldstein, 1944).

In sum, early vocalizations, such as call sounds, are dominated by an affective-preferential attitude. Subsequent forms involve more of a referential quality, and denote or represent something for someone else. It is sometimes difficult to specify precisely whether an utterance is of the attitudinal or referential variety. One guideline is that the former is associated with wanting the object or attempting to grasp it and mouth it, and the latter is associated with pointing without an attempt to grasp or mouth. The same vocal form can go through both stages. Initially it is a call sound, functioning not to represent but to demand something;

subsequently it is associated with pointing; and finally the form takes on the special function of designating a certain quality of objects. Thus, there is a progression from the nonrepresentational use of the form, to denotation (that is, simply locating an object for another person), to characterizing a quality.

Multicomponent Utterances

FROM NAMES TO WORDS

Linguistic development is described in terms of the degree of dissimilarity and nonimmediacy of the verbal form from the referent. There are two aspects associated to this process: the development of words from names and the formation of sentences.

The first referents of vocalizations are the affectively salient occurrences involving actions of an infant in a particular context, such as the feeding situation. Later, the single-component verbal forms used to designate these complex events are applied in a more discriminating way. They may be used to designate a delimited aspect of the context in which they were first elaborated, or they may be generalized to different contexts that include similar activities of the infant. When generalized in this way, a verbal form ceases to be a name for a particular event and becomes a word that can be used to designate a class of referents. It also begins to serve a grammatical function within a larger utterance. That is, with the use of combinations of words in syntactically organized patterns, verbal units are lifted out of specific contexts, cease to be names that primarily refer to individual objects, and begin to function as words.

In a sense, then, the initial single-component utterances function as sentences, with one name, such as "mah," expressing desire to be fed when the milk bottle is observed and the mother is in the room. With multicomponent utterances, each component refers to a specific aspect of the situation originally designated by one utterance. Thus, in sentences, the components are words (rather than names), for each refers to a given aspect of several complex situations (note Braine's, 1963, pivot-class distinction).

THE DIFFERENTIATION OF VOCAL EXPRESSIONS

Multicomponent utterances have been studied more from the linguistic point of view than in terms of the associated vocal and gestural expressions. However, these expressions are also important (Lewis, 1936). The vocal expression, for instance, may characterize one quality of the referent while the words denote another.

The vocal component which accompanies any verbalization can be described as one of several categories: one that is characteristic of requesting an object, one associated with puzzlement and surprise at a novel stimulation, and one for denoting an object or person. The significance of the various parts of a multicomponent utterance can be determined by independently characterizing the associated vocal expression. Thus, a two-component utterance may be enunciated with a denoting voice for the first vocable and a requesting one for the second vocable. Alternatively, the first vocable, such as "da," may vocally express denotation and the second one, surprise. Vocal expressions can be used to order the developmental sequence of two-component utterances. Initially, both parts of two-component utterances have identical vocal expressions; for example, they both indicate demand or surprise. Subsequently, the child uses a different type of vocal expression with each component, so the two parts designate either two different attitudes or an attitude plus a denotative orientation toward the object. In short, the verbalizations of an infant begin to denote, demand, and express puzzlement through efficient combinations of verbal and nonverbal behavior. Sometimes repetition is used to characterize the attitudinal component. For example, repetition of the same unit can indicate speed, size, or the intensity of affect toward the referent.

THE DIFFERENTIATION OF VERBAL CONTENTS

Another developmental quality of multicomponent utterances is seen when new words are acquired. Some two-component utterances employ an earlier single-component utterance in conjunction with a newly acquired word. This combination still specifies the complex event originally implied by the single vocable. For instance, the vocable "goo-goo" is used by an infant to describe his mother tapping water from a faucet into a pot. The two-component utterance "Mama goo-goo" he uses later indicates that "goo-goo" refers more specifically to the action of tapping water, while the mother's role is indicated by "Mama." Thus, earlier single-component utterances that designate objects, and others that designate actions, are used in combinations to refer to an action-object situation. One specific index of such development is the use of the same action word in conjunction with different object words, or vice versa (Braine, 1963).

Two-component utterances can be categorized into three types. First, two components can refer to the same thing, with one sound, such as "da" or "ta", denoting the referent and the second vocable characterizing it more specifically. Second, there may be a differentiation of the agent from his action, one vocable referring to the agent and the other referring to his action. Third, there can be a differentiation between the object and some quality of the object, so one vocable designates the referent and the second describes one of its specific attributes. The first form is illustrated by "da ball," the second by "Mama goo-goo," and the third form by "da bum," meaning "That think is broken." These three types are developmentally ordered.

Let us examine the precursors of some two-component utterances that differentiate between the agent and the action. A child begins to denote an agent or a person by orienting toward it. Later, he uses a single utterance to refer to the composite of an agent-in-action. For example, an object that has a characteristic sound associated with its motion is referred to with a single utterance. Subsequently that single utterance is used to designate the specific object rather than the object plus the movement and sound.

On the other hand, single utterances referring to specific actions evolve from a child's response to sudden changes, intense or affect arousing movements or noises, or his own movement. As these utterances become progressively specific, they are used by the child to request action from others, and subsequently to refer to an agent-action relationship in a concrete context. For example, a parent asks a baby "What am I doing?" while he rocks him in a crib, and the child responds with his utterance to designate rocking movement. After having separated the two components from the complex situation of an agent acting, the child is in the position to juxtapose the two units of utterance to represent an agent acting upon an object, such as "Mama goo-goo" meaning "Mother is washing."

Attributes are differentiated out of an emotionally salient situation in an analogous manner. An important early form of attribution is possession. A child names an object while pressing it to himself, expressing a desire to have it. Later on he expresses the relationship of possession by simply calling the name of the owner, such as a brother or sister, and pointing out the object. Or, he uses a demonstrative plus the name of the owner while pointing to the object. Later, the demonstrative is replaced with the name of the object, such as "Mama shoe." Such expressions provide the basis for subsequent utterances in which possession is still the implied relation but the verbal form approaches adult usage, as "paper white."

RELATIONS

Expressions of relations can be ordered in terms of their coordinate, sequential, simultaneous, antithetical or dependent quality. In adult language, these relations are expressed respectively with *and, then, while, but,* and *if . . . then. . . .* Coordinate utterances are exemplified by "these chairs" and "this table," in which both components refer to the same entity. Sequential utterances reflect the sequence of occurrences in the referent in a one-to-one fashion, such as "Daddy home eat" meaning "Daddy, take me home to eat." The expression of simultaneity is more advanced than in the preceding two: verbalizations are of necessity sequential in quality, therefore simultaneity requires greater dissimilarity between the order of the utterance and that of the referent. Finally, antithetic relations are initially expressed with a negation of one thing plus an assertion of something else, such as "No milk . . . chocolate" meaning "I don't want milk. I want chocolate."

Vocal Expressions of Relations. The telegraphic speech of children does not contain the connectives that can effectively characterize the syntactic relationships among the various components in an expression (Brown and Fraser, 1963). Therefore, the child expresses these relations using vocal expressions and rhythm. At times, filler sounds, such as "ah" or "mah" are also used to clarify the dependency relation. Some of these fillers are precursors of the verbal conjunctions and, when consistently combined with vocal expressions and other nonverbal acts, imply relationships of *so that, because,* and *which.* Utterances in which a child inverts the correct grammatical order of words are clearly understood anyway due to the concomitant vocal expression. The child also uses pauses to express certain relationships such as *what* or *and.*

Verbal Contents: Relations. At a more advanced level of development, vocal expressions lose ground to words for communicating dependency relations. The first words used for expressing these relations are conjunctions, such as *and* or *then.* In these initial stages, the child reduces dependency relations to conjunctive ones so that cause-effect relations are verbalized as if they were sequential. Examples are, "We did not sit down—the benches were wet," meaning "We did not sit down because the benches were wet." Again, the conjunction *and* is frequently used to express causal relations. A typical developmental sequence of expressions of dependency is "The toy is broken—it doesn't move," to "It doesn't move because it is broken," to "Because it is broken, it doesn't move." In the first instance the utterance parallels the observed event. In the second the outcome is observed and its cause is sought; therefore the outcome is stated first. In the last, the relation is logical rather than temporal.

THE ACTION MODEL

One of the major problems in the study of syntax and its relation to semantics is to find a model that provides a basis of correspondence of a string of words on one hand and the structure of the referents on the other. It can be argued that Indo-European languages employ the "human action model," in which an agent acts on an object. This model is readily evident in descriptions of concrete happenings (for example, "The boy struck the cat"). However, it describes other relations as well, such as "My stomach hurts" (which is an abbreviation for "My stomach hurts me"), or more abstract statements, such as "X is equal to Y."

These transformations in the application of the action model are explained in terms of a primary tenet of developmental theory: language develops through the application of familiar and concrete forms in conjunction with metaphors to characterize the less familiar and the more abstract (Cassirer, 1953–57). Thus, a syntax that is developed to describe concrete and perceptually available events is subsequently employed to represent those more abstract referents in which total significance cannot be represented but may be illustrated with a specific perceptual configuration. Consider, for example, the statement, "I have digested the food." Here, the action model is implied, but the referents are rather abstract in quality. Thus, the available forms (in this case, syntax corresponding to the action model), which initially served a concrete function, later are used to serve a more abstract one. Once the form takes on its new function, it becomes partially modified and more independent of the concrete referents from which it evolved.

Let us consider some examples to illustrate this trend. Children frequently use action models in their verbal behavior, as evidenced in such animistic expressions as "The window is crying," referring to condensation on the window, or "My car is hurt," referring to a broken toy car. They also tend to characterize the less familiar and more abstract with descriptions analogous to the more familiar and concrete, such as calling a large tree "Daddy tree" and a small one "baby tree."

Finally, it is interesting to note the development of such formal elements as articles, prepositions, or conjunctions as a syntactic structure assumes its new and more abstract function. These elements initially served the function of reference in and of themselves, denoting concrete occurrences. Subsequently, they were used to portray more abstract syntactic relationships (for example, conjunctions initially served as words to refer to combined entities, but now perform only a syntactic function).

It is interesting to consider the limits imposed by the character of our languages on the degree to which abstract relationships can be represented (Whorf, 1956). For example, the description of very abstract and complex relations in mathematics in large part hinged upon the development of a system of notation which was independent of language and the metaphor of human action.

Summary

Any communication situation is characterized by the similarity and immediacy of its four components: the communicator, the addressee, communication behavior, and the referent.[1] The development of child communication is described in terms of increasing degrees of dissimilarity and/or nonimmediacy among the various components, particularly between the communication behaviors and the referent. Unlike adults,

This section contains a rewritten paragraph from my article "Measures of Vocabulary and Grammatical Skills for Children up to Age Six," *Developmental Psychology*, 2 (1970), 439–46. Copyright (1970) by the American Psychological Association. Reproduced by permission.

children exhibit greater similarity and immediacy among these components due to ability limitations. Adults who sometimes behave in similar ways do so as a matter of choice, since they are also able to produce other forms. For instance a one-year-old child denotes things only by pointing, whereas an adult can do the same as well as locate something verbally.

A second general principle about child communication is that more advanced forms of communication are derived from behaviors that are already available in the repertoire of the child and that have been used to express simpler relations. Thus, pointing emerges from reaching to touch. Reaching to touch expresses the desire for something but pointing denotes it for another. Again, in expressing relations of causality, juxtaposition, or conjunction, utterances that are already available in the child's repertoire are used together with vocal expressions to show dependency.

The present approach provides guidelines for the investigation of correlated prelinguistic and early linguistic behaviors (Mehrabian, 1970f; Mehrabian and Williams, 1971). Various forms of nonverbal (delayed) imitation and anticipatory behavior are all indicative of a capacity to represent a referent in some other medium, such as gesturally. Our framework also specifies how such representations can be ordered developmentally. Thus, in imitation, more advanced forms are associated with the greater dissimilarity of the gestural behavior from the referent being imitated. It is also associated with nonimmediacy of the imitating gesture from the referent, since it implies an internalized schema or model that guides the imitation.

Some linguists (for example, Chomsky, 1965; Lenneberg, 1967; McNeill, 1966) have suggested that children's early linguistic development is not compatible with their cognitive skills. A child of four years, while not possessing an elaborate vocabulary, can exhibit the fully developed grammatical competence of an adult. Thus, one problem of primary concern is the relationship between early cognitive development and grammatical competence. These linguists contend that the relatively incomplete and somewhat irregular linguistic data in the child's social environment and the limits of his cognitive abilities do not provide a basis for his acquisition of grammar. They suggest that the child selects one of many innately given grammars which fits his linguistic data (for example, Chomsky, 1965, pp. 30–33; Lenneberg, 1967).

In contrast, the present approach evolved from one which attempts to relate children's nonlinguistic and linguistic skills. According to our view, the initial forms of communication rely most heavily on nonverbal gestures, vocal activity, movements, and postures. These nonverbal representational abilities of children are certainly not incompatible with their level of cognitive development, and provide the basis for the development of verbal representational skills.

10

Overview

How Can There be Consensus in Implicit Communication?

There are two pervasive traditions of western society that bear on the understanding of implicit communication. Although either one may be found in any culture, the occurrence of both within the same culture produces a unique significance for implicit behaviors. The first, and probably more important, of these traditions is restraint in the expression of feelings, particularly negative ones, outside the sphere of intimate relationships. The second is the absence of explicit instruction on the subject of implicit messages within the framework of formal education. The continued emphasis on language skills both at home and in school is a sharp contrast to the neglect of implicit communication.

How do these two traditions relate to one another in affecting communication? It is assumed that the human organism cannot totally "conceal" emotion—that emotions that are denied expression in one channel find another outlet (Ekman and Friesen, 1969a; Feldman, 1959; Mehrabian, 1971a). Both negative feelings (frustration, irritation, anger, hostility) and positive feelings (pleasure, liking, love) are part of social life, so if the expression of either is discouraged, it is conveyed less deliberately with implicit behaviors. Such means for expression, while more subtle, nonetheless assume similar significance for many. The de-emphasis of implicit communication in education helps to perpetuate a situation where "socially unacceptable" feelings must be expressed in behaviors other than speech and must not be recognized "officially" as part of a person's com-

Acknowledgment is given to Wadsworth Publishing Company, Belmont, California, for their permission to include in this chapter a small modified segment from Chapter 7 of my book, *Silent Messages*, published in 1971.

munication: we learn to express a variety of feelings in these more subtle ways to avoid being accused of transgressing the social norms.

Any behavior that is observable can serve as an outlet for feeling and is thus, in principle, communicative. Behaviors as diverse as the eye blink, the crossing of legs while seated, postures, gestures, facial and vocal expressions, tension in the muscles, and twitches are all potentially significant in communication, although of course, some are more communicative than others (for example, facial expressions compared to foot movements). One of the biggest stumbling blocks in the study of communication is precisely this fact; there are so many behaviors one can observe and study that it becomes difficult to know where to start, what to exclude, or how to order the priorities. In desparation, some investigators turned to a physical characterization of movements. Birdwhistell (1952) described movements of each body part in terms of their width and extent, or velocity. Others (Pittenger, Hockett, and Danehy, 1960; Trager, 1958) attempted to categorize implicit behaviors without much regard for the significance of these cues in social situations. In dance, where one would expect at least some reliance on feeling and intuition for describing movements, it is discouraging to find that the only comprehensive system of notation describes movements merely as motion, with no reference to what they signify (Hutchinson, 1970). Such reliance on physical description alone for nonverbal and implicit verbal behavior is inadequate. It fails to take into account the similar significance of unlike movements that emanate from different body parts (for example, approval given with a head nod or a pat on the back). Even more important, it fails to provide guidelines for identifying socially significant implicit behaviors.

The approach proposed for the study of implicit communication is not evident in early literature. I will not trace its meandering development, but only state the tentative conclusions. Feelings that are communicated nonverbally (or even verbally) can be characterized in terms of three independent dimensions: like-dislike, potency or status, and responsiveness. The first of these dimensions requires little definition; the second dimension, potency, refers to dominant and controlling versus submissive and dependent attitudes. Extreme examples are the "dignified" postures and movements of a monarch, or those of a snob who exudes a feeling of aloofness, in contrast to the hunched posture of a submissive person.

Responsiveness refers to the extent of awareness of, and reaction to, another. Alternatively, it is the extent to which someone else is salient for us. Extreme examples are the withdrawn schizophrenic standing in a hospital hallway oblivious to the people around him, in contrast to expressions of anger or joy, both of which indicate high responsiveness.

Various combinations of these three dimensions can be used to characterize any subtle nuance of feeling. For instance, a *disdainful* attitude conveys moderate dislike, high potency, and low responsiveness.

What categories of implicit behavior relate to each of these three dimensions? Behaviors relating to the like-dislike dimension are metaphorically expressed in proxemics (Hall, 1963, 1966) or immediacy (Wiener and Mehrabian, 1968). Immediacy or closeness in an interaction between two individuals (or between an individual and an object) involves greater physical proximity and/or increasing perceptual availability of two persons (or an object to a person). Approach and immediacy indicate preference, positive evaluation, and liking; avoidance and nonimmediacy indicate lack of preference, dislike and, in extreme cases, fear (Miller, 1964). The immediacy metaphor helps to identify behaviors that are communicative and relate to expressions of like-dislike. For instance, closer positions to another, the turning of the head so that it is in a face-to-face position and allows mutual observation, leaning forward toward another while seated, and touching all reflect more positive feelings (Mehrabian, 1969b).

The heuristic value of the immediacy metaphor is evidenced in some of the diverse behaviors that it has helped identify. The employer who fires his employee through an intermediary uses a less immediate means of communication than does the employer who talks with the employee himself. The "Dear John" letter is another common example of nonimmediate communication. Media of communication range from the most immediate, face-to-face situation, to video tape communications received on a monitor screen, telephone conversations where not only verbal contents but also vocal expressions are available to the listener, on to written communications where the subtle qualities of the voice are absent. Given a choice of all these media, the one that someone actually selects is an indicator of his positive-negative feelings. If we choose to use the telephone or write a letter when it is equally feasible to communicate face-to-face, our nonimmediacy can indicate dislike of the addressee, of the contents of communication, or of the act of communicating those contents to that particular addressee.

There are many subtle variations of immediacy in speech as well. For instance, I could say to a visitor, "I have been writing a paper" or "I am writing a paper." The second statement is temporally more immediate and implies greater liking of my activity. Or I could say, "I'm writing this paper for those people who. . . ." versus "I'm writing this paper for these people who. . . ." Again, the closeness implied by *these* instead of *those* reflects a more positive feeling.

Indicators of potency and status are observed in metaphorical expressions of strength and fearlessness. Strength is metaphorically implied by large-small (strutting versus shuffling, expansive versus small and controlled quality), high-low (standing upright versus bowing), and fast-slow movements. Absence of fear is metaphorically implied by relaxation versus tension and by turning one's back to another. For instance, a tradition in historic Middle Eastern cultures was for a person of lower standing to back out of a room rather than turn around and walk out. Abbreviated versions of such backing out are observed even today. This is frequently combined with bowing and a low speech volume—the latter being consistent with the metaphorical expression of weakness.

There is considerable evidence on relaxation-tension and its relation to status, since it is a frequent vehicle for conveying status variations in our culture (Mehrabian, 1969b). When two persons are together, the one of higher status is more relaxed. His limbs and trunk tend to be asymmetrically positioned (legs crossed, leaning sideways, or reclining). Interestingly, rocking while seated indicates relaxation, but rocking while standing indicates the opposite, tension.

The third dimension, responsiveness, is expressed metaphorically through greater nonverbal, and implicit verbal, activity (for example, facial expressiveness that includes positive and negative cues, vocal activity, speech rate as measured by the number of words uttered per minute, and speech volume). In those situations where the speaker must influence his listener (political campaigns or advertising) but cannot express liking, lest his motive be questioned as manipulative or insincere, there is a sharp increase in responsiveness but only a slight increase in implicit positiveness (Mehrabian and Williams, 1969).

Metaphorical expressions of liking, potency, and responsiveness are sometimes formalized and explicit (in the Orient, bowing is part of the high-low metaphor for status); but usually they remain implicit (as in our culture where relaxation-tension conveys variations in status). The fact that there can still be consensus within, and even between, cultures (Ekman, 1972; Ekman and Friesen, 1971), when the communication codes are implicit, supports our thesis that much of implicit communication draws upon these shared metaphors that are inherent in human experience.

Our analysis of communication in terms of metaphors illustrates their more general function in human thought. Metaphors draw upon the elementary and familiar aspects of sensory-perceptual experience, whose rich connotations provide the basis for understanding the novel (as in science) and the unfamiliar (as in learning). Philosophers Cassirer (1953–57) and Pepper (1942) discussed the function of metaphors in human culture; Mehrabian (1968e) illustrated the specific application of metaphors in social science. The frequent use of metaphors is also evident in art (when the poet likens a human being to a tree) and in the altogether familiar realm of advertising.

The Interpretation of Inconsistent Messages

If feelings can be described in terms of three basic dimensions, then inconsistency is readily characterized for each dimension. What happens when someone expresses varying degrees of liking in different behaviors?

Our studies have produced an answer for most cases in the form of a simple linear model (Mehrabian and Ferris, 1967; Mehrabian and Wiener, 1967):

Total liking = 7% verbal liking + 38% vocal liking + 55% facial liking

Thus, in the case of inconsistency, facial expressions are the most dominant, the vocal component ranks second, and words are the least significant. In other words, one would be hesitant to rely on what is said when the facial, or the vocal, expression contradicts the words. In sarcasm, for instance, the negative voice determines the meaning of the entire message even though the words are positive.

Does the equation also apply to the other two dimensions, potency and responsiveness? Argyle, Salter, Nicholson, Williams, and Burgess (1970) found that, indeed, implicitly communicated potency dominated over contradictory degrees of potency conveyed verbally in the same message. There are as yet no findings bearing on inconsistent communications of responsiveness. However, a similar dominance of implicit channels over the verbal one seems likely. A fast-talking auctioneer or trader whose facial or vocal expressions are bland seems quite unresponsive to his listener. We can therefore extrapolate from the findings and rewrite the equation for any feeling (for example, responsiveness, dominance, elation-depression or distress).

Total feeling = 7% verbal feeling + 38% vocal feeling + 55% facial feeling

Besides its bearing on inconsistent messages, the equation indicates that redundancy leads to the intensification of a message. When the verbal component in a message conveys dislike while the remaining components are neutral, the total dislike computed from the equation is less than if all three channels were to be negative. This suggests that any form of redundancy or repetition of the same message yields greater intensity, such as when a child says "big, big teddy bear" to emphasize size. Indeed, in some African languages the successive repetition of the same word is formalized as a grammatical rule to indicate more of whatever the repeated word denotes (Werner and Kaplan, 1963).

Reasons and Conditions for the Use of Inconsistent Messages

With this preliminary understanding of how inconsistent and consistent messages are interpreted, we proceeded to explore the somewhat more complex questions involving the use of inconsistent messages. The first question was why a person uses an inconsistent message when he can use a consistent message of comparable attitudinal impact. The second, and related, question was whether inconsistent messages of liking occur more frequently in families with more maladjusted members.

In four experiments, Mehrabian (1970e) used four kinds of messages and asked subjects about their preference for each of these messages in a variety of social situations. In all the experiments, two channels of communication, verbal and vocal, were employed. The inconsistent positive communications involved positive vocal and negative verbal components. The inconsistent negative communications involved negative vocal and positive verbal components. The control stimuli for these two sets of messages consisted of moderately positive verbal and vocal communications on one hand and moderately negative verbal and vocal communications on the other. Several instances of each of the four types of communication were recorded on tape. Subjects listened and indicated preferences for these while imagining a variety of social situations.

The results of each experiment showed that consistent communications of attitude are preferred over inconsistent ones, and that, among inconsistent communications, positive communications are less preferred than are negative ones. The implication is that, due to their less frequent use, inconsistent messages are more difficult to produce, and that the less frequent use reflects a lower preference for them. An observation during preparation of stimuli was that inconsistent communications of attitude frequently rely on facial expressions. For instance, when subjects were instructed to say something negative with a positive vocal component, they actually used a neutral vocal component but assumed a positive facial expression, so that audio recordings of their statements did not really reflect the intended inconsistency. It thus seems that any further exploration of preference for inconsistent messages should include facial as well as verbal and vocal expressions.

The second generalization that emerged from the Mehrabian (1970e) study was that inconsistent communications were preferred more in the less formal communication settings.

Without exception, the remaining results from the four experiments were consistent with the following general conclusions: (1) The verbal component of an inconsistent message conveys evaluation of an addressee's action, and therefore is the basis for selecting a message when the addressee behaves pleasantly versus unpleasantly. (2) The nonverbal component of an inconsistent message conveys evaluation of the addressee's person, and therefore is the basis for selecting a message when the addressee is liked versus disliked.

Also, without exception, the significant effects indicated that the more anxious subjects had more preference for positive inconsistent messages and less preference for negative inconsistent messages. This finding showed that more anxious persons were less willing to convey negative feelings to the person of the addressee, since they preferred messages with positive nonverbal components and avoided those with negative non-verbal components. There were no consistent results for communicator approval-seeking tendency.

With these results for the uses of inconsistent messages in the general population, Beakel and Mehrabian (1969) proceeded to explore the frequency of occurrence of consistent and inconsistent attitude communications of parents toward their more or less disturbed adolescent children. According to the double-bind hypothesis, it is expected that parents of the more disturbed children communicate inconsistency in attitude more frequently than do parents of less disturbed children.

In the Beakel and Mehrabian (1969) experiment, inconsistency of communication was assessed from the attitudes conveyed verbally and posturally. Postural, rather than facial or vocal, cues were selected because of their more subtle quality. We could have relied on facial cues, but in the presence of an "evaluative" therapist it seemed that parents would be less able to censor their communication of attitude via postural cues than to censor or control their facial expressions.

A sample of 21 families who had a disturbed adolescent member were the subjects who provided the communications analyzed in the experiment. Verbalizations and postures were measured from audio and video recordings of adolescents and their parents as they discussed a family problem stemming from the child's disturbance. The results of the experiment did not support the double-bind hypothesis; there was no greater incongruity in the postural-verbal communications of parents of more disturbed adolescents than in the communications of parents of less disturbed adolescents. These findings that contradicted the double-bind hypothesis were consistent with the conclusions that Schuham (1967) drew from his review.

The most interesting finding of the study was that the parents of the more disturbed adolescents showed more negative attitudes toward these adolescents than did the parents of the less disturbed adolescents. Thus, the study showed that exploration of the overall quality of positive-negative attitude, rather than inconsistency in attitude communication, is a more useful avenue for investigating the relationship between communication patterns and psychopathology.

Our Approach and Methods

The rationale for the research we have reviewed and reported here differs from earlier approaches to the study of nonverbal and subtle verbal behaviors. In contrast to the earlier approaches, which sought discrete nonverbal behaviors and explored their specific referents or conversely identified the discrete behaviors associated with certain feelings, our approach relied on a multidimensional characterization of the referents of implicit communication as variations in liking, potency, and responsiveness. It has thus been possible to identify, in a variety of channels, the behaviors that consistently convey varying degrees of each of these referents.

The advantage of our approach is that encoding paradigms can be used readily to identify large numbers of behaviors associated with each of these referential dimensions. The disadvantage is that the approach does not permit the identification of specific feelings that may convey varying degrees of each of the referential dimensions. Thus, just as the general characterization of the referents of speech in terms of evaluation, potency, and activity accounts for only about 65 per cent of the referential significance of speech (for example, Osgood, Suci, and Tannenbaum, 1957, p. 61), likewise the use of a multidimensional framework certainly does not exhaust the referents of implicit behavior. Nevertheless, such a description accounts for about half of the variance in the significance of nonverbal and implicit verbal cues.

The reliance on a multidimensional framework does seem desirable at this point because it provides a reasonably simple and general scheme with which to identify and study quite diverse sets of behaviors. As more work relating to each of these referential dimensions becomes available, it will be not only possible, but desirable, to identify the specific behaviors that convey more subtle shades of feeling (for example, the Mona Lisa smile), and to place them as points in this three-dimensional semantic space.

This being a volume on communication research, it seems appropriate to include a note on methodology. There are two complementary avenues for exploring communication phenomena. In the first, *decoding*, subjects are presented with prepared stimuli and are instructed to infer feelings and attitudes from those stimuli. Such a method is advantageous since it allows a comparison of the effects of a number of cues, singly or in combination, on inferred attitudes. It also allows the investigation of the relative effects of these cues for various communicator and addressee groups (for example, different sex or personality). Finally, possible confounding effects of communications in other channels (for example, facial expressions, verbalizations, or gestures) can be eliminated. A decoding method yields considerable information because it makes possible the systematic control of a large number of variables.

In the second method, *encoding*, subjects are placed in experimental situations which elicit different kinds of attitude-related behavior. Typical encoding methods employ role-playing, in which a subject is requested to assume a certain role or attitude toward his addressee (for example, Rosenfeld, 1966a, 1966b). Occasionally there are studies which take advantage of existing likes and dislikes or status differences among subjects, and other studies which actually induce like or dislike in a subject toward the addressee (Exline and Winters, 1965).

Thus, an encoding method, unlike a decoding one, cannot include the systematic study of interactions among communication cues. But a decoding study requires factorial designs for the study of the interactions, and thus limits the number of cues that can be investigated, since a design involving more than six or seven factors is unmanageably large. In an encoding method, although it is possible to study the interactive effects of only one cue at a time with communicator and addressee characteristics, there is no limit to the number of communication cues that can be readily included and interpreted in the design. The use of regression or discriminant analyses (for example, Anderson and Bancroft, 1955) in conjunction with an encoding method can provide the relative strengths of the various communication cues that connote attitudes.

Almost all communication research is based on either the encoding or decoding method. There would be some value in a third methodology which encompasses the major advantages of both encoding and decoding methods. In one such method, stimuli are prepared as they would be with a decoding method. They are then presented to subjects who are asked to indicate their preference for using these stimuli in various social situations. There are several advantages to this third method. First, if the experimenter prepares a series of stimuli that are inappropriate for the communication of the particular referents he is studying, subjects will characteristically show very low preference scores for the use of those stimuli. This informs the experimenter just how well suited his stimuli actually are for the communication of the particular referents—an inference which is not possible when the decoding method is used. This third method allows a systematic control of the communication cues that are employed. Factorial designs can be used to assess the independent and interactive effects of various communication cues in determining a referent, an advantage that is not available with encoding methods. Mehrabian's (1970e) study of inconsistent messages illustrates the use of this third encoding-decoding method.

This third method does not require the experimenter to possess an advanced understanding of the phenomenon he is about to explore. Extensive knowledge is, however, required to prepare an appropriate set of stimuli when one uses a decoding method. Thus, whereas encoding methods are appropriate in the beginning stages of communication research, the proposed encoding-decoding method is appropriate for intermediate stages, and decoding methods are appropriate during the highly developed phases of such research.

Applications

In a variety of contexts, we have seen that nonverbal behaviors are more important or basic (possibly because they are more difficult to censor) than are verbal ones: untrained observers assign greater weight to the feelings communicated nonverbally in vocal and facial expressions than to the feelings expressed verbally.[1] Further, some nonverbal channels are more subtle than others. For instance, communications of attitude or status with posture and position cues are more subtle and probably less subject to censorship or deliberate control than are the same attitudes when expressed facially or vocally. Finally, some of the findings show individual differences in channel preference for the expression of unacceptable feelings (Zaidel and Mehrabian, 1969).

The preceding generalizations can serve as a basis for applying the findings of implicit communication in both everyday and experimental situations. In social psychological experiments, it is sometimes important to obtain valid indexes of a communicator's feelings and attitudes toward a certain group of persons, beliefs, or experiences, but the experimenter may not feel confident about his subject's verbal reports. For example, if the topic of experimentation deals with prejudice, honest and explicit verbal responses may be confounded by a subject's approval-seeking tendency or by the general social discouragement of openly expressing certain attitudes or feelings (for example, males are discouraged from admitting they are afraid or feel threatened). Consequently, the researcher must rely on more subtle measures. Some of the nonverbal or implicit verbal cues that have been considered in this study lend themselves readily to the assessment of attitudes in such experimental situations. Suppose, for instance, that an experimenter wishes to explore prejudice toward blacks, and creates a situation to test the effects of cooperative or competitive interaction on attitude change. Verbal and postural immediacy measures could be obtained both before and after the subject's interaction. Changes in the degree of postural or verbal immediacy would serve as indexes of attitude change and also provide a basis for assessing the generalization of new attitudes toward other blacks as well.

Nonverbal and implicit verbal cues can also be used in everyday situations; for example, to assess candidates' attitudes as expressed in their political speeches. Exploring these findings for persons from different cultures may yield valuable applications in the context of diplomatic negotiations as well. These would not only provide clues to determine which nonverbal behaviors inadvertently communicate misleading attitudes (Hall, 1959), but also ways to assess the attitudes of various participants in negotiations where the verbal communications are not sufficiently informative. A by-product of the less controlled nature of implicit cues is that they help not only to identify feelings or attitudes that a communicator is hesitant to express due to social pressure or conformity, but also to detect deceit.

The subtle quality of nonverbal cues has been used intuitively in vari-

---

1. This section contains rewritten segments from my article "A Semantic Space for Nonverbal Behavior," *Journal of Consulting and Clinical Psychology,* 35 (1970), 248–57, copyright (1970) by the American Psychological Association. Reproduced by permission.

ous forms of advertising to induce particular attitudes toward various products. These cues can be used yet more systematically, since they lend themselves in a variety of ways toward maximizing the persuasive impact of communications (Mehrabian and Williams, 1969).

The concepts of reinforcement-learning theory are receiving increasing attention and application in behavior modification. When one uses the principles of instrumental learning to modify interpersonal behaviors, the choice of reinforcers is quite critical. This is especially the case when the person being influenced is not dependent upon the person who reinforces or influences (that is, he is not a child, a hospital patient, or a prison inmate). When the client and the modifying agent are of equal status, having potentially equal power to materially reinforce each other, social reinforcers can serve as important vehicles for the modification of behavior (Mehrabian, 1970c). Social reinforcers may be viewed as ways of communicating liking or respect and higher status to a person whose behaviors are being shaped. For instance, head nodding is a way of communicating respect to the addressee, as in agreement with him. Thus, it is expected that both cues should function as reinforcers, and the findings show this to be the case (Krasner, 1958; Matarazzo, Wiens, and Saslow, 1965). Communications of agreement and head nodding show respect, but the analysis and groupings of nonverbal cues in terms of liking and status differences (respect) suggest that the cues that primarily express liking are also quite relevant and important in the shaping of interpersonal behavior. The findings we have reported provide a basis for the experimental control of the level and kind of social reinforcers that can be used to explore nonverbal cues in behavior modification. Experimenters could select from a diversity of nonverbal cues those which are best suited to their particular experimental requirements. For instance, they could explore the differential effectiveness of the communication of respect versus the communication of liking in shaping the behaviors of different types of subjects, such as children versus adults.

The use of inconsistent reinforcers in the shaping of behavior may also be of some interest here. What, if any, is the value of using inconsistent messages, such as positive or negative inconsistent messages, in the process of social influence? Haley (1963) suggested that one way to view the typical psychodynamic therapy is in terms of inconsistent messages to the client. For example, the therapist verbally asserts an unwillingness to be directive, because being directive would imply his higher status in the situation and might be resented by the client. But both informal observations and recent experimental findings have shown that even those who completely deny a directive therapeutic role nevertheless use nonverbal cues to shape their clients' behaviors (Truax, 1966). Since they have denied the use of shaping in their procedures, psychodynamically-oriented therapists have not presented a theoretical analysis of the rationale for such a method. The choice of this method is nevertheless significant and requires analysis. Why is it that such inconsistency is used? Mehrabian (1970c) suggested a possible rationale for the use of inconsistent messages among psychoanalytic or Rogerian therapists. This same technique can be experimentally explored with a variety of simple methods by shaping a subject's behaviors through systematic use of in-inconsistent cues: the experimenter's nonverbal cues being used for shaping while his verbal cues are neutral or even contradictory. The differential effectiveness of such inconsistent messages in shaping the behaviors of different types of subjects should be of considerable interest. It would seem that when the verbal component includes a denial of manipulative intent, but the nonverbal cues nevertheless systematically communicate liking or respect, more effective shaping of another person's behavior will result, particularly when that person is openly resistant to influence or manipulation by a peer.

Some additional applications of findings from studies of implicit communication can occur in the exploration of characteristic attitude communications. Concern for individual differences in nonverbal behavior (expressive qualities) was partially responsible for the study of nonverbal behavior in the first place. Conceptualizing the referents of nonverbal behavior in terms of evaluation, potency and responsiveness, it is expected that (1) affiliative dispositions correlate with more immediate nonverbal behaviors toward others; (2) dominant personality dispositions correlate with relaxation; (3) anxious or disturbed individuals exhibit less relaxation and, depending on the form of psychopathology, possibly less immediacy, as in the case of withdrawn schizophrenia; and (4) empathic tendency is correlated with characteristic responsiveness; and depressive tendencies, which are associated with withdrawal and less responsiveness to people in general, are reflected in low levels of activity.

Individual differences can also be explored by investigating preferences for expressing negative feelings in more or less obvious channels. It is assumed that the various channels of attitude communication convey increasingly obvious negative feelings in this order: verbal nonimmediacy (Wiener and Mehrabian, 1968), postural nonimmediacy, negative vocal, negative facial, and negative verbal communications. For instance, Zaidel and Mehrabian (1969) found that, in the relatively obvious facial and vocal channels, higher approval seekers were less able to communicate variation in negative feelings.

In general, then, individual differences in the use of implicit communication cues can be conceptualized in three ways: (1) in terms of the three-dimensional framework (that is, consistent individual differences in the expression of positive feelings and differences in the expression of dominance and responsiveness); (2) in terms of a person's tendency to use implicit and nonobvious, versus more obvious and explicit, channels to express his feelings; and (3) as one aspect of social skills—the appropriate communication of attitude and status through nonverbal cues. At one extreme, pathology can be detected from grossly inappropriate manifestations of immediacy or tension-relaxation, as when a communicator is too immediate with an unfamiliar addressee or when his tension level communicates fear to an addressee who is not actually threatening. Variations in the effectiveness of more normal individuals in their social dealings may be partially due to the attitude or status which they typically convey. For instance, an individual who indiscriminately assumes a generally high level of postural relaxation with addressees of different status may experience persistent but puzzling problems with high-status others. Finally, individual differences in persuasive ability may be due partially to the ability to communicate appropriate levels of positive attitude and status to different kinds of addressees.

The relation of characteristic attitude communications to level of psychopathology of the communicator can also be explored. Attitudes could be experimentally assessed from both verbal and nonverbal behaviors, thus yielding not only a measure of the inconsistency in the communication of liking but also the extent of total negative attitude conveyed to addressees. Such measures could be related in turn to the level of psychopathology of children who are frequent recipients of such attitudes, or to their personalities.

The implicit communications of like or dislike, or the characteristic implicit communications of a more or less dominant attitude, may contribute to inaccuracy in communications (Mehrabian and Reed, 1968). Thus, knowledge of implicit cues can also assist in a variety of settings where inaccuracy detracts from effective communication, such as between supervisors and employees, or between teachers and students.

Scoring Criteria for Some Categories of Nonverbal and Implicit Verbal Behavior

The following criteria were derived after considerable modification based on a variety of experimental findings. They are designed to provide a reasonably comprehensive description of the nonverbal and subtle (or non-content) aspects of verbal interaction. Although a larger set of cues has been explored, only those that yielded significant relations to the independent variables in various experiments are summarized below. Scoring reliability estimates for most measures are given within parentheses.

Criteria for Scoring the Positions and Postures of Standing or Seated Communicators

IMMEDIACY DIMENSION

Touching. Touching involves bodily contact between the communicator and the addressee, as would be the case in holding hands, or of shoulders touching. In the case of this measure and that of eye contact noted below, the duration of touching (or of eye contact), expressed as a fraction of the total time when the communicator and the addressee are in each other's presence, is the appropriate measure. For all the remaining measures, average values over time are used (for example, average distance during a five-minute conversation between the communicator and addressee).

Distance (0.95). Physical distance separating the communicator from the addressee. In two studies involving seated communicators (Mehrabian, 1968b; Mehrabian and Friar, 1969) distance was specifically scored as follows. Total distance is, of course, the relevant measure. It is based on the following straight-ahead and lateral distance scores:

1. Straight-ahead distance: The distance from the front of the addressee's chair to the center spoke of the communicator's chair. This is measured by

the 9″ × 9″ tiles on the floor, starting with the tile immediately below the front of the addressee's chair. The distance is measured to the nearest one-half tile.

2. Lateral distance: The distance the communicator is to the right or left of an imaginary plane which would cut the addressee's chair bilaterally in half. This distance is measured by the tiles on the floor from the imaginary plane to the center spoke of the communicator's chair. The distance is measured to the nearest one-half tile.

In one study involving standing communicators (Mehrabian, 1968a) the following criteria were used for distance:

1. Straight-ahead distance: Measured from the front line of the addressee in terms of number of tiles to the nearest one-half up to a line that is perpendicular to the straight-ahead and that passes near the center portion of the foot on which the communicator is resting. If he is resting on both feet, then a point in between the two feet is used.

2. Lateral distance: Measured similarly to the straight-ahead distance.

Forward Lean (0.87). The number of degrees that a plane from the communicator's shoulders to his hips is away from the vertical plane. Angles are measured in units of 10 degrees; whereas reclining angles are scored as negative, forward-leaning angles are scored as positive.

Eye Contact (0.65). Fraction of the duration of interaction (that is, when the communicator and the addressee are in each other's presence) when the communicators look into each other's eyes.

Observation (0.84). Sometimes scored instead of eye contact, observation is the fraction of the duration of interaction when the communicator looks into the face of his addressee, whether or not it can be ascertained that the addressee is looking back.

Orientation (0.90). The number of degrees a plane perpendicular to the plane of the communicator's shoulders is turned away from the median plane of the addressee. This angle is estimated to the nearest 10 degrees, and cannot exceed 180 degrees.

NOTE: The preceding criteria are listed in order of their importance. More touching, forward lean, and eye contact, and less distance and smaller orientation angles are more immediate. With the exception of the forward-lean angle, which is not scored for standing positions, all the criteria above are scored for both seated and standing positions.

RELAXATION DIMENSION

Arm-Position Asymmetry (0.87).

0: Symmetrical position of the arms: for example, hands clasped at the midsection, arms folded symmetrically, or both arms hanging straight down or akimbo while standing.

1: Slight asymmetry in the position of the arms: for example, both hands resting on the lap of the communicator, but one hand from two to five inches more forward than the other, or one hand clasping the other at the wrist.

2: Moderate asymmetry in the position of the arms: for example, one hand holds an elbow or the upper arm whereas the other hand is free, one arm hanging loosely and the other hanging by a finger which is stuck in a pocket.

3: Extreme asymmetry in the position of the arms: for example, one arm in the lap and the other hooked over the back of the chair, one hand stuck in a pocket and the other resting on a knee or hanging loosely, or only one arm akimbo.

Sideways Lean (0.63). The number of degrees that a plane cutting the communicator's torso bilaterally in half is away from the vertical. This angle is estimated to the nearest 10 degrees, and cannot exceed 90 degrees.

Leg-Position Asymmetry (0.96).

0: Symmetrical position of the legs with both feet flat on the floor and the insteps touching.

1: Symmetrical position of the legs with both feet flat on the floor and the insteps *not* touching.

2: Asymmetrical stance of the legs with both feet resting flat on the floor, such as when one foot is moved to a more forward position.

3: Asymmetrical stance of the legs with one or both feet partially lifted off the floor, as when there is a bend at the ankle and only an edge of the foot is resting on the floor, or when the legs are crossed while seated.

Hand Relaxation (0.66).

0: Very tense: hands or fists are tightly clenched, or hands are clasping something tightly, or hands are in motion, such as drumming fingers.

1: Moderately tense: loosely clasped or in loose fists or loosely clasping any object or part of the body.

2: Relaxed: fingers are extended but not stiffly; hands are in pockets.

Neck Relaxation (0.70).

0: The head is not supported and the line of vision is pointing 10 degrees or more above the horizontal.

1: The head is not supported and the line of vision is within 10 degrees of the horizontal.

2: The head is supported, as when resting on the back of a couch, or is hanging so that the line of vision forms 10 or more degrees below the horizontal.

Reclining Angle (0.87). The number of degrees that a plane from the communicator's shoulders to his hips is away from the vertical plane. Angles are measured in units of 10 degrees. Reclining angles are scored as positive; forward leaning angles are scored as negative.

NOTE: The preceding criteria are listed in approximate order of their importance. Increasing degrees of each of the preceding criteria indicate more relaxation. With the exception of reclining angles, which are not scored for standing positions, all the criteria listed above are scored for both seated and standing positions.

194

Criteria for Scoring Movements, Facial Expressions, and Verbalizations

MOVEMENTS

Trunk Swivel Movements (0.89). Number of times S swivels his body on a swivel chair. Score all movements that involve a rotation greater than 10 degrees. If motions are cyclical rather than unidirectional, each complete cycle is scored as one unit.

Rocking Movements (0.91). Number of times S changes his angle of forward-back lean (and also of sideways lean while standing) by 10 degrees or more. Again, cyclical movements (for example, a forward-back rock) are scored as one unit. (Caution: Note that rocking while standing has the opposite connotation to the relaxation connoted by rocking while seated.)

Head Nodding Movements (0.80). Number of cyclical up and down movements of the head, each of which is scored as one unit. This is scored when the head nodding is clearly directed at the addressee, either during the speech of the addressee or as a nonverbal response to or acknowledgment of something the addressee has said.

Head Shaking Movements (0.86). Number of cyclical sideways movements of the head, each of which is scored as one unit. The remaining criteria are the same as those for head nodding.

Gesticulation (0.94). Number of movements of hands or of fingers, excluding the self-manipulatory movements scored below. This includes side-to-side, forward-back, and up-and-down movements. Cyclical movements (for example, raising and lowering a finger) are scored as one unit each.

Self-Manipulation (0.90). "Motion of a part of the body in contact·with another—either directly or mediated by an instrument. Examples are scratching, rubbing, or tapping an arm or leg with finger or pen" (Rosenfeld, 1966b, p. 67), which are scored as in Gesticulation. In other words, single brief movements in one direction are scored once, and cyclical movements are scored once each. A brief (that is, less than five seconds) scratching movement is scored once only. Continuous movements are scored once every five seconds.

Object-Manipulation (0.89). This is scored like self-manipulation, except that the action is primarily on an object that is *not* used to mediate stimulation of the communicator's own body (for example, writing with a piece of chalk or rearranging objects in the room).

Leg Movement (0.97). Number of movements of the leg at the knee joint (for example, placing one foot onto the other or crossing the legs). Again, any cyclical movements are scored as one unit each. Do not include in this measure any movements that are incidental to trunk swivel or rocking movements.

Foot Movement (0.87). Number of movements of feet or number of times ankle is twisted (rotated). Again, cyclical movements (for example, turning the foot from side to side) are each scored as one unit. Do not score movements incidental to leg movements.

Per cent Duration of Walking (0.96). For a standing position, this is simply that percentage of the duration of interaction when the communicator walks about.

FACIAL EXPRESSIONS

Facial Pleasantness (*0.79*). Number of positive expressions, such as smiles, minus number of negative expressions, such as frowns, glares, or sneers. Continuous expressions of either a positive or negative quality are scored once every five seconds.

Facial Activity (*0.65*). Total number of facial expressions, both positive and negative. Thus, any movements of the facial muscles to a non-neutral expression, such as raising of the eyebrows in surprise or biting of the lips, are scored. Continuous expressions are scored once every five seconds.

Facial Dominance (*0.83*). Assessed from semantic differential ratings using the scales of Table A.1, which are taken from Mehrabian and Russell (1972).

Table A.1. Semantic differential scales for rating nonverbal cues.

Pleasantness

Happy	Unhappy
Pleased	Annoyed
Satisfied	Unsatisfied
Contented	Melancholic
Hopeful	Despairing
Relaxed	Bored

Responsiveness

Stimulated	Relaxed
Excited	Calm
Frenzied	Sluggish
Jittery	Dull
Wide awake	Sleepy
Aroused	Unaroused

Dominance

Controlling	Controlled
Influential	Influenced
In control	Cared for
Important	Awed
Dominant	Submissive
Autonomous	Guided

NOTE: These scales can also be used to rate any subset of nonverbal behaviors (postures, movements, vocal expressions).

VERBALIZATIONS

Communication Length (*0.91*). Measured in terms of number of words or, slightly less satisfactorily, in terms of duration, which is considerably easier to score. Sometimes it is convenient to score the communicator's speech duration as a fraction of the total time when the communicator and addressee are in each other's presence. In this case, it is referred to as "per cent speech duration."

Number of Statements (*0.90*). The total number of simple sentences and independent clauses uttered by a communicator while in the presence of the addressee. When the interaction duration between the communicator and addressee varies slightly for different pairs, then the number of statements per minute of the communicator is the more convenient measure. (Verbal reinforcers, defined below, are not counted as statements, since they are not simple sentences in general.)

Number of Questions (*0.95*). Total number of questions asked of the addressee. Once again a rate measure may be used as in measuring "Number of Statements."

Verbal Reinforcers (*0.74*). Comments from the communicator that convey acknowledgment of, agreement with, or identity with a statement of the addressee, or with the addressee himself. Examples are *yeah, uh-huh, really? hmmm, me too,* or *same here.*

Pleasantness of Vocal Expressions (*0.76*). The degree of positive versus negative quality that is inferred from paralinguistic features alone, based on the following scale. For this purpose a Krohn-Hite model 3500 electronic filter can be used to eliminate the higher frequencies (above 200 cps) of speech and render it incomprehensible, while retaining the paralinguistic features.

+2: Extreme enthusiasm, pleasure, amusement, or sympathetic interest in the addressee.

+1: Noticeable amount of enthusiasm, pleasure, amusement, or sympathetic interest in the addressee.

  0: Neither positive nor negative quality, or a balance between instances of positive and negative quality.

−1: Sarcasm, annoyance, boredom, or suspicion (noticeable).

−2: Extreme sarcasm, annoyance, boredom, or suspicion.

Positive Verbal Content (*0.86*). The extent to which the communicator's words convey a positive feeling to the addressee; ranging from no suggestions of interest in the addressee, to statements about the impersonal aspects of the setting, to statements indicating interest in and liking of the addressee.

0: No verbal response, or brief replies to the addressee's statements.

1: Verbal references to the setting in which the interaction occurs, showing some interest or approval.

2: Verbal references to the setting with moderate to strong interest or approval.

3: Questions directed to the addressee that are of a personal nature, such as what he is studying, or where he is from. Verbal immediacy indicators such as *us* or *we*, which suggest common experiences with the addressee, are helpful in assigning statements to this level.

4: Questions and comments such as those cited in the preceding paragraph that indicate a moderate to strong interest in the addressee.

Negative Verbal Content (*0.86*). The extent to which the communicator's words convey a negative feeling to the addressee; ranging from no suggestions of disinterest in the addressee or disapproval of the setting, to statements of a negative quality about the setting, to negative statements directed to the addressee himself.

0: No verbal references, or brief replies to the addressee's statements.
1: Verbal references to the setting in which the interaction occurs, showing small degrees of disinterest or disapproval.
2: Verbal references to the setting, showing moderate to strong degrees of displeasure about being in the situation, or disinterest in or disapproval of the general situation, provided no explicit mention is made of the addressee himself.
3: One or more instances where a question of the addressee is left unanswered, or two or more instances where the communicator does not follow through initial comments made by the addressee. Also, statements by the communicator that indicate an inappropriate or disrespectful attitude toward the addressee, such as telling the addressee what to do. Finally, statements that imply that being in the same situation with the addressee is unpleasant or boring.
4: More frequent and more pronounced instances of categories cited in the preceding paragraph. Profanity is assigned to this category.

Speech Error Rate (0.78). Based on the number of speech disruptions per unit time. Kasl and Mahl (1965) and Mahl's (1959, Table 1) criteria for "sentence change," "repetition," "stutter," "sentence incompletion," "tongue slips," and "intruding incoherent sounds" provide a reliable basis for scoring speech disruptions.

Halting Quality of Speech (0.70). This is the variability of speech rate and can be computed from speech rate figures obtained for 15-second intervals of speech. Alternatively, it can be estimated on a five-point scale by listening to an audio recording of a communication. Such judgments can be anchored by assigning a score of zero to "radio announcer" quality speech and a score of four to stammering speech. Judges can initially be provided with such examples. The inter-observer reliability given is for the latter case.

Speech Rate (0.77). Measured in terms of words per minute. Alternatively, it can be estimated on the following scale with the reliability indicated:

0: Very slow
1: Slow
2: Average
3: Fast
4: Very fast

Speech Volume (0.88). Measured, for instance, with the calibrated scale of an audio recorder. Alternatively, it can be estimated on the following scale with anchor stimuli that are also provided to judges, in which case the preceding reliability applies.

0: A whisper, or the lowest volume at which the communicator could have been heard.
1: Soft
2: Average
3: Loud
4: Very loud

Vocal Activity (0.44). A sound spectrum analyzer (for example, Bell Telephone Laboratories Spectrograph No. 2) can be used first to obtain the values of fundamental frequency range and intensity range for a recorded speech sample. Huttar used such equipment to make "Broad-band (300 Hz band width) and narrow-band (45 Hz band width) spectrograms and continuous amplitude displays (logarithmic setting) of each utterance" (Huttar, 1967, p. 96), and he used these records to measure fundamental frequency range and intensity range. An equally weighted composite of the latter two measures can then be used as the index of vocal activity. Alternatively, it may be estimated on a five-point scale with the reported reliability. The latter judgments can be anchored by assigning a score of zero to the "flat or affectless" vocal component associated with private reading, and a score of four to "radio announcer," or angry, speech. These are intially provided to judges as examples.

Personality Measures Relating to Affective Communication

The measures of affiliative tendency and sensitivity to rejection are based on studies by Mehrabian (1970b, 1970d, 1971b), Mehrabian and Diamond (1971a, 1971b) and Mehrabian and Ksionzky (1971a, 1972). Validity and reliability data for the measure of empathic tendency are given by Mehrabian and Epstein (1972). The measures of achieving tendency are based on the studies by Mehrabian (1968f, 1969a). Additional validational data for the latter were provided by Weiner, Johnson, and Mehrabian (1968) and Weiner and Kukla (1970).

The (+) and (−) signs preceding each item indicate the direction of scoring. To compute a total score for each scale, first change the sign of a subject's responses on the negative (−) items, then obtain an algebraic sum of all items of that scale.

Of course, in actual use of the tests, the signs for the direction of scoring would be omitted and answer spaces provided for subjects. Further, the items from the varying scales should be mixed together in random order to minimize a subject's awareness of the attributes being measured.

Mean = 30, *Standard Deviation* = 23, for the Affiliative Tendency scale; and *Mean* = −6, *Standard Deviation* = 23, for the Sensitivity to Rejection scale.

For the measure of empathic tendency, *Mean* = 41 and *Standard Deviation* = 26. However, since males and females differ significantly on this measure, separate statistics may be necessary in some cases. For males, *Mean* = 26, *Standard Deviation* = 22; for females, *Mean* = 56, *Standard Deviation* = 21.

For the Male Achievement scale, *Mean* = 9, *Standard Deviation* = 18. For the Female Achievement scale, *Mean* = 5, *Standard Deviation* = 19.

INSTRUCTION TO SUBJECTS

Please use the following scale to indicate the degree of your agreement or disagreement with each of the statements on the following page. Record your answers in the spaces provided below.

+4 = Very strong agreement
+3 = Strong agreement
+2 = Moderate agreement
+1 = Slight agreement
 0 = Neither agreement nor disagreement
−1 = Slight disagreement
−2 = Moderate disagreement
−3 = Strong disagreement
−4 = Very strong disagreement

Measure of Affiliative Tendency

(−) 1. When I'm introduced to someone new, I don't make much effort to be liked.

(+) 2. I prefer a leader who is friendly and easy to talk to over one who is more aloof and respected by his followers.

(+) 3. When I'm not feeling well, I would rather be with others than alone.

(−) 4. If I had to choose between the two, I would rather be considered intelligent than sociable.

(+) 5. Having friends is very important to me.

(+) 6. I would rather express open appreciation to others most of the time than reserve such feelings for special occasions.

(−) 7. I enjoy a good movie more than a big party.

(+) 8. I like to make as many friends as I can.

(−) 9. I would rather travel abroad starting my trip alone than with one or two friends.

(+) 10. After I meet someone I did not get along with, I spend time thinking about arranging another, more pleasant meeting.

(−) 11. I think that fame is more rewarding than friendship.

(−) 12. I prefer independent work to cooperative effort.

(+) 13. I think that any experience is more significant when shared with a friend.

(+) 14. When I see someone I know walking down the street, I am usually the first one to say hello.

(−) 15. I prefer the independence which comes from lack of attachments to the good and warm feelings associated with close ties.

(+) 16. I join clubs because it is such a good way of making friends.

(+) 17. I would rather serve in a position to which my friends had nominated me than be appointed to an office by a distant national headquarters.

(−) 18. I don't believe in showing overt affection toward friends.

(−) 19. I would rather go right to sleep at night than talk to someone else about the day's activities.

(−) 20. I have very few close friends.

(−) 21. When I'm with people I don't know, it doesn't matter much to me if they like me or not.

(+) 22. If I had to choose, I would rather have strong attachments to my friends than have them regard me as witty and clever.

(−) 23. I prefer individual activities such as crossword puzzles to group ones such as bridge or canasta.

(+) 24. I am much more attracted to warm, open people than I am to stand-offish ones.

(−) 25. I would rather read an interesting book or go to the movies than spend time with friends.

(+) 26. When traveling, I prefer meeting people to simply enjoying the scenery or going places alone.

Measure of Sensitivity to Rejection

(−) 1. I sometimes prefer being with strangers than with familiar people.

(−) 2. If I don't enjoy a party, I don't mind being the first one to leave.

(+) 3. I would be very hurt if a close friend should contradict me in public.

(−) 4. When a group is discussing an important matter, I like my feelings to be known.

(+) 5. I tend to associate less with people who are critical.

(−) 6. I often visit people without being invited.

(−) 7. I don't mind going some place even if I know that some of the people there don't like me.

(+) 8. I try to feel a group out before I take a definite stand on a controversial issue.

(−) 9. When two of my friends are arguing I don't mind taking sides to support the one I agree with.

(+) 10. If I ask someone to go someplace with me and he refuses, I'm hesitant to ask him again.

(+) 11. I am cautious about expressing my opinions until I know people quite well.

(+) 12. If I can't understand what someone says in a discussion, I will let it pass rather than interrupt to ask him to repeat it.

(−) 13. I enjoy discussing controversial topics like politics and religion.

(+) 14. I feel uneasy about asking someone to return something he borrowed from me.

(−) 15. I criticize people openly and expect them to do the same.

(−) 16. I can still enjoy a party even if I find that I am not properly dressed for the occasion.

(+) 17. I sometimes take criticism too hard.

(+) 18. If someone dislikes me, I tend to avoid him.

(−) 19. It seldom embarrasses me to ask someone for a favor.

(+) 20. I seldom contradict people for fear of hurting them.

(+) 21. I am very sensitive to any signs that a person might not want to talk to me.

(+) 22. Whenever I go somewhere where I know no one, I always like to have a friend come along.

(−) 23. I often say what I believe, even when it alienates the person with whom I am speaking.

(−) 24. I enjoy going to parties where I don't know anyone.

Measure of Empathic Tendency

(+)   1. It makes me sad to see a lonely stranger in a group.
(−)   2. People make too much of the feelings and sensitivity of animals.
(−)   3. I often find public displays of affection annoying.
(−)   4. I am annoyed by unhappy people who are just sorry for themselves.
(+)   5. I become nervous if others around me seem to be nervous.
(−)   6. I find it silly for people to cry out of happiness.
(+)   7. I tend to get emotionally involved with a friend's problems.
(+)   8. Sometimes the words of a love song can move me deeply.
(+)   9. I tend to lose control when I am bringing bad news to people.
(+) 10. The people around me have a great influence on my moods.
(−) 11. Most foreigners I have met seemed cool and unemotional.
(+) 12. I would rather be a social worker than work in a job training center.
(−) 13. I don't get upset just because a friend is acting upset.
(+) 14. I like to watch people open presents.
(−) 15. Lonely people are probably unfriendly.
(+) 16. Seeing people cry upsets me.
(+) 17. Some songs make me happy.
(+) 18. I really get involved with the feelings of the characters in a novel.
(+) 19. I get very angry when I see someone being ill-treated.
(−) 20. I am able to remain calm even though those around me worry.
(−) 21. When a friend starts to talk about his problems, I try to steer the conversation to something else.
(−) 22. Another's laughter is not catching for me.
(−) 23. Sometimes at the movies I am amused by the amount of crying and sniffling around me.
(−) 24. I am able to make decisions without being influenced by people's feelings.
(+) 25. I cannot continue to feel OK if people around me are depressed.
(−) 26. It is hard for me to see how some things upset people so much.
(+) 27. I am very upset when I see an animal in pain.
(−) 28. Becoming involved in books or movies is a little silly.
(+) 29. It upsets me to see helpless old people.
(−) 30. I become more irritated than sympathetic when I see someone's tears.
(+) 31. I become very involved when I watch a movie.
(−) 32. I often find that I can remain cool in spite of the excitement around me.
(−) 33. Little children sometimes cry for no apparent reason.

Measure of Male Achieving Tendency

(−)   1. I worry more about getting a bad grade than I think about getting a good grade.

(+)   2. I would rather work on a task where I alone am responsible for the final product than one in which many people contribute to the final product.

(+)   3. I more often attempt difficult tasks that I am not sure I can do than easier tasks I believe I can do.

(−)   4. I would rather do something at which I feel confident and relaxed than something which is challenging and difficult.

(+)   5. If I am not good at something, I would rather keep struggling to master it than move on to something I may be good at.

(−)   6. I would rather have a job in which my role is clearly defined by others and my rewards could be higher than average, than a job in which my role is to be defined by me and my rewards are average.

(+)   7. I would prefer a well-written informative book to a good movie.

(+)   8. I would prefer a job which is important, difficult, and involves a 50 per cent chance of failure to a job which is somewhat important but not difficult.

(−)   9. I would rather learn fun games that most people know than learn unusual skill games which only a few people would know.

(+) 10. It is very important for me to do my work as well as I can even if it means not getting along well with my co-workers.

(−) 11. For me, the pain of getting turned down after a job interview is greater than the pleasure of getting hired.

(−) 12. If I am going to play cards I would rather play a fun game than a difficult thought game.

(−) 13. I prefer competitive situations in which I have superior ability to those in which everyone involved is about equal in ability.

(+) 14. I think more of the future than of the present and past.

(−) 15. I am more unhappy about doing something badly than I am happy about doing something well.

(+) 16. In my spare time I would rather learn a game to develop skill than for recreation.

(+) 17. I would rather run my own business and face a 50 per cent chance of bankruptcy than work for another firm.

(−) 18. I would rather take a job in which the starting salary is $10,000 and could stay that way for some time than a job in which the starting salary is $5,000 and there is a guarantee that within five years I will be earning more than $10,000.

(−) 19. I would rather play in a team game than compete with just one other person.

(+) 20. The thing that is most important for me about learning to play a musical instrument is being able to play it very well, rather than learning it to have a better time with my friends.

(−) 21. I prefer multiple-choice questions on exams to essay questions.

(+) 22. I would rather work on commission which is somewhat risky but where I would have the possibility of making more than working on a fixed salary.

(−) 23. I think that I hate losing more than I love winning.

(+) 24. I would rather wait one or two years and have my parents buy me one great gift than have them buy me several average gifts over the same period of time.

(+) 25. If I were able to return to one of two incompleted tasks, I would rather return to the difficult than the easy one.

(−) 26. I think more about my past accomplishments than about my future goals.

Measure of Female Achieving Tendency

(+) 1. I think more about getting a good grade than I worry about getting a bad grade.

(+) 2. I more often attempt difficult tasks that I am not sure I can do than easier tasks I believe I can do.

(−) 3. I would rather do something at which I feel confident and relaxed than something which is challenging and difficult.

(+) 4. If I am not good at something, I would rather keep struggling to master it than move on to something I may be good at.

(−) 5. I would rather have a job in which my role is clearly defined by others and my rewards could be higher than average, than a job in which my role is to be defined by me and my rewards are average.

(−) 6. My strongest feelings are aroused more by fear of failure than by hope of success.

(+) 7. I would prefer a well-written informative book to a good movie.

(+) 8. I would prefer a job which is important, difficult, and involves a 50 per cent chance of failure to a job which is somewhat important but not difficult.

(−) 9. I would rather learn fun games that most people know than learn unusual skill games which only a few people would know.

(+) 10. It is very important for me to do my work as well as I can even if it means not getting along well with my co-workers.

(−) 11. For me, the pain of getting turned down after a job interview is greater than the pleasure of getting hired.

(−) 12. If I am going to play cards I would rather play a fun game than a difficult game.

(−) 13. I prefer competitive situations in which I have superior ability to those in which everyone involved is about equal in ability.

(+) 14. I think more of the future than of the present and past.

(−) 15. I am more unhappy about doing something badly than I am happy about doing something well.

(+) 16. I worry more about whether people will praise my work than I do about whether they will criticize it.

(−) 17. If I had to spend the money myself I would rather have an exceptional meal out than spend less and prepare an exceptional meal at home.

(+) 18. I would rather do a paper on my own than take a test.

(−) 19. I would rather share in the decision-making process of a group than take total responsibility for directing the group's activities.

(+) 20. I would rather try to make new and interesting meals that may turn out badly than make more familiar meals that frequently turn out well.

(−) 21. I would rather do something I enjoy than do something that I think is worthwhile but not much fun.

(−) 22. I would rather try to get two or three things done quickly than spend all my time working on one project.

(−) 23. If I am ill and must stay home, I use the time to relax and recuperate rather than try to read or work.

(+) 24. If I were rooming with a number of girls and we decided to have a party, I would rather organize the party myself than have one of the others organize it.

(+) 25. I would rather cook for a couple of gourmet eaters than for a couple who simply have huge appetites.

(+) 26. I would rather that our women's group be allowed to help organize city projects than be allowed to work on the projects after they have been organized.

Bibliography

Allport, G. W., and P. E. Vernon. 1967. *Studies in expressive movement*. New York: Hafner.

Anastasi, A. 1958. *Differential psychology*. New York: Macmillan.

Anderson, N. H. 1962. Application of an additive model to impression formation, *Science, 138*, 817–18.

———. 1964. Note on weighted sum and linear operator models, *Psychonomic Science, 1*, 189–90.

Anderson, R. L., and T. A. Bancroft. 1955. *Statistical theory in research*. New York: McGraw-Hill.

Ardrey, R. 1966. *The territorial imperative*. New York: Atheneum.

Argyle, M. 1969. *Social interaction*. New York: Atherton.

Argyle, M., F. Alkema, and R. Gilmour. 1971. The communication of friendly and hostile attitudes by verbal and nonverbal signals. Unpublished Manuscript, Institute of Experimental Psychology, Oxford University.

Argyle, M., and J. Dean. 1965. Eye contact, distance, and affiliation, *Sociometry, 28*, 289–304.

Argyle, M., and A. Kendon. 1967. The experimental analysis of social performance, in L. Berkowitz (ed.), *Advances in experimental social psychology*, Vol. 3. New York: Academic Press, 55–98.

Argyle, M., V. Salter, H. Nicholson, M. Williams, and P. Burgess. 1970. The communication of inferior and superior attitudes by verbal and nonverbal signals, *British Journal of Social and Clinical Psychology, 9*, 222–31.

Aronson, E., and B. Golden. 1962. The effect of relevant and irrelevant aspects of communicator credibility on opinion change, *Journal of Personality, 30*, 135–46.

Bach, G. R., and P. Wyden. 1968. *The intimate enemy*. New York: William Morrow.

Baker, E. E., and W. C. Redding. 1961. The effects of perceived tallness in persuasive speaking: An experiment, *Journal of Communication, 12*, 51–53.

Bales, R. F. 1950. *Interaction process analysis*. Reading, Mass.: Addison-Wesley.

Bateson, G., D. D. Jackson, J. Haley, and J. H. Weakland. 1956. Toward a theory of schizophrenia, *Behavioral Sciences, 1*, 251–64.

Baxter, J. C. 1970. Interpersonal spacing in natural settings, *Sociometry, 33*, 444–56.

Beakel, N. G., and A. Mehrabian. 1969. Inconsistent communications and psychopathology, *Journal of Abnormal Psychology, 74*, 126–30.

Bellugi, U., and R. Brown. 1964. The acquisition of language, *Monographs of the Society for Research in Child Development, 29* (1, Serial No. 92).

Bentler, P. M. 1969. Semantic space is (approximately) bipolar, *Journal of Psychology, 71,* 33–40.

Birdwhistell, R. L. 1952. *Introduction to kinesics.* Louisville: University of Kentucky Press.

———. 1963. The kinesic level in the investigation of the emotions, in P. H. Knapp (ed.), *Expression of the emotions in man.* New York: International Universities Press, 123–39.

———. 1970. *Kinesics and context: Essays on body motion communication.* Philadelphia: University of Pennsylvania Press.

Boomer, D. S. 1963. Speech disturbance and body movement in interviews, *Journal of Nervous and Mental Disease, 136,* 263–66.

Braatoy, T. F. 1954. *Fundamentals of psychoanalytic technique.* New York: Wiley.

Braine, M. D. S. 1963. The ontogeny of English phrase structure: The first phase, *Language, 39,* 1–13.

Brown, R. 1958. *Words and things.* New York: Free Press.

Brown, R., and C. Fraser. 1963. The acquisition of syntax, in C. N. Cofer and B. S. Musgrave (eds.), *Verbal behavior and learning.* New York: McGraw-Hill, 158–97.

Bugental, D. E., J. W. Kaswan, and L. R. Love. 1970. Perception of contradictory meanings conveyed by verbal and nonverbal channels, *Journal of Personality and Social Psychology, 16,* 647–55.

Byrne, D. 1969. Attitudes and attraction, in L. Berkowitz (ed.), *Advances in experimental social psychology,* Vol. 4. New York: Academic Press, 35–89.

Calhoun, J. B. 1962. *The ecology and sociology of the Norway rat.* Bethesda, Md.: Public Health Service.

Cassirer, E. 1953–57. *The philosophy of symbolic forms,* 3 vols. New Haven, Conn.: Yale University Press.

Chappell, W. N. 1929. Blood pressure changes in deception, *Archives of Psychology, 17,* No. 105.

Cherry, C. 1966. *On human communication.* Cambridge, Mass.: M. I. T. Press.

Chomsky, N. 1965. *Aspects of the theory of syntax.* Cambridge, Mass.: M.I.T. Press.

Cohen, A. R. 1964. *Attitude change and social influence.* New York: Basic Books.

Cohen, J. 1968. Multiple regression as a general data-analytic system, *Psychological Bulletin, 70,* 426–43.

Condon, W. S., and W. D. Ogston. 1966. Sound film analysis of normal and pathological behavior patterns, *The Journal of Nervous and Mental Disease, 143,* 338–47.

———. 1967. A segmentation of behavior, *Journal of Psychiatric Research, 5,* 221–35.

Coss, R. G. 1970. The perceptual aspects of eye-spot patterns and their relevance to gaze behaviour, in C. Hutt and S. J. Hutt (eds.), *Behaviour studies in psychiatry.* Oxford, England: Pergamon, 121–47.

Crowne, D. P., and D. Marlowe. 1960. A new scale of social desirability independent of psychopathology, *Journal of Consulting Psychology, 24,* 349–54.

———. 1964. *The approval motive.* New York: Wiley.

Crystal, D., and R. Quirk. 1964. *Systems of prosodic and paralinguistic features in English.* The Hague: Mouton.

Darwin, C. 1965. *The expression of the emotions in man and animals.* Chicago: The University of Chicago Press.

Davitz, J. R. (Ed.) 1964. *The communication of emotional meaning.* New York: McGraw-Hill.

——. 1969. *The language of emotion.* New York: Academic Press.

Deutsch, F. 1947. Analysis of postural behavior, *Psychoanalytic Quarterly, 16,* 195–213.

——. 1952. Analytic posturology, *Psychoanalytic Quarterly, 21,* 196–214.

Deutsch, F., and W. F. Murphy. 1955. *The clinical interview,* Vols. 1 and 2. New York: International Universities Press.

Dittmann, A. T. 1971. Kinesics and Context by Ray L. Birdwhistell, *Psychiatry, 34,* 334–342.

Dittmann, A. T., and L. G. Llewellyn. 1968. Relationship between vocalizations and head nods as listener responses, *Journal of Personality and Social Psychology, 9,* 79–84.

——. 1969. Body movements and speech rhythm in social conversation, *Journal of Personality and Social Psychology, 11,* 98–106.

Dittmann, A. T., M. X. Parloff, and D. S. Boomer. 1965. Facial and bodily expression: A study of receptivity of emotional cues, *Psychiatry, 28,* 239–44.

Dollard, J., and N. E. Miller. 1950. *Personality and psychotherapy.* New York: McGraw-Hill.

Duncan, S., Jr. 1969. Nonverbal communication, *Psychological Bulletin, 72,* 118–37.

Duncan, S., Jr., and R. Rosenthal. 1968. Vocal emphasis in experimenters' instruction reading as unintended determinant of subjects' responses, *Language and Speech, 11,* 20–26.

Efran, J. S. 1968. Looking for approval: Effects on visual behavior of approbation from persons differing in importance, *Journal of Personality and Social Psychology, 10,* 21–25.

Efran, J. S., and A. Broughton. 1966. Effect of expectancies for social approval on visual behavior, *Journal of Personality and Social Psychology, 4,* 103–107.

Efron, D. 1941. *Gesture and environment.* New York: King's Crown.

Ekman, P. 1964. Body position, facial expression and verbal behavior during interviews, *Journal of Abnormal and Social Psychology, 68,* 295–301.

——. 1965. Differential communication of affect by head and body cues, *Journal of Personality and Social Psychology, 2,* 726–35.

——. 1972. Universals and cultural differences in facial expressions of emotion, in J. K. Cole (ed.), *Nebraska symposium on motivation, 1971,* Lincoln, Nebr.: University of Nebraska Press.

Ekman, P., and W. V. Friesen. 1967. Head and body cues in the judgment of emotion: A reformulation, *Perceptual and Motor Skills, 24,* 711–24.

——. 1969a. Nonverbal leakage and clues to deception, *Psychiatry, 32,* 88–106.

——. 1969b. The repertoire of nonverbal behavior: Categories, origins, usage, and coding, *Semiotica, 1,* 49–98.

——. 1971. Constants across cultures in the face and emotion, *Journal of Personality and Social Psychology, 17,* 124–29.

Ellsworth, P. C., and J. M. Carlsmith. 1968. Effects of eye contact and verbal content on affective response to a dyadic interaction, *Journal of Personality and Social Psychology, 10,* 15–20.

Escalona, S. K. 1945. Feeding disturbances in very young children, *American Journal of Orthopsychiatry, 15,* 76–80.

Exline, R. V. 1962. Effects of need for affiliation, sex, and the sight of others upon initial communications in problem-solving groups, *Journal of Personality, 30,* 541–56.

——. 1963. Explorations in the process of person perception: Visual interaction in relation to competition, sex, and need for affiliation, *Journal of Personality, 31*, 1–20.

——. 1972. Visual interaction—the glances of power and preference, in J. K. Cole (ed.), *Nebraska symposium on motivation, 1971*, Lincoln, Nebr.: University of Nebraska Press.

Exline, R. V., and C. Eldridge. 1967. Effects of two patterns of a speaker's visual behavior upon the perception of the authenticity of his verbal message. Paper presented at the meetings of the Eastern Psychological Association, Boston, April, 1967.

Exline, R. V., D. Gray, and D. Schuette. 1965. Visual behavior in a dyad as affected by interview content and sex of respondent, *Journal of Personality and Social Psychology, 1*, 201–209.

Exline, R. V., and D. Messick. 1967. The effects of dependency and social reinforcement upon visual behavior during an interview, *British Journal of Social and Clinical Psychology, 6*, 256–66.

Exline, R. V., and L. C. Winters. 1965. Affective relations and mutual glances in dyads, in S. Tomkins and C. Izard (eds.), *Affect cognition and personality*. New York: Springer, 319–30.

Eysenck, H. J., and S. B. Eysenck. 1963. *Manual for the Eysenck Personality Inventory*. San Diego: Educational and Industrial Testing Service.

Feldman, S. S. 1959. *Mannerisms of speech and gestures*. New York: International Universities Press.

Felipe, N. J., and R. Sommer. 1966. Invasions of personal space, *Social Problems, 14*, 206–14.

Fischer, C. T. 1968. Social schemas: Response sets or perceptual meanings? *Journal of Personality and Social Psychology, 10*, 8–14.

Fisher, R. L. 1967. Social schemas of normal and disturbed school children, *Journal of Educational Psychology, 58*, 88–92.

Flavell, J. H. 1963. *The developmental psychology of Jean Piaget*. New York: Van Nostrand.

Freedman, N., and S. P. Hoffmann. 1967. Kinetic behavior in altered clinical states: Approach to objective analysis of motor behavior during clinical interviews, *Perceptual and Motor Skills, 24*, 527–39.

Freud, S. 1938. The psychopathology of everyday life (1904), in *The basic writings of Sigmund Freud*. New York: Random House.

——. 1959. Fragment of an analysis of a case of hysteria (1905), in *Collected papers*, Vol. 3. New York: Basic Books.

Frijda, N. H. 1969. Recognition of emotions, in L. Berkowitz (ed.), *Advances in experimental social psychology*. New York: Academic Press, 167–223.

Fromm-Reichmann, F. 1950. *Principles of intensive psychotherapy*. Chicago: The University of Chicago Press.

Garfinkel, H. 1964. Studies of the routine grounds of everyday activities, *Social Problems, 11*, 225–50.

Gates, G. S. 1927. The role of the auditory element in the interpretation of emotion, *Psychological Bulletin, 24*, 175. (Abstract)

Gitin, S. R. 1970. A dimensional analysis of manual expression, *Journal of Personality and Social Psychology, 15*, 271–77.

Goffman, E. 1961. *Encounters: Two studies in the sociology of interaction*. Indianapolis: Bobbs-Merrill.

Golding, P. 1967. Role of distance and posture in the evaluation of interactions, *Proceedings of the 75th Annual Convention of the APA. 2*, 243–44.

Goldman-Eisler, F. 1968. *Psycholinguistics: Experiments in spontaneous speech*. New York: Academic Press.

Gottlieb, R., M. Wiener, and A. Mehrabian. 1967. Immediacy, discomfort-relief quotient, and content in verbalizations about positive and negative experiences, *Journal of Personality and Social Psychology, 7,* 266–74.

Haley, J. 1963. *Strategies of Psychotherapy.* New York: Grune & Stratton.

Hall, E. T. 1959. *The silent language.* Garden City, N. Y.: Doubleday.

———. 1963. A system for the notation of proxemic behavior, *American Anthropologist, 65,* 1003–26.

———. 1964. Silent assumptions in social communication, *Disorders of Communication, 42,* 41–55.

———. 1966. *The hidden dimension.* Garden City, N. Y.: Doubleday.

Hanfmann, E., M. Rickers-Ovsiankina, and K. Goldstein. 1944. Case Lanuti: Extreme concretization of behavior due to damage of the brain cortex, *Psychological Monographs, 57* (Whole No. 264).

Hearn, G. 1957. Leadership and the spatial factor in small groups, *Journal of Abnormal and Social Psychology, 54,* 269–72.

Henderson, E. H., B. H. Long, and R. C. Ziller. 1965. Self-social constructs of achieving and non-achieving readers, *The Reading Teacher,* 114–18.

Holt, E. B. 1931. *Animal drive.* London: Williams & Norgate.

Horowitz, I. A., and B. H. Rothschild. 1970. Conformity as a function of deception and role playing, *Journal of Personality and Social Psychology, 16,* 224–26.

Hovland, C. I., I. L. Janis, and H. H. Kelley. 1953. *Communication and persuasion.* New Haven, Conn.: Yale University Press.

Hutchinson, A. 1970. *Labanotation: The system for recording movement.* New York: Theater Arts Books.

Huttar, G. L. 1967. *Some relations between emotions and the prosodic parameters of speech.* Santa Barbara, Cal.: Speech Communications Research Laboratory.

Insko, C. A. 1967. *Theories of attitude change.* New York: Appleton-Century-Crofts.

Jackson, D. N. 1967. *Personality research form manual.* Goshen, N. Y.: Research Psychologists Press.

James, W. T. 1932. A study of the expression of bodily posture, *Journal of General Psychology, 7,* 405–37.

Jesperson, O. 1922. *Language; its nature, development, and origin.* London: Allen and Unwin.

Jones, E. E. 1964. *Ingratiation: A social psychological analysis.* New York: Appleton-Century-Crofts.

Jourard, S. M. 1966. An exploratory study of body accessibility, *British Journal of Social and Clinical Psychology, 5,* 221–31.

Jourard, S. M., and J. E. Rubin. 1968. Self-disclosure and touching: A study of two modes of interpersonal encounter and their inter-relation, *Journal of Humanistic Psychology, 8,* 39–48.

Jung, C. G. 1905. Diagnostisch assoziationsstudien, *Journal fur Psychologie und Neurologie, 4,* 1–36.

Kahl, J. A. 1964. *The American class structure.* New York: Holt.

Kasl, S. V., and G. F. Mahl. 1965. The relationship of disturbances and hesitations in spontaneous speech to anxiety, *Journal of Personality and Social Psychology, 1,* 425–33.

Keller, H. 1903. *The story of my life.* New York: Doubleday.

Kendon, A. 1967a. Some functions of gaze direction in social interaction, *Acta Psychologica, 26,* 22–63.

———. 1967b. Some observations on interactional synchrony. Unpublished Manuscript, Western Psychiatric Institute and Clinic, Pittsburgh, Pa.

Knower, R. H. 1945. Studies in the symbolism of voice and action: V. The use of behavioral and tonal symbols as tests of speaking achievement, *Journal of Applied Psychology, 29,* 229–35.

Krasner, L. 1958. Studies of the conditioning of verbal behavior, *Psychological Bulletin, 55,* 148–70.

Kuethe, J. L. 1964. Prejudice and aggression: A study of specific social schemata, *Perceptual and Motor Skills, 18,* 107–15.

Lampel, A. K., and N. H. Anderson. 1968. Combining visual and verbal information in an impression-formation task, *Journal of Personality and Social Psychology, 9,* 1–6.

Leipold, W. D. 1963. Psychological distance in a dyadic interview. Unpublished doctoral dissertation, University of North Dakota.

Lenneberg, E. H. 1967. *The biological foundations of language.* New York: Wiley.

Levitt, E. A. 1964. The relationship between abilities to express emotional meanings vocally and facially, in J. R. Davitz (ed.), *The communication of emotional meaning.* New York: McGraw-Hill, 87–100.

Levy, P. K. 1964. The ability to express and perceive vocal communications of feeling, in J. R. Davitz (ed.), *The communication of emotional meaning.* New York: McGraw-Hill, 43–56.

Lewin, K. 1935. *A dynamic theory of personality: Selected papers.* New York: McGraw-Hill.

Lewis, M. M. 1936. *Infant speech.* London: Kegan Paul.

Little, K. B. 1965. Personal space, *Journal of Experimental Social Psychology, 1,* 237–47.

———. 1968. Cultural variations in social schemata, *Journal of Personality and Social Psychology, 10,* 1–7.

Lombroso, P. 1909. Das Leben der Kinder, *Pedogogische Monographien.* Leipzig: Nemrich.

Long, B. H., and E. H. Henderson. 1968. Self-social concepts of disadvantaged school beginners, *Journal of Genetic Psychology, 113,* 41–51.

Long, B. H., R. C. Ziller, and E. H. Henderson. 1968. Developmental changes in the self-concept during adolescence, *The School Review, 76,* 210–30.

Lorenz, K. 1966. *On aggression* (trans. by M. K. Wilson). New York: Harcourt, Brace & World.

Lott, D. F., and R. Sommer. 1967. Seating arrangements and status, *Journal of Personality and Social Psychology, 7,* 90–95.

Lowen, A. 1958. *Physical dynamics of character structure: Body form and movement in analytic therapy.* New York: Grune & Stratton.

Luria, A. R. 1930. The method of recording movements in crime detection, *Zeitschrift fur angewandte psychologie, 35,* 139–83.

Machotka, P. 1965. Body movement as communication, *Dialogues: Behavioral Science Research, 2,* 33–66.

Mahl, G. F. 1959. Measuring the patient's anxiety during interviews from "expressive" aspects of his speech, *Transactions of the New York Academy of Sciences, 21,* 249–57.

Mahl, G. F., B. Danet, and N. Norton. 1959. Reflection of major personality characteristics in gestures and body movement. Paper presented at Annual Meeting, American Psychological Association, Cincinnati, Ohio, September, 1959.

Mahl, G. F., and G. Schulze. 1964. Psychological research in the extra-linguistic area, In T. A. Sebeok, A. S. Hayes, and M. C. Bateson (eds.), *Approaches to semiotics*. The Hague: Mouton, 51–124.

Malamud, D. I., and S. Machover. 1965. *Toward self-understanding: Group techniques in self-confrontation*. Springfield, Ill.: Charles C Thomas.

Maltzman, I. 1967. Individual differences in "attention": The orienting reflex, in R. M. Gagne (ed.), *Learning and individual differences*. Columbus, Ohio, Charles E. Merrill, 94–112.

Mandler, G., and S. B. Sarason. 1952. A study of anxiety and learning. *Journal of Abnormal and Social Psychology*, 47, 166–73.

Marston, W. M. 1920. Reaction-time symptoms of deception, *Journal of Experimental Psychology*, 3, 72–87.

Matarazzo, J. D., A. N. Wiens, and G. Saslow. 1965. Studies in interviewer speech behavior, in L. Krasner and L. P. Ullmann (eds.), *Research in behavior modification*. New York: Holt, Rinehart and Winston, 179–210.

McBride, G. 1964. *A general theory of social organization and behavior*, St. Lucia, Austr.: University of Queensland Press.

McNeill, D. 1966. Developmental psycholinguistics, in F. Smith and G. A. Miller (eds.), *The genesis of language*. Cambridge, Mass.: The M.I.T. Press, 15–84.

McQuown, N. A. 1957. Linguistic transcription and specification of psychiatric interview material, *Psychiatry*, 20, 79–86.

Mehrabian, A. 1964. Differences in the forms of verbal communication as a function of positive and negative affective experience. Unpublished doctoral dissertation, Clark University.

——. 1965. Communication length as an index of communicator attitude, *Psychological Reports*, 17, 519–22.

——. 1966a. Attitudes in relation to the forms of communicator-object relationship in spoken communications, *Journal of Personality*, 34, 80–93.

——. 1966b. Immediacy: An indicator of attitudes in linguistic communication, *Journal of Personality*, 34, 26–34.

——. 1967a. Orientation behaviors and nonverbal attitude communication, *Journal of Communication*, 17, 324–32.

——. 1967b. Attitudes inferred from non-immediacy of verbal communications, *Journal of Verbal Learning and Verbal Behavior*, 6, 294–95.

——. 1967c. Attitudes inferred from neutral verbal communications, *Journal of Consulting Psychology*, 31, 414–17.

——. 1967d. Substitute for apology: Manipulation of cognitions to reduce negative attitude toward self, *Psychological Reports*, 20, 687–92.

——. 1968a. Inference of attitudes from the posture, orientation, and distance of a communicator, *Journal of Consulting and Clinical Psychology*, 32, 296–308.

——. 1968b. Relationship of attitude to seated posture, orientation, and distance, *Journal of Personality and Social Psychology*, 10, 26–30.

——. 1968c. The effect of context on judgments of speaker attitude, *Journal of Personality*, 36, 21–32.

——. 1968d. Communication without words, *Psychology Today*, 2, 52–55.

——. 1968e. *An analysis of personality theories*, Englewood Cliffs, N. J.: Prentice-Hall.

———. 1968f. Male and female scales of the tendency to achieve, *Educational and Psychological Measurement, 28,* 493–502.

———. 1969a. Measures of achieving tendency, *Educational and Psychological Measurement, 29,* 445–51.

———. 1969b. Significance of posture and position in the communication of attitude and status relationships, *Psychological Bulletin, 71,* 359–72.

———. 1969c. Some referents and measures of nonverbal behavior, *Behavior Research Methods and Instrumentation, 1,* 203–207.

———. 1970a. A semantic space for nonverbal behavior, *Journal of Consulting and Clinical Psychology, 35,* 248–57.

———. 1970b. Some determinants of affiliation and conformity, *Psychological Reports, 27,* 19–29.

———. 1970c. *Tactics of social influence,* Englewood Cliffs, N. J.: Prentice-Hall.

———. 1970d. The development and validation of measures of affiliative tendency and sensitivity to rejection, *Educational and Psychological Measurement, 30,* 417–28.

———. 1970e. When are feelings communicated inconsistently? *Journal of Experimental Research in Personality, 4,* 198–212.

———. 1970f. Measures of vocabulary and grammatical skills for children up to age six, *Developmental Psychology, 2,* 439–46.

———. 1971a. Nonverbal betrayal of feeling, *Journal of Experimental Research in Personality, 5,* 64–73.

———. 1971b. Verbal and nonverbal interaction of strangers in a waiting situation, *Journal of Experimental Research in Personality, 5,* 127–38.

———. 1971c. *Silent messages.* Belmont, Cal.: Wadsworth.

———. 1972. Nonverbal communication, in J. K. Cole (ed.), *Nebraska symposium on motivation, 1971.* Lincoln, Nebr.: University of Nebraska Press.

Mehrabian, A., and S. G. Diamond. 1971a. Seating arrangement and conversation, *Sociometry, 34,* 281–89.

———. 1971b. The effects of furniture arrangement, props, and personality on social interaction, *Journal of Personality and Social Psychology, 20,* 18–30.

Mehrabian, A., and N. Epstein. 1972. A measure of emotional empathy, *Journal of Personality.*

Mehrabian, A., and S. R. Ferris. 1967. Inference of attitudes from nonverbal communication in two channels, *Journal of Consulting Psychology, 31,* 248–52.

Mehrabian, A., and J. T. Friar. 1969. Encoding of attitude by a seated communicator via posture and position cues, *Journal of Consulting and Clinical Psychology, 33,* 330–36.

Mehrabian, A., and S. Ksionzky. 1970. Models for affiliative and conformity behavior, *Psychological Bulletin, 74,* 110–26.

———. 1971a. Anticipated compatibility as a function of attitude or status similarity, *Journal of Personality, 39,* 225–41.

———. 1971b. Factors of interpersonal behavior and judgment in social groups, *Psychological Reports, 28,* 483–92.

———. 1972. Categories of social behavior, *Comparative Group Studies.*

Mehrabian, A., and H. Reed 1968. Some determinants of communication accuracy, *Psychological Bulletin, 70,* 365–81.

Mehrabian, A., and J. Russell. 1972. *An approach to environmental psychology.* Unpublished manuscript, UCLA.

Mehrabian, A., and M. Wiener. 1966. Non-immediacy between communicator and object of communication in a verbal message: Application to the inference of attitudes, *Journal of Consulting Psychology, 30,* 420–25.

———. 1967. Decoding of inconsistent communications, *Journal of Personality and Social Psychology, 6,* 109–14.

Mehrabian, A., and M. Williams. 1969. Nonverbal concomitants of perceived and intended persuasiveness, *Journal of Personality and Social Psychology, 13,* 37–58.

———. 1971. Piagetian measures of cognitive development for children up to age two, *Journal of Psycholinguistic Research, 1,* 113–26.

Menyuk, P. 1969. *Sentences children use.* Cambridge, Mass.: M.I.T. Press.

Miller, D. E. 1966. Individual differences in the communication of emotion. Unpublished doctoral dissertation, University of Utah.

Miller, N. E. 1964. Some implications of modern behavior therapy for personality change and psychotherapy, in P. Worchel and D. Byrne (eds.), *Personality change.* New York: Wiley, 149–175.

Mills, J. 1966. Opinion change as a function of the communicator's desire to influence and liking for the audience, *Journal of Experimental Social Psychology, 2,* 152–59.

Mills, J., and E. Aronson. 1965. Opinion change as a function of the communicator's attractiveness and desire to influence, *Journal of Personality and Social Psychology, 1,* 173–77.

Mowrer, O. H. 1950. On the psychology of "talking" birds—A contribution to language and personality theory, in O. H. Mowrer (ed.), *Learning theory and personality dynamics; selected papers.* New York: Ronald, 688–726.

Nachshon, I., and S. Wapner. 1967. Effect of eye contact and physiognomy on perceived location of other person, *Journal of Personality and Social Psychology, 7,* 82–89.

Nakazima, S. 1965–66. A comparative study of the speech developments of Japanese and American English in childhood (2), *Studia Phonologica, 4,* 38–55.

Newman, S. 1933. Further experiments in phonetic symbolism, *American Journal of Psychology, 45,* 53–75.

Norum, G. A., N. J. Russo, and R. Sommer. 1967. Seating patterns and group task, *Psychology in the Schools, 4(3),* 276–80.

Osgood, C. E. 1966. Dimensionality of the semantic space for communication via facial expressions, *Scandinavian Journal of Psychology, 7,* 1–30.

Osgood, C. E., G. J. Suci, and P. H. Tannenbaum. 1957. *The measurement of meaning.* Urbana: The University of Illinois Press.

Patterson, M. L., and D. S. Holmes, 1966. Social interaction correlates of the MPI extroversion-introversion scale, *American Psychologist, 21,* 724–25 (Abstract).

Pepper, S. C. 1942. *World hypotheses.* Berkeley: University of California Press.

Phillips, L. 1968. *Human adaptation and its failures.* New York: Academic Press.

Piaget, J. 1960. *Psychology of intelligence.* Paterson, N. J.: Littlefield, Adams.

Pittenger, R. E., C. F. Hockett, and J. J. Danehy. 1960. *The first five minutes.* Ithaca, N. Y.: Martineau.

Pittenger, R. E., and H. L. Smith, Jr. 1957. A basis for some contributions of linguistics to psychiatry, *Psychiatry, 20,* 61–78.

Reece, M. M., and R. N. Whitman. 1962. Expressive movements, warmth and verbal reinforcement. *Journal of Abnormal and Social Psychology, 64,* 234–36.

Reich, W. 1945. *Character analysis* (Trans. by T. P. Wolfe). New York: Orgone Institute Press.

Riesman, D. 1950. *The lonely crowd.* New Haven: Yale University Press.

Roe, A. 1956. *The psychology of occupations.* New York: Wiley.

Rogers, C. R. 1959. A theory of therapy, personality, and interpersonal relationships, as developed in the client-centered framework, in S. Koch (ed.), *Psychology: A study of a science,* Vol. 3. New York: McGraw-Hill, 184–256.

Rosenfeld, H. M. 1965. Effect of an approval-seeking induction on interpersonal proximity, *Psychological Reports, 17,* 120–22.

———. 1966a. Approval-seeking and approval-inducing functions of verbal and nonverbal responses in the dyad, *Journal of Personality and Social Psychology, 4,* 597–605.

———. 1966b. Instrumental affiliative functions of facial and gestural expressions, *Journal of Personality and Social Psychology, 4,* 65–72.

———. 1966c. Relationships of ordinal position to affiliation and achievement motives: Direction and generality, *Journal of Personality, 34,* 467–80.

Rosenthal, R. 1966. *Experimenter effects in behavioral research.* New York: Appleton-Century-Crofts.

Rosnow, R. L., and E. J. Robinson. 1967. *Experiments in persuasion.* New York: Academic Press.

Rubenstein, L., and D. E. Cameron. 1968. Electronic analysis of nonverbal communication, *Comprehensive Psychiatry, 9,* 200–208.

Scheflen, A. E. 1964. The significance of posture in communication systems, *Psychiatry, 27,* 316–31.

———. 1965. *Stream and structure of communicational behavior: Context analysis of a psychotherapy session.* Behavioral Studies Monograph No. 1. Philadelphia: Eastern Pennsylvania Psychiatric Institute.

———. 1966. Natural history method in psychotherapy: Communicational research, in L. A. Gottschalk and A. H. Auerbach (eds.), *Methods of research in psychotherapy,* New York: Appleton-Century-Crofts, 263–89.

Schlosberg, H. 1954. Three dimensions of emotion, *Psychological Review, 61,* 81–88.

Schuham, A. 1967. The double-bind hypothesis a decade later, *Psychological Bulletin, 68,* 409–16.

Shipley, W. C. 1939. *Shipley institute of living scale for measuring intellectual impairment.* Norton, Mass.: Mrs. W. C. Shipley.

Slobin, D. I. (ed.) 1967. *A field manual for cross-cultural study of the acquisition of communicative competence.* Berkeley: University of California Press.

Smith, G. H. 1953. Size-distance of human faces (projected images), *Journal of General Psychology, 49,* 45–64.

———. 1954. Personality scores and personal distance effect, *Journal of Social Psychology, 39,* 57–62.

Snider, J. G., and C. E. Osgood. (eds.) 1969. *Semantic differential technique.* Chicago: Aldine.

Sommer, R. 1959. Studies in personal space, *Sociometry*, *22*(3), 247–60.
———. 1967. Small group ecology. *Psychological Bulletin, 67*, 145–51.
———. 1969. *Personal space*. Englewood Cliffs, N. J.: Prentice-Hall.
Starkweather, J. A. 1964. Variations in vocal behavior, in D. M. Rioch (ed.), *Disorders of communication*. Proceedings of ARNMD, Vol. 42. Baltimore: Williams & Wilkins.
Stern, C., and W. Stern. 1920. *Die Kindersprache*. Leipzig: Barth.
Strongman, K. T., and B. G. Champness. 1968. Dominance hierarchies and conflict in eye contact, *Acta Psychologica, 28*, 376–86.
Tomkins, S. S., and R. McCarter. 1964. What and where are the primary affects? Some evidence for a theory, *Perceptual and Motor Skills, 18*, 119–58.
Trager, G. L. 1958. Paralanguage: A first approximation, *Studies in Linguistics, 13*, 1–12.
Truax, C. B. 1966. Reinforcement and nonreinforcement in Rogerian psychotherapy, *Journal of Abnormal Psychology, 71*, 1–9.
Vigotsky, L. S. 1939. Thought and speech, *Psychiatry, 2*, 29–54.
Watson, O. M., and T. D. Graves. 1966. Quantitative research in proxemic behavior, *American Anthropologist, 68*, 971–85.
Weakland, J. H. 1961. The "double bind" hypothesis of schizophrenia and three-party interaction, in D. D. Jackson (ed.), *The etiology of schizophrenia*. New York: Basic Books, 373–388.
Weiner, B., P. Johnson, and A. Mehrabian. 1968. Achievement motivation and the recall of incompleted and completed exam questions, *Journal of Educational Psychology, 59*, 181–85.
Weiner, B., and A. Kukla. 1970. An attributional analysis of achievement motivation, *Journal of Personality and Social Psychology, 15*, 1–20.   ·
Weinstein, L. 1965. Social schemata of emotionally disturbed boys, *Journal of Abnormal Psychology, 70*, 457–61.
Weisbrod, R. M. 1965. Looking behavior in a discussion group. Term paper submitted for Psychology 546, under the direction of Professor Longabaugh, Ithaca, N. Y.: Cornell University.
Weiss, W. 1957. Opinion congruence with a negative source on one issue as a factor influencing agreement on another issue, *Journal of Abnormal and Social Psychology, 54*, 180–86.
Werner, H. 1957. *Comparative psychology of mental development* (Rev. ed.). New York: International Universities Press.
Werner, H., and B. Kaplan. 1963. *Symbol formation*. New York: Wiley.
Whorf, B. L. 1956. *Language, thought, and reality*. Cambridge, Mass.: M.I.T. Press.
Wiener, M., and A. Mehrabian. 1968. *Language within language: Immediacy, a channel in verbal communication*. New York: Appleton-Century-Crofts.
Wiens, A. N., R. H. Jackson, T. S. Manaugh, and J. D. Matarazzo. 1969. Communication length as an index of communicator attitude: A replication, *Journal of Applied Psychology, 53*, 264–66.
Williams, F., and B. Sundene. 1965. Dimensions of recognition: Visual vs. vocal expression of emotion, *Audio Visual Communications Review, 13*, 44–52.
Williams, J. L. 1963. Personal space and its relation to extroversion-introversion. Unpublished M.A. thesis, University of Alberta.

Willis, F. N., Jr. 1966. Initial speaking distance as a function of the speakers' relationship, *Psychonomic Science*, 5, 221–22.

Winer, B. J. 1962. *Statistical principles in experimental design*. New York: McGraw-Hill.

Woodworth, R. S., and H. Schlosberg. 1954. *Experimental Psychology*. New York: Holt.

Zaidel, S. F., and A. Mehrabian. 1969. The ability to communicate and infer positive and negative attitudes facially and vocally, *Journal of Experimental Research in Personality*, 3, 233–41.

Name Index

Subject Index